SURPRISE HEIRS

Volume 1

Illegitimacy, Patrimonial Rights, and Legal Nationalism
in Luso-Brazilian Inheritance, 1750-1821

SURPRISE HEIRS

Volume 1

———◆—◆—◆———

Illegitimacy, Patrimonial Rights, and Legal Nationalism in Luso-Brazilian Inheritance, 1750-1821

———◆—◆—◆———

LINDA LEWIN

STANFORD UNIVERSITY PRESS

STANFORD, CALIFORNIA

2003

Stanford University Press
Stanford, California
© 2003 by the Board of Trustees of the
Leland Stanford Junior University
Printed in the United States of America

Library of Congress Cataloging-in-Publication Data

Lewin, Linda.
  Surprise heirs, vol. 1 : illegitimacy, patrimonial rights, and legal
nationalism in Luso-Brazilian inheritance, 1750–1821 / Linda Lewin.
    p.   cm.
  Includes bibliographical references and index.
  ISBN 0-8047-3881-5 (cloth : alk. paper) —
    1. Illegitimacy—Brazil—History—19th century.   2. Brazil—
Social conditions—19th century.   I. Title.

KHD520 .L49   2003
346.8105′2—dc21   2002010019

This book is printed on acid-free, archival-quality paper.

Original printing 2003

Last figure below indicates year of this printing:
        12   11   10   09   08   07   06   05   04   03

Designed and typeset at Stanford University Press in 10/13 Minion

For a new generation of historians of Brazil, who write the history of the family from the archives and frame their inquiry within a transatlantic perspective

Acknowledgments

Writing this book has been a great source of personal satisfaction not only because I gained a new perspective on the history of the family in Brazil but also because, initially, I did not believe I could write eighteenth-century legal history. The difficulty of mastering a legal literature that has become obsolete was more than matched by the challenge of locating rare legal commentaries authored between the 1780s and the 1820s. Precisely those works defining the major primary source for this analysis were widely scattered over a number of libraries in Brazil, Portugal, and the United States. For that reason, this book owes its existence to the generosity and the tireless professionalism of librarians who worked with me to locate an obscure legal literature. Far beyond the assistance one normally expects, several librarians offered me the extraordinary help that literally made this book a reality.

Martha Siqueira Cavalcanti, at the old library of the Faculdade de Direito do Recife (FDR), unearthed a treasure of nineteenth-century commentaries, treatises, and dissertations and put them at my disposal during several visits in the early 1990s. For her cheerfulness and willingness to search the darkest corners of that wonderful and most unforgettable of Brazil's earliest libraries, I will be eternally grateful. Thanks to her, the pivotal writings of Manoel de Almeida e Souza de Lobão came into my hands, together with commentaries by half a dozen other Portuguese jurists. For quite a while, Lobão's *Notas à Mello* offered my only access to the primary source that was fundamental for the interpretive approach followed in this book, Paschoal José de Mello Freire's *De jure personarum*, Book 2 of his *Institutiones civilis juris lusitani*. That is, until Rachel Barreto Edensword, former librarian of the Oliveira Lima Library, at Catholic University of America in Washington, D.C., surprised me with an extremely rare copy of the earliest Brazilian translation of *De jure personarum*. The fact that Francisco Pereira Freire, its author-annotator, had been a professor at Recife's famous law faculty, and produced his translation for his students, seemed very appropriate.

Thanks are also due to Maria Lucia Horta de Mello, of the Fundação Casa Rui Barbosa, in Rio de Janeiro, the archivist who brought me into the private world of Brazil's most famous republican jurist. She acquainted me with Rui's *pareceres*, or legal opinions, and one in particular that he authored on the fine points of matrimonial impediments. Iêda Siqueira Wiarda, librarian in charge of Brazilian sources at the Hispanic Collection of the Library of Congress, generously assisted me in obtaining timely access to selected volumes of the *Anais do Parlamento Brasileiro* and searched as far as Brasília for others. Those minutes of legislative debates made clear the historical significance of the eighteenth-century legacy of legal nationalism fashioned by jurists Mello Freire and Lobão. I am also very grateful to Ida Lewcowicz, of the History Department of the Universidade Estadual de São Paulo, Franca, who enabled me to use the library of former justice minister Alfredo Buzaid, recently acquired by her institution. During a brief and rewarding residence as a visiting professor, I found the final texts outstanding for this book among Min. Buzaid's impressive collection of legal commentaries. Thanks also go to Pedro Tórtima of the Instituto Histórico e Geográfico Brasileiro, Rio de Janeiro; and to both Eliane Pereira, of the Biblioteca Nacional's Rare Book Room, and José Gabriel Pinto, of the Arquivo Nacional, of Rio de Janeiro. Each of them helped me find elusive documentation.

Throughout the writing of this book, I often felt like a student of the law, because I approached my subject matter from the alien legal tradition of English common law. As my admiration grew for the jurists whose commentaries revealed the importance of Portugal's legal nationalism, I began to appreciate the irony that most of what I was reconstructing no longer mattered in contemporary Brazilian private law. The circumstance that there were no law professors who could explain all of the complexities of eighteenth-century inheritance law—for private law in Brazil has changed substantially since the advent of a republic in 1889—prompted me to approach my task as someone determined to solve a gigantic cross-word puzzle. An early and stimulating late-night conversation that I was fortunate to share with four professors from the University of São Paulo, all of whom wrote pioneering studies in Brazil's family history, furnished the spark that made me determined to solve that cross-word puzzle. Maria Luiza Marcílio, Laima Mesgraves, Eni Mesquita Samara, and Lia Fukui collectively pointed out that the position of non-legitimate individuals in family and inheritance law, as Brazil had moved from colony to independence, remained obscure. A clear picture of their evolutionary position within the overarching inheritance system was needed. I am particularly grateful to Maria Luiza Marcílio, of USP's History Department, who sponsored me as a visiting fellow at her institution in the initial phase of this project. She introduced me to the scholars who made the Centro de Demografia Histórica de América Latina (CEDHAL) that she founded the premier center for family history in Latin America. In São Paulo I also drew on the nineteenth-century library holdings of the FDR's sister institution, the Faculdade de Direito de São Paulo.

I have incurred many debts to my fellow scholars over the course of two decades. Several stand out for the tutoring and encouragement they offered me in the project's early stage. I am especially grateful to Mary Ann Glendon, of Harvard University Law School, and to Boston College Law School, for jointly sponsoring me as a visiting scholar in residence, when Mary Ann was teaching there. As an expert in comparative family law, she initiated me into the special features of a civil law tradition applying to the inheritance system. Without her guidance and personal interest in my project, I could not have unraveled the knotty complexities of Portugal's eighteenth-century legal tradition. To Ann Twinam of the University of Cincinnati, as one historian of Latin America to another, I am extremely indebted. She not only read the drafts of both volumes of this study and offered me the most valuable set of comments and criticisms one could hope to receive for undertaking revisions but she also proved an enthusiastic and encouraging collaborator. Through countless discussions on the subjects of crown legitimization and the Iberian context of legal bastardy, she helped me more than anyone else to delineate and clarify the central arguments in this study.

I have also benefited from the willingness of other historians of Brazil to offer me examples from their research in inheritance documents. Especially Hendrik Kraay, of the University of Calgary, and Kathleen Higgins, of the University of Iowa, deserve thanks, together with Dimas José Batista, formerly a graduate student at Unesp/Franca. They generously supplied the texts of wills that serve as illustrative examples in several chapters of this book. Hendrik Kraay also gave me extracts from imperial legal documents treating military law that clarified a great deal. Donald Ramos, of Cleveland University, assisted by providing the texts of several Pombaline laws. Anthropologist Mariza Corrêa, of the University of Campinas, who invited me to present some of the arguments of this book to her graduate seminar, deserves singular credit for inspiring my use of the *"herdeiro de surpresa"* for the title for this book. Paloma Fernández Pérez, my former graduate student who now teaches at the University of Barcelona, helpfully shared her own research and clarified the regional strands of Spanish inheritance law for me. Finally, Norris Pope, Editorial Director of Stanford University Press, deserves singular recognition and my deep appreciation as a collaborator who believed in the value of this book from the start. His encouragement, suggestions, and willingness to entertain two books on the subject of illegitimacy and inheritance law in Brazil was a constant inspiration.

A very special kind of appreciation is due fellow historians who gave generously of their time to offer me detailed, written comments on chapter drafts: Muriel Nazzari, Brian Juan O'Neill, Ted Riedinger, Patricia Seed, Mary Karasch, Dauril Alden, Keith Rosenn, Charles Hale, Hendrik Kraay, Marty Jay, Donna Guy, Jeff Needell, Bert Barickman, Paloma Fernández Pérez, and Sandra Lauderdale Graham. Keith Rosenn set me straight on Roman law and clarified my understanding of "legal nationalism," while calling the appropriateness of that term to my attention. Marty Jay brought Continental liberalism into a more finely tuned focus vis-à-vis its Brazilian variant. Any errors I have made in failing to heed their invaluable written comments and conversational pointers are strictly my own responsibility.

The financial support I received for this two-volume project was generous, extensive, and indispensable. A Tinker Post-Doctoral Fellowship, in tandem with a research travel grant from the Social Science Research Council and the American Council of Learned Societies, initially enabled me to spend an academic year as a research fellow in residence at Boston College Law School and the University of São Paulo. A Humanities Research Fellowship from the University of California, Berkeley, and a research travel award from the American Philosophical Society later offered me opportunity for a sabbatical semester of leave for follow-up research, as a visiting research scholar at the Fundação Casa de Rui Barbosa, Rio de Janeiro. Another Humanities Research Fellowship from UCB contributed toward a year of sabbatical leave for write-up in the mid-1990s and enabled me to expand the project's focus to what is now a two-volume study. Assistance from my department's Shepard Fund permitted me to work at the Oliveira Lima Library and the Library of Congress for nearly a month. The Shepard Fund also contributed to publication of this study. I especially wish to thank my friends and colleagues in the History Department, University of California, Berkeley, for believing in the merits of this book and for showing me infinite patience in waiting for its publication. At all of these institutions, I benefited from faculty, research staff, and graduate students, who as friends and colleagues shared their enthusiasm for a project that for me has been as much an amazing intellectual journey as the authorship of a book. It was a journey that made many disparate pieces of Brazil's history fit meaningfully together for the first time. I hope this book proves worthy of their kindness, support, and curiosity.

Contents

Preface

In the late eighteenth century, Sir William Blackstone proudly defended the English legal precept laid down by the Statute of Merton in 1234: "Once a bastard, always a bastard." The immutability of bastardy had formed part of a royal response to a question put forward by some of the same barons who several decades earlier had challenged the king over Magna Carta. The steadfastness of English law in upholding the Statute of Merton until Blackstone's day etched a cardinal difference in how two legal traditions, both originating in western Europe, treated illegitimate birth and defined bastardy. Furthermore, as Blackstone boasted, England's thirteenth-century statute admitted almost no loopholes, another circumstance leading him to draw a favorable contrast between his own legal tradition and that of the civil law countries of western Europe, where law offered ample opportunity to transform bastardy into legitimacy.[1]

In two respects, Blackstone's boast suggests the diverging line of inquiry pursued in this book, one that English-speaking readers will find alien to their own legal tradition. First, Blackstone's prideful assertion extolled the moral superiority of what essentially stood as the aberrant position of English law. In rejecting the principal loophole offered by Roman and canon law for mitigating bastard birth, late medieval law in Catholic England had diverged significantly from the rest of Catholic Europe. Thus Blackstone's exceptionalist position repudiated an important feature of the civil law tradition that had evolved throughout western Europe, above all in the Iberian countries of Spain and Portugal. Yet his tone of moral superiority continued to resonate within what by the close of the eighteenth century amounted to an Anglo-American legal tradition, one where illegitimacy assumed the proportions of an aberrant phenomenon rather than a commonplace occurrence. Although a post-colonial North America admitted some divergences from English legal practice, Blackstone essentially defined the stark judgment that would continue to color the moral evaluations of North Americans who shared the same, broad legal tradition.[2]

The second respect in which Blackstone's boastful pronouncement converges with the focus of this book rests precisely on how and why a Luso-Brazilian legal tradition failed to bifurcate individuals as "legitimate" or "illegitimate" and then impose those legal identities as permanent conditions. Instead, individuals born outside wedlock occupied a continuum ranging from quasi-legitimacy to bastardy, while law generously offered several ways for them to be legitimized. The availability of legitimization as the remedy for equipping individuals born outside marriage on a par with legitimate individuals explained the principal divide between how English and Portuguese legal traditions treated non-legitimate birth. Consequently, Iberian countries depended on a legal tradition that responded very differently to the question that a group of English barons put to Henry III at Merton in 1234. Nowhere is the contrast between the English and Iberian traditions more strikingly confirmed than in Portugal during the late eighteenth century. What by then amounted to a Luso-Brazilian legal tradition generously favored those born outside wedlock and carefully accorded them rights as individuals on the basis of whether they were born in either illicit or spurious unions.

Unlike Blackstone, who deserves to be read as the consummate spokesman for England's legal nationalism, the jurists who were his nationalistic counterparts in late eighteenth-century Portugal approached illegitimacy very differently. They sought to blur distinctions of birth deriving from unions unsanctified by matrimony and to liberalize, even to reverse, the "stain" of bastard birth in their legal tradition. Consequently, this book ventures into a realm of legal history unfamiliar to readers from an Anglo-American legal tradition, one that by Blackstone's time reflected pronounced dissonance over the treatment of illegitimate individuals in heirship. Blackstone preferred to condemn what in a civil law tradition Portuguese jurists attempted to enhance. From the 1750s onward, as jurisconsults and ministers of the crown, they devised or honed the juridical arguments that underlay important royal legislation removing illegitimate birth as a barrier to employment in crown civil service and judiciary, to university entrance, or even to contracting marriage. Equally important, their legal commentaries elaborated the juridical reasoning intended for use in royal courts, where the standing in inheritance law of individuals born outside wedlock would be generously reinterpreted. Portuguese jurists, for example, undermined their own legal tradition when they began to insist that "infamy" (*infame*) no longer intrinsically derived from the fact of bastard birth. Drawing on the

Enlightenment, they insisted that infamy resulted only from an individual's freely committed criminal acts against the state—from treason.

From a different perspective, this is a book resting on the commonplace of illegitimate birth in late colonial Brazil. Therefore, its stands as a history of the family taking law as the pivot. The attention paid to rights in heirship enjoyed by a population born outside wedlock complements the impressive amount of scholarly research undertaken by historians of the family in Brazil over the last three decades. Their digging in archives to unearth inheritance documents and parish records has produced a sophisticated picture of family life confirming the importance of unions that did not depend on the sacrament of matrimony. Moreover, what were late colonial or early imperial patterns of Brazilian family organization reflected significant continuities with Portuguese practices and attitudes about customary marriage and concubinage. Both of the latter were implied in the consensual unions generically identified as "*mancebia.*" More appropriately, the higher incidence of out-of-wedlock births associated with Luso-Brazilian family organization deserves appreciation as part of a Mediterranean, or southern European, pattern of family constitution that stands in marked contrast to either an English or a northern European pattern.[3]

Legal rights in heirship proceeded directly from an individual's "quality" of birth—what Brazilians of all walks of life identified as "*qualidade*" whenever they inquired if someone was of legitimate, illicit, or spurious birth. The history of the family in late colonial and imperial Brazil thus resonates with concepts deriving from a civil law tradition that penetrated vernacular speech. Central attention is paid throughout this book to the mutability of individual *qualidade*, thanks to rules of heirship that generously rewarded both the fact of paternal recognition and the great legal "equalizer" of legitimization. By the same token, legal notions about nobility, whether by descent or, as civil nobility, imposed "by the law," receive parallel emphasis as neglected criteria of heirship that operated in tandem with *qualidade*.

The "surprise heirs" featured in the titles of this two-volume study underscore both the suddenness and the unanticipated consequences of a Luso-Brazilian inheritance system whenever it disrupted the private sphere of legitimate family life. They also capture the impact of a juridical movement known as legal nationalism that gradually mitigated the position of natural and spurious offspring in positive law. Although surprise heirs figure more prominently in the second volume of this study, where illegitimacy, heirship, and legal reform are examined within the context of the Brazilian Empire (1822–1889), they nonetheless deserve consideration as intrinsic actors within the rules of heirship that occupy this volume's major focus. Legal change and juridical clarification throughout the second half of the eighteenth century enabled more individuals born outside marriage to assert claims to a parent's, usually a father's, patrimony. To do so, they increasingly went to court to petition for either paternal recognition or crown legitimization. Alternatively, illegitimate individuals aggressively contested the claims of a deceased parent's legitimate heirs, whether those heirs were children born in wedlock or other close collateral relatives.

"Surprise heirs" was a cliché that emerged only in the second half of the nineteenth century, to connote the appearance of an unexpected heir whose non-legitimate birth had either been concealed or denied by the dead parent. Although the fact of his or her existence was not always a surprise, the assertion of a claim to legitimate patrimony definitely was. Thus the cliché might subtly imply that a family strategy for denying patrimonial claims on the part of the legitimate heirs had gone awry. In fiction, the more literal meaning of the term prevailed, as when a previously unknown offspring who was not legitimate suddenly revealed his or her identity at the parent's funeral or the reading of the will. In the eighteenth century, of course, surprise heirs also appeared as actors in family dramas devoted to patrimonial issues. Although they did so in the context of legal change favorable to their claims, demanding rights in heirship that reached to medieval times, they were not as numerous as their successors in post-independence Brazil. Consequently, this volume anticipates and accounts for the emergence of the surprise heir as a more familiar challenger to legitimate family patrimony in imperial Brazil, by virtue of legal change. Surprise heirs were identified and resisted prior to Brazilian independence in terms other than the nineteenth-century cliché. If not scorned as "impostors," then they were disparaged as akin to "outsiders" (*estranhos*), the same term used to deprecate and withdraw rules of heirship that favored distant cousins, especially those so geographically far flung that they were not recognized as kin within the kindred's inner core.

This book began as an introductory chapter about the position of non-legitimate individuals in Brazil's inheritance system on the eve of independence, in 1822. Subsequently, it metamorphosized into the first of a two-volume study devoted exclusively to their position in heirship during the final seven decades of Brazil's colonial history. The decision to pay major attention to both the inheritance system and the position that non-legitimate individuals occupied in inheritance law followed from a discovery made in analyzing the first three decades of the *Anais do Parlamento Brasileiro*. This record of parliamentary debates dating to 1823 revealed that political discourse on illegitimacy and inheritance matter-of-factly articulated reference to "*direito pátrio*," or national law. Better identified as "legal nationalism," the term's narrowest application pertained to key positive national law adopted in Portugal during the era of the king's first minister, the marquis of Pombal (Sebastião José de Carvalho e Mello), from 1750 to 1777. Brazilian legislators, however, invoked "*direito pátrio*" in terms of its fundamentally broader connotation of legal culture. They accepted Pombaline legal nationalism as their juridical heritage whenever they debated reforming features of inheritance law, frequently, because they had imbibed it as politico-legal culture at the Law Faculty of Coimbra University. In doing so, they followed the interpretive lead of that institution's most distinguished law professor and Portugal's foremost proponent of legal nationalism, Paschoal José de Mello Freire dos Reys (1738–1798).

Sharing the homogeneity of a late colonial legal tradition inherited from Portugal, Brazil's early imperial lawmakers also sought to fulfill what had been a Pombaline political agenda of reform that encompassed key features of the inheritance system, including the legal position of illegitimate offspring in heirship. Furthermore, those legislators depended on legal commentaries until the 1850s that continued to be authored by Portuguese jurists. Consequently, this volume represents an effort to capture a legal tradition overlooked by historians of imperial Brazil as much as it offers a reconstruction of the position of non-legitimate individuals in the inheritance system so profoundly recast by legal nationalism.

The Introduction offers readers, especially those who are Anglophone, a brief summary of the evolution of the Luso-Brazilian legal tradition within which inheritance and family law are situated throughout this book. It presents the features of a civil law tradition common to both Portugal and Spain, one that originated in the *jus comun* shared by western European countries formerly governed by Rome. The Introduction also offers a valuable explanation of the sources of law that, by the fifteenth century, found their way into Portugal's first national law code, known as the *Ordenações do Reino*. The multiple strands of national positive law, that is, all law in force, whether written or customary, receive initial emphasis. Historically, the tension between Roman and canon law on the one hand, and, on the other, between both of the latter and what became identified as "*direito pátrio*," punctuated the efforts of Portugal's monarchs to centralize their political power vis-à-vis both church and nobility. Custom proved an important and controversial source of law in Portugal, especially where marriage, dowry, and matrimonial property mattered. The ambiguous toleration of forms of customary and de facto marriage—immortalized in popular speech as "marriage according to the *Ordenações*"—simultaneously with the sacrament of matrimony, figured importantly in high rates of out-of-wedlock births in both Portugal and Brazil.

Codes, a central feature of the civil law tradition, figure in the introductory discussion as important repositories of Roman law as well as projects of state that reflected the Portuguese crown's growing reliance on the figure of the jurist trained in Roman civil law. The sources of law, codification, and, eventually, the reception of the Articles of the Council of Trent, all signified the expanding role that law played in consolidating Portugal's national monarchy from the late Middle Ages through the eighteenth century. The tension between church and state historically exerted a profound impact on how legal marriage—and, by extension, illegitimacy—would be defined over the long run. Finally, in concluding with the emergence of the movement of legal nationalism in the 1750s, the Introduction briefly connects eighteenth-century legal culture to the eve of Brazilian independence.

Chapter 1 reconstructs the broad features of what, by the time the Portuguese court emigrated to Rio de Janeiro, in 1808, was a Luso-Brazilian inheritance system. It introduces readers to what republican jurist Clovis Bevilaqua described at the end of the nineteenth century as the "dense forest" of Brazil's system of succession. In fact, it introduces readers to what were *two* discrete and parallel systems of succession, one *ab intestato* and legitimate, or natural, and the other testamentary.[4] Relying on Jack Goody's apt construct, that the intergenerational transmission of property amounts to a mechanism of "diverging devolution," this chapter surveys the major features of the inheritance system. Thus it ties rules of succession, as well as the disposition of testamentary bequests, to related arrangements of dowry, matrimonial property, and gifts inter vivos.[5] Beyond laying out the elementary operation of the inheritance system, discussion illustrates how, under the impact of legal nationalism, the inheritance system was reformulated between 1754 and 1821. The ladder of intestate succession that remained in effect in Brazil until 1907 is given central attention as the embodiment of the basic rules of heirship that Pombaline Portugal recast in 1754. The more conceptually complex operation of testamentary succession, with its subset of universal heirship, similarly figures prominently in this chapter, due to its central relevance for heirs who enjoyed crown legitimization. Given that family and inheritance law represented a major concern of the movement known as legal nationalism, this introductory overview ties the post-1754 reform of the inheritance system to the ideological imperatives of the absolutist state.

Chapters 2 and 3 respectively explain and illustrate the position of natural and spurious offspring within the dual system of succession elaborated from

Portugal's national code of laws, the *Ordenações Filipinas* of 1603. Each chapter in turn focuses on the key variables of birth and gender that defined patrimonial rights. They attempt to clarify a historiography that often has confused paternal recognition with crown legitimization or, otherwise, has not apprehended how the latter rested on procedures depending on a Pombaline revision of the *Ordenações Filipinas*. Chapter 2 underscores the importance of natural offspring, and their uniqueness in a European civil law tradition, as the possessors of a discrete identity in heirship following from parental recognition. From a historiographical perspective, this chapter considers natural offspring "a lost population of heirs" and offers an innovative analysis of their distinctive position in inheritance law that ties their legal position to popularly validated social norms. Consequently, paternal recognition, because it conferred patrimonial rights on natural offspring, occupies central attention. By the same token, the right to a judicial recognition of paternity, the cornerstone of their position in heirship, is evaluated within a historical context of late eighteenth-century legal change. By bringing this enormous population of heirs to center stage, the chapter foreshadows the growing significance of natural offspring in post-independence Brazil and, therefore, anticipates the surprise heir.

Chapter 3, by analogously visiting the position that spurious offspring enjoyed in law, takes their uniqueness as legal bastards for a starting point. Beyond discriminating discrete sub-categories of spurious birth and examining how law denied each succession rights, this chapter elaborates how law nonetheless implied differential access to patrimonial rights on the basis of gender as well as birth. The remedy of crown legitimization enabled many spurious individuals to "repair" their "defect" of birth, whenever conferred by the monarch's "grace and mercy." However, discussion pursues several contexts where parents used testamentary devices that contravened law, on the assumption that merely their simple legitimization would convey rights in inheritance. The engendered position of the child of unknown father receives central attention, both in terms of matrilineal inheritance rights and as a prototype for the "surprise heir."

Crown legitimization, the legal loophole for those whose quality of birth denied them succession rights, receives important scrutiny in a chapter exclusively devoted to clarifying its application as a royal "dispensation" that conveyed profound social advantages as well as succession rights. Chapter 4 dissects how law defined and mediated quality of birth when it was attached to either parent's nobility. Consequently, the discussion offers an important reassessment of how historians of Brazil have treated the subject of nobility, by revising the excessive emphasis placed on titleholding. It draws directly on late eighteenth- and early nineteenth-century laws that expanded what this study construes throughout as "minimal" nobility and connects the latter to the mechanism of crown legitimization before the Tribunal of the Desembargo do Paço. The analysis situates the "defect" of color as a social criterion, vis-à-vis the "defect" of birth, in order to ascertain if the latter acquired related and new meaning as a social marker by independence. Minimal nobility, it is argued in Volume 2, would closely correspond to the "active" citizenship introduced by Brazil's Constitution of 1824. By linking the importance of minimal nobility, especially Pombaline "civil nobility," to crown legitimization, this chapter anticipates the bills that Brazil's imperial legislators introduced to reform the position of natural and spurious offspring.

The last chapter takes legal nationalism as its subject matter. Chapter 5 assumes the career and writings of Portugal's most distinguished eighteenth-century jurist, Paschoal José de Mello Freire dos Reys, as central for retrieving the statist ideology that penetrated Portugal's juridical culture. The political means for achieving a fundamental reformulation of national law during the ministry of the marquis of Pombal is analyzed in terms of the dual pillars on which it rested: the 1769 Lei da Boa Razão, or Law of Right Reason, and the curricular reform of Coimbra University's Law Faculty that the latter both anticipated and authorized. As this chapter makes clear, the *Ordenações Filipinas* came under substantial revision after 1750, suggesting for historians of the family that the law relevant to their research could no longer necessarily be found in that famous code of 1603, but in the statutory legislation that supplanted it. Mello Freire's reformulation of law, especially the private law of family and inheritance, is appraised according to his classic text, especially Book 2 of the *Institutiones juris civilis lusitani*, published on the cusp of the French Revolution. His interpretations of legitimization, bastardy, and the "*quaesito*" of unknown father receive emphasis as constructs that found their way into the legal commentaries providing Brazil's first legislators with their basic understanding of illegitimacy and heirship.

The Conclusion pursues Mello Freire's significance in post-independence Brazil for liberal reformers who continued to depend on the legal nationalism he articulated, as well as for the Portuguese jurists who, as disseminators of that cultural tradition, subsequently authored nineteenth-century commentaries that were authoritatively received until the 1850s. By stressing the continuity in politico-legal culture, it ties Brazil's early liberalism to eighteenth-century legal nationalism.

As an indispensable primary source, the legal commentary, along with its counterparts, the treatise and the dissertation, offers the key for decoding inheritance documents and reading the social history they unlock for a given time or place. The historian who consults the legal commentaries used as primary sources throughout this book will discover that they were not written for beginners. They assume more knowledge of a civil law tradition than anyone brought up in an Anglo-American legal tradition could easily apprehend. They also leave a great deal implicit. Yet even a Brazilian conversant with the civil law and the notion of forced heirship will find those legal commentaries initially intimidating. Brazil's "return" to Roman law in the last quarter of the nineteenth century increased the intellectual distance between the essentially Pombaline texts used as evidence in this book and the new juridical discourse popularized by the Pandectists who reaffirmed the utility of Roman law in the second half of the century. What civil law jurists termed "doctrine," the accepted precepts in national jurisprudence that turned on both philosophical and logical assumptions, and also implied precise procedures, again began to shift. Thanks to Augusto Teixeira de Freitas' *Consolidações das leis civis* (1857), Brazilian jurists rediscovered the utility of Roman law so extolled by European Pandectists. The consequent abandonment, after a century, of much of the eclectic approach inherent in eighteenth-century legal nationalism still matters today, wherever historians who are Brazilian consult legal commentaries published prior to 1860.

Some readers of this book will be "hands-on" researchers pursuing the task of archival research in eighteenth- and nineteenth-century inheritance documents in Brazil. In deciphering a documentary arcana that spanned the gamut of inventories, estate divisions known as *partilhas*, wills, contracts for dowry and dower, and notarized affidavits declaring paternity—but very rarely, maternity—they work empirically with discrete pieces of an overarching system of inheritance. Yet its dynamic evolution is not always known to them. Nor are the ways the parts fit together necessarily transparent. I have tried to take their task of interpretation into account, even as I wondered if those "front-line" historians might object that the attention paid to the rules of heirship in these pages is misplaced. What really matters, they may insist, is practice: What did inheritance documents *say*? Not were they written in compliance with law. In this respect, the crotchety voice of "Lobão"—Manuel de Almeida e Souza de Lobão—has echoed in my ear. He spent the first twenty-five years of his career working as a lawyer in the royal courts. Impatient with the abstractions of his law professors, and their legal commentaries, he took them to task in his *Notas à Mello* for their ignorance of how law was applied in the courtroom.[6] Like Lobão's "Notes of Practical and Critical Use," this book offers a utilitarian dimension that accompanies a

fundamental interpretation. Only by becoming familiar with rules of heirship and their implications for a *system* of inheritance can historians who
work with the archival documents accurately interpret them.

The approach offered herein does not assume that legal documents pertaining to inheritance necessarily conformed to the letter of the law. Nor
should historical researchers using those documents assume they were deliberately executed in fulfillment of law. Quite the contrary. Documents could
be and were drawn up in direct contradiction of law. Consequently, I have
tried to articulate and explain rules of heirship pertaining to those who were
not legitimate, knowing very well that the rules could be ignored. My assumption throughout is that, unless the historian has a firm grasp of both the
rules of heirship and how the logic of the overarching system of inheritance
worked, then neither accurate nor meaningful conclusions can be drawn
from documents to produce a richly nuanced interpretation. Thus the historian's first task in interpreting a document is to decide whether it was written
to comply with law or to evade it. The lacunae in documents, often deliberate omissions, are what ought to draw the attention of the historian who
reads them.

Put differently, the texts of those documents should be read with an eye
to eliciting specific strategies in heirship. Where documents deviated from
what law prescribed, we must ask whether the historical significance of such
a deviation did not lie more in validating social practice. Practically speaking,
invalid wills and *partilhas* could frequently dispose of patrimony as long as
the co-heirs concurred in the dispositions. Probably in no other area of law
than rules of heirship applying to those born outside legitimate wedlock is
such inquiry more worth pursuing. Any accurate extraction of inferences
about social behavior derived from those documents, however, must pre-
suppose a fairly sophisticated understanding of juridical concepts, rules, and
legal language over time.[7]

Throughout this book, a Brazilian context is situated within a broader,
Latin American context. Much of the discussion of the inheritance system, as
well as the contours of family formation discussed herein, holds analogous
relevance for Spanish America, despite the differences prescribed by national
codes of law. Those codes nonetheless drew on many common sources of
law, not to mention a dynastic collaboration that over centuries implied a
certain convergence in national law. Legal nationalism flourished in Bourbon Spain as well as Pombaline Portugal, although it found much bolder ar-
ticulation under the Bragança monarchy.[8] Furthermore, Portuguese organizational patterns of family and concubinage, like the legal position of individuals born outside wedlock, will be very familiar to scholars of Spanish

America as variants on a common Iberian theme.⁹ Portugal's inheritance system and historically high incidences of non-legitimate births bear direct comparison with those of Spain, but both suggest they deserve greater incorporation within the scholarly literature treating "the European family." The Iberian historical context establishes that neither "illegitimacy" nor "bastardy" could be reduced to a common denominator that inscribed all of western Europe.¹⁰

Beyond providing a comprehensive understanding of a Luso-Brazilian inheritance system, and a finely nuanced analysis of the respective positions of natural and spurious individuals within that system, this volume offers the new and crucial dimension of evolutionary legal change that recast the inheritance system during the final seven decades of Portugal's colonial rule of Brazil. Furthermore, statist ideology *cum* legal nationalism provided the raison d'être for the legal change that Brazil's early liberal legislators promoted after 1822, in their efforts to establish a modern and secularized inheritance system. Consequently, this book offers an interpretation tying the Brazilian liberal attack on distinctions of estate or birth that is the subject of Volume 2 to the preceding age of absolutism in Portugal. This approach innovates by declining to respect the conventional divide of Brazilian independence. Instead, it suggests the notion of "a middle period" running roughly from the 1750s to the 1840s, during which a great deal of both late colonial structures and absolutist ideology endured. Therefore, the era of independence offered a timely and compelling opportunity for liberal legislators to extend and expand currents of reform that had first been fostered in the eighteenth century as part of a crown agenda of legal nationalism, but it also witnessed the survival of many features inherent in the political ethos of the age of absolutism.

Fundamentally an interpretation of family in late colonial Brazil, this book takes as its inspiration an assumption held by the jurists who propounded legal nationalism, that, *entre outras coisas*, national law served as the repository of "our customs." In other words, social practices and values determining the nature of family, concubinage, or marriage at a popular level acquired the legitimacy of national positive law. Furthermore, they defined the essence of what it meant to be either "Portuguese" or "Brazilian." Therefore, all that is left to say is that the task of writing the history of the family in late colonial and early imperial Brazil should turn on locating within the realities of social attitudes and behaviors that defined the meaning of "family" those very abstractions of private law that presumed to validate them.

A Note on Legal Language and Brazilian Orthography and Names

Language, especially the language of law in the eighteenth and nineteenth centuries, plays a central role in this study. The terms used in this book frequently differ from legal terminology currently in use in Brazil. Deviation often reflects more than merely a linguistic shift, however. Today, the legal concepts have often changed from what they were two hundred years ago. Consequently, English cannot always supply precise equivalents. If they exist in Anglo-American law, equivalent terms may imply different outcomes. Consequently, I have sometimes used archaic English to render language derived from a Luso-Brazilian legal tradition, as in the practice of "calling" the legitimate heirs to succeed. Otherwise, Brazilian readers will discover constructs that are central to discussion, such as "*qualidade*," an individual's quality of birth, no longer matter in their inheritance system. In matters of inheritance, Jack Goody has reminded us, "It is not easy to be precise unless we are technical."[1] Although I have translated Portuguese legal terms into English wherever they do correspond to Anglo-American legal concepts, there is a strong case to be made for retaining Portuguese where English "synonyms" either do not exist or imply different constructs, meanings, or outcomes. Rather than trying to harmonize linguistically what are really notions fundamentally alien to Anglo-American usage today, I have deliberately left a small number of those terms dissonant by retaining Portuguese terms. To do otherwise would be to blunt, to distort and misrepresent, or to confuse analysis of change over the century this book addresses.

Readers may initially be puzzled as to why I have not spoken consistently throughout the book of "illegitimacy" and "illegitimate" offspring, and, instead, alternated the latter with terms like "non-legitimate" or "out-of-wedlock." One reason is to avoid reliance on the dichotomy familiar from Anglo-American law that rigidly opposes "legitimate" to "illegitimate." Luso-Brazilian legal tradition demonstrated a spectrum of intermediate positions rather than a bifurcation of legal birth status. Another is to favor deliberate usage of "natural" and "spurious" offspring, as opposed to merging both as "illegitimate offspring." Sometimes even much finer discrimination is warranted, for alternate terms were operative in Brazil and Portugal until the twentieth century: *incestuosos, adulterinos,* and *sacrílegos,* as well as *quaesitos* and *expostos.* Basically, however, I have retained the language Brazilians used to designate those born out of wedlock for the period under study, because I wanted to convey how individuals from all walks of life labeled and thought about people who lacked legitimate birth. Although, historically, Anglo-American legal tradition has not discriminated finely among those who were illegitimate, it is also the case today that even Brazilians are much less likely to apply the finely tuned discrimination that was second nature to their grandparents or great-grandparents.

"Illegitimate" is a term taken from the civil law. Normally, Brazilian vernacular speech during the Empire and colonial period preferred the finer discrimination supplied by canon law. Although "illegitimacy" and "illegitimate" were not alien to the vocabulary of either jurists or ordinary people throughout the period this book spans, the language of canon law supplied the analytical constructs of an individual's "quality of birth." Those constructs, received in national positive law, underlay the social categories people regularly used in vernacular speech. Therefore, a crown jurist in Pombal's Lisbon and an illiterate farmer in Brazil's era of independence spoke the same language when they identified an individual as a "natural" child rather than an "illegitimate" child. In other words, religion, as much as inheritance law, inculcated the vocabulary of heirship used in this book and accounted for why the language of canon law penetrated popular speech. Rather than applying constructs of illegitimacy contemporary with the twenty-first century, I have tried to suggest those appropriate to the context spanning 1750 to 1821. The result is greater nuance and cultural shading, not to mention legal precision.

In one case, I have opted to retain a Latin term as the equivalent for Portuguese usage when a perfectly acceptable English equivalent exists: *ab intestato.* The reason that I have not adopted "intestate" as a translation is that it would only distract North American and British readers from appreciating the fundamental difference between their system of succession and the Luso-Brazilian system analyzed in this book. My initial effort to isolate the essence of what nineteenth-century legal commentators usually wrote as "*abintestado*" led me to discard "intestate," the better to focus on what a Luso-Brazilian context implied. The term conjures up a fundamental difference in an Anglo-American legal tradition—nearly the opposite meaning in a Luso-

Brazilian legal tradition. "*Ab intestato*" is synonymous with "legitimate" or "natural" succession and it presumes the natural order of events in Luso-Brazilian succession. That order is one where a will is unnecessary, because the rules of forced heirship determine the division of an estate and offer re-assurance that the identity of the heirs is already known. In Anglo-American legal tradition, on the other hand, "intestate" implies a lapse—the failure to write a will. "Intestate" therefore can imply a family catastrophe, or at least a dissonant order of events that threatens to overturn normative expectations about heirship.

Finally, "intestate" implies the state's intervention is needed to identify and verify the authenticity of the heirs in an Anglo-American legal tradition. Those heirs, like wills, must be proved in a court of law. In the Luso-Brazilian legal tradition relevant to this book, the state remained rather marginal to legitimate or natural succession. Certainly succession took place without its intervention, a circumstance largely explaining why no tax was levied on *ab intestato* heirs in Brazil until the second half of the nineteenth century.

Ab intestado succession in Luso-Brazilian law was also carefully distinguished from testamentary succession, the latter being the exception rather than the rule—and again, the opposite of Anglo-American practice. Hence, by relying on the device of "*ab intestato*" throughout the text, I am encouraging North American and British readers to stop thinking in terms of the assumptions, concepts, and rules of Anglo-American succession. I am asking them to don the mentality of an eighteenth-century civil law tradition, one where the heirs were already known and the lack of a will frequently defined the best scenario.

Brazilian orthography has varied considerably since the eighteenth century. The text of this book has modernized the spelling of archaic legal terms as well as the titles of legal codes, but left them unaltered in the notes and bibliographies. I have, however, spelled the names of individuals mentioned in the text of this book according to the usage in vogue when they were alive, meaning that names have usually been left consistent with the orthography specific to the sources cited in the notes. Given the latest orthographic reform that removes many diacritical marks from Portuguese, early nineteenth-century spelling now more closely approximates early twenty-first-century spelling. Because historically there were no firm rules governing how people in Portugal and Brazil projected their names, not only the spelling of names but also the ways that individuals idiosyncratically manipulated their discrete name sets varied considerably. To a much lesser extent, this phenomenon continues to be true in Brazil down to the present. This is to say that Portuguese often prefers first names, even nicknames, wherever they are sufficiently uncommon or unique to obviate use of a concatenation of family names. Consequently, sometimes I have applied a lone rule of thumb that is still used in Brazil today. Individuals with uncommon or unique first names are often identified on a first-name basis, just as in the 1980s the Brazilian press referred to Prime Minister Margaret Thatcher as "Margaret."

Frequently, I have shortened jurists' complex string of family names to the forms they used to refer to each other in their legal commentaries. Therefore, they are identified initially in terms of their full names and then only mentioned by the short forms. Thus Manoel de Almeida e Souza de Lobão was universally identified simply as "Lobão," and Lafayette Rodrigues Pereira became "Lafayette." In homage to Candido Mendes de Almeida, imperial Brazil's great jurist, he is identified obliquely in this book by the name Brazilians still use to refer to him, given his fame and the uniqueness of his first, Brazilian edition of the *Philippine Code*: "Candido Mendes." The list of Legal Primary Sources Cited, found at the end of this book, facilitates the referencing of jurists' full names for readers.

Individuals are identified by their noble titles, although their full names are offered initially. I have retained the honorific "*dom*" and "*dona*," which both Portuguese and Brazilians employed in lieu of the title "King" or "Queen," abbreviated as in "D. João VI" and "D. Maria I." Otherwise, I have followed standard usage and applied "*dom*" to several prelates of the Brazilian church. As this volume clarifies, the honorific "*dom*" also applied widely to individuals who were either noble by descent or ennobled by the monarch. Women were analogously identified as "*dona*." This designation inscribed all military officers and their wives. However, those whose nobility was merely civil, conferred by the law and therefore "secondary," did not enjoy the right to be addressed as "*dom*."

The laws that comprise the primary sources for this volume are identified in terms of a myriad of designations originally dictated by usage employed by the Portuguese crown. Statutory law, the most important source cited herein, was attributed to the sovereign and identified as "legislation," notwithstanding the absence of a legislature. Statutes were issued in the form of an *alvará* synonymous with "law" in English. After Brazilian independence, either "law" (*lei*) or "decree" (*decreto*), and even "decree-law" (*decreto-lei*), supplanted "*alvará*." The indiscriminate use of both "law" and "decree," sometimes applied to the same statute, may confound readers. It also confounded jurists, who understood that "law" and "decree" were virtually synonymous. In Portugal, lamented legal historian João Gomes B. Câmara, "the inexplicable distinction between 'law' and 'decree' was not resolved until

1936," when "law" triumphed. He offered a fine point doubtlessly accounting for the persistence of a dual nomenclature. A decree emanated from the legislature, but only the monarch's sanction, or signature, made it a "law."[2] In Brazil's case, the abolition of the monarchy in 1889 brought this duality to a close.

The other main source of law cited in this volume is, of course, the *Ordenações do Reino*, the four, successive compilations of Portuguese positive law that were promulgated as national codes of law between 1446 and 1603. References to the *Ordenações Filipinas* of 1603 herein refer to Candido Mendes de Almeida's monumental 14th edition, published in 1870, the first to offer juridical commentary in terms of Brazilian law: *Codigo Philippino ou Ordenações do Reino de Portugal . . . .*[3] Otherwise, law in both colonial and early imperial Brazil consistently drew on administrative orders and clarifications, such as *avisos*, that were issued by the king's ministers or, in imperial Brazil, by the cabinet ministers associated with parliamentary government. Procedural law, such as that pertaining to high crown courts like the Tribunal of the Mesa do Desembargo do Paço, usually was defined in discrete "*regimentos*" or sets of regulations having the force of law. By the same token, the decisions of high crown courts, termed "*estilos*," frequently were cited as law throughout colonial and imperial centuries. A list of abbreviations for these administrative and judicial forms of law has been prepared for readers.

In order to facilitate readers' access to the legal sources employed in writing this volume, they have been gathered in a separate list entitled Legal Primary Sources Cited. It consists of legal commentaries, treatises, dissertations, and notarial manuals, as well as law codes and collections of statutory law. The lengthy nature of legal titles means that some have been abbreviated. Where relevant to discussion in the text, occasionally the first editions of legal commentaries have been included in the Legal Primary Sources Cited, especially when I consulted a different edition. Footnotes herein employ what usually were the standard abbreviations devised by jurists to cite legal commentaries in terms of their titles and discrete parts: books, volumes, chapters, titles, sections, and so forth. I have inserted the relevant page numbers in parentheses to assist readers who want to locate specific references, because most legal commentaries used for this book ran to many editions, meaning that their pagination varied, and the textual sub-divisions and lengthy footnotes spilled over many pages. Legal histories have been included in the Other Sources Cited, as have the wills in manuscript lent to me by several scholars.

SURPRISE HEIRS

Volume 1

Illegitimacy, Patrimonial Rights, and Legal Nationalism in Luso-Brazilian Inheritance, 1750-1821

Today, no one can ignore how much *direito pátrio*, or its study, is altered from what it was. The laws of the last two monarchies and the new form given to the Law Faculty of Coimbra University, thanks to His Majesty, D. José, will produce a revolution among us.
                    Antonio Joaquim Antonio de Gouvêa Pinto, 1813

Legislation and jurisprudence took a new direction. The laws acquired a vainglorious air, their language devoid of meaning and convoluted by irrelevancies. What was singular was that Roman law, which had been the vehicle for transporting the absolutist regime for centuries, was, with notable ingratitude, pronounced ruinous.
                    Candido Mendes de Almeida, 1870

Introduction

———————•◆◆◆•———————

> From the beginning of the monarchy until His Majesty, D. Afonso
> V, laws applying to wills were almost not used, only customs
> adapted to canon and Roman law. D. Afonso V was the first to
> have these customs written down, adding to them many things de-
> duced from Roman law, which he put in his Code. They can be
> found in Book Four . . . what passed afterward into the Manueline
> and Philippine Codes.
>
> Desembargador Antonio Joaquim de Gouvêa Pinto,
> <i>Tratado Pratico de testamentos e successões</i> (1813)[1]</div>

Only since the late 1970s have historians considered the features and evolution of Brazil's inheritance system, including dowry and the marriage regulation.[2] They have done so as researchers concerned with uncovering common
practices among groups owning varying amounts of property, and primarily
through documents found in local archives, especially for the provinces of
São Paulo, Rio de Janeiro, Minas Gerais, and Bahia. When attention has been
paid to law, ecclesiastical law has received deserving emphasis. Considerable
interest has continued to focus on episcopal visits dedicated to enforcing
canon law in eighteenth-century contexts, with the result that social behavior
and community values often have been revealed to differ markedly from ecclesiastical law.[3]

More recently, greater attention has been paid to marriage and concubinage in Brazilian history, bringing to light the growing significance of a large
population born outside wedlock. In bringing marriage and concubinage
under historical scrutiny, scholars have singled out how law regulated the
private sphere of family life and paid emphasis to the provisions of the *Ordenações do Reino*, Portugal's national code of law, as well as to the *Constituições primeiras do arcebispado da Bahia*, which eventually acquired authority as an ecclesiastical "constitution" for all of Brazil. Where marriage was
concerned, canon law carried legal effect in Brazil until 1889. The intersection of positive and canon law—above all, the ambiguous incorporation in
positive law of the articles on marriage adopted by the Council of Trent

(1545–1563)—has enjoyed growing interest in the historical literature, causing historians to explore patterns of consensual cohabitation that fell short of sacramental marriage. Consensual cohabitation, ambiguously denominated "*mancebia*," was remarkably tolerated, and, in certain contexts, it admitted de jure recognition as customary and de facto marriage, forms sanctioned by the *Ordenações*. Clandestine marriage, explicitly prohibited at Trent, defined yet another variant of *mancebia*. Alternatively, when *mancebia* denoted concubinage, whether lay or clerical, it received similar toleration in the community.[4]

Yet where the broad subject of inheritance is concerned, historical research rarely has reflected the interaction of changing legal rules and social behavior over time. Nor, for that matter, do we know much about the reasons why inheritance law changed between adoption of the *Ordenações Filipinas* in 1603 and promulgation of Brazil's first civil code in 1916. Scholarship on Brazil's past has not taken sufficient account of the importance of the inheritance system per se for a plethora of social, economic, and political arrangements.[5] For the agrarian society that defined Brazil on the eve of independence, the inheritance system offers the master key for unlocking economic organization and social arrangements. Many nuances of individual behavior remain undetected in documents simply because those who read them continue to be misinformed or unfamiliar with the law's basic rules of heirship. Only when those rules become central to analyses of change will the social history of Brazil be written as a more subtle and complex undertaking.[6]

How individuals approached the disposition of their patrimony in ingenious ways that intentionally circumvented law needs to be taken directly into account, if historical imagination is to recapture the subtle features of social life in imperial Brazil. Not only the situation of individuals born outside wedlock is subject to ignorance or misunderstanding, but also the basic rules of heirship applying to those who were of legitimate birth have too frequently been overlooked. Those rules held crucial implications for patterns of land tenure and sales or transfers of real property, in addition to commercial or capital investments, business partnerships, and, eventually, the issuance of stocks and bonds and the establishment of mortgage banks.

Rules of heirship drew on Roman and canon law as well as customary arrangements, the latter frequently being articulated by Germanic law, given the Visigothic and Swabian presence in the Iberian peninsula during the early Middle Ages. Yet what became a Luso-Brazilian system of inheritance underwent substantial modification during the second half of the eighteenth century, thanks to a juridical movement known as legal nationalism. Familiarity with the civil law tradition within which Portugal's inheritance system evolved, consequently, is essential as a preliminary step for grasping rules of heirship that largely derived from Roman law. Codification, for instance, sets off the European countries sharing a civil law tradition from the British Isles, Canada, and the United States. So does a partitive system of inheritance, one where heirs are "forced" and inheritance portions are "equal." Furthermore, canon law directly determined individual quality of birth, and thus rights in heirship for a civil law tradition, according to rules that were not always received in Anglo-American positive law. Consequently, the ways in which a Luso-Brazilian inheritance system depended on a civil law tradition differed from an Anglo-American inheritance system grounded in the common law. The differences between those two legal traditions largely accounted for the vastly different position individuals born outside marriage occupied in each inheritance system.

LUSO-BRAZILIAN LEGAL TRADITION

Roman Law and the Civil Law Tradition

Law in imperial Brazil drew fundamentally on a Portuguese legal tradition, accounting for why it is appropriate to situate analysis of Brazil's juridical evolution within what was a "Luso-Brazilian" legal tradition. By the second half of the eighteenth century, that tradition still rested fundamentally on Portugal's late sixteenth-century law code known as the *Ordenações Filipinas*, or Philippine Code. However, it also reflected considerable and recent legal change directed toward modifying or discarding the latter. Promulgated in 1603, the *Ordenações Filipinas* had been compiled by Spanish and Portuguese jurists appointed by Philip II in 1595. The last in a series of four national codes reaching to the late Middle Ages, the Philippine Code nevertheless conserved essentially Portuguese legal features. It endured in Brazil until 1916, when adoption of a civil code finally fulfilled the mandate of Brazil's 1824 Constitution. On the other hand, Brazil's imperial legislators lost no time in revising or annulling provisions of the *Ordenações Filipinas*, starting in the 1820s. They did so mindful of the legal tradition they shared with the former metropole, for they were obliged to rely exclusively on legal commentaries authored by Portuguese jurists for the first three decades of their independence.

As a western European nation once part of the Roman Empire, Portugal acquired a legal tradition that both retained Roman law after Roman rule collapsed and acquired it anew as part of a European revival initiated in the eleventh century. This circumstance would set the former colony of Brazil apart from the common law tradition of the Anglo-American world. By the same token, the revival of Roman law would explain why Brazil shared many features common to the legal tradition of its Spanish American neighbors. Portugal's civil law tradition drew fundamentally on the revival of Roman law that began in Bologna and reintroduced the late imperial legal texts produced by Emperor Justinian's jurists. What is called the *Corpus Juris Civilis* consisted of a core of four works produced during the sixth century under Justinian's supervision: the Digest (also the Pandects), Institutes, second Code, and Novels, or New Constitutions. Although these texts fell into disuse during the Germanic invasions, their impact continued to be felt in law codes adopted by the peoples who supplanted Roman power in western Europe. The civil law systems that emerged, consequently, have often been regarded as "Romano-Germanic," rather than merely "Roman" or "Romanist."[7]

Although the codes adopted by the Germanic successors of the Romans came to be regarded as "barbarian legislation," they, too, bore the stamp of Roman law. For instance, Portugal's Visigothic Code, the *Lei Wisigodo,* or *Lex Gothorum,* better known as the *Liber Judicorum* (654) and promulgated in final form in 694, was the Germanic code most heavily influenced by Roman law. Yet it also diverged from the written law of the Romans that medieval scholars construed as *ratio scripta,* or "written reason," and considered more prestigious. The Visigothic Code incorporated what came to be regarded as "vulgar" Roman law—what amounted to much of the "living law" practiced in the former Roman territories by peoples the Romans had conquered. This circumstance, that initially a great deal of the Germanic law in practice was not written, but exerted the force of custom in the early Middle Ages, accounts for why regalist jurists in eighteenth-century Portugal returned to the Visigothic Code, in reaction against a preceding, excessive reliance on late imperial Roman law. They saw in Visigothic law one of the repositories for "our customs," a source of law favorable to their movement of legal nationalism.[8]

The *Corpus Juris Civilis* possessed significance as an expression of late imperial Roman law, although the most important work it embraced, the Digest, stood as a treatise representing a valuable distillation of the best Roman legal texts for all Roman periods. The Digest authoritatively restated Roman law from earlier centuries, given that none of the texts on which it was based had survived. Legal scholarship in Portugal during the second half of the eighteenth century would exploit the historical diversity of Roman law, because the pre-Justinian heritage reaching to the classical era facilitated political interpretations deviating from the *Corpus Juris Civilis.* The Institutes, originally adopted by Justinian as a statute, simultaneously served as an introductory textbook for law students. Their organizational structure provided the model for European commentaries on national law that emerged during the early modern era. Eighteenth-century Portuguese legal commentaries, as well as the earliest ones authored by Brazilian jurists, perpetuated the formula of "institutes of civil law," a circumstance discernible from their titles through the 1850s. The second Code was a systematic collection of Roman legislation, while the Novels, or New Constitution, presented later imperial legislation enacted after compilation of the Code and Digest.[9]

The Glossators, who were the prime movers of the revival of Roman law in the eleventh and twelfth centuries, played a special role in national codification in Portugal, and they continued to be cited authoritatively by Portuguese jurists into the eighteenth century. They had discovered, collected, and reconciled extant glosses for legal texts that defined the Roman heritage, in addition to producing glosses of their own. The glosses were comments or commentaries on a word, a phrase, or a text inserted into a manuscript containing an original legal work, such as Justinian's Code or Digest. Eventually, the works produced by the Glossators rendered secondary the original texts they elucidated, elevating legal commentary and scholarship to a new plane. Although the Glossators acquired considerable authority, derived from their rediscovery and interpretation of Roman texts, they fell under criticism for failing to treat legal systems as evolving, organic entities. The literalism of their method made future generations of legal scholars critical of their utility, for they failed to apply principles and rules from Roman law appropriate to contemporary society.[10]

The thirteenth-century successors of the Glossators, the Commentators, carried the *Corpus Juris Civilis* from Italy to the courts of princes, bishops, and municipalities. A student of Bartolus Saxoferrato (1314–1357), the most famous Commentator, first took Roman law to Lisbon. The Commentators pushed forward what became identified as legal science, because they were inclined to engage in a speculative dialectic appropriate to rational inquiry. The legal science on which they depended for consolidating a civil law tradition, grounded in the *Corpus Juris*, gradually came to embody the common law of Europe—known as the *jus commune*.[11] The role played by the Commentators in developing and interpreting a *jus commune* that unified law gained significance as the princes appreciated the value of Roman law for their projects of political consolidation. Eventually, the Commentators broadened the *jus commune* to inscribe both canon and commercial law. The jurist, especially when connected directly to the court of the monarch as a counselor—who sometimes bore the reappropriated Roman designation of "jurisconsult"—discharged a function within a civil law tradition that approximated that of the judge in the legal tradition of Anglo-American common law. Both rendered interpretations of statutes and made law, but the civil law jurist often did so theoretically as well as in terms of actual cases.[12] As the author of a legal treatise or dissertation, he was consulted as an authoritative source for interpreting law in the context of the courtroom.

Early Portuguese Codification of National Law

The relatively early attainment of national legal codification, in the 1440s, distinguished Portugal's juridical evolution as a civil law country and brought into prominence the special role that Roman law played in both codification and national consolidation. The process reflected the success of Portugal's early political unification under the House of Aviz, testifying to that dynasty's deliberate promotion of a precocious legal codification on behalf of the sovereign's power. Beginning in the twelfth century, when Gratian transformed canon law into a unified system, the latter began to be taught in conjunction with Roman civil law in European universities. In Portugal, the position canon law enjoyed until the thirteenth century was considerable. Its earlier reception presented an obstacle to the reception of Roman law. The latter arrived relatively late and, initially, only indirectly, from Castile. The vehicle for introducing Roman law into Portugal was the famous, mid-thirteenth-century law code known as the *Ley de las Siete Partidas* (1256–1265), or "the Law of Seven Parts." However, so strong was the force of local custom as law that this enduring code, originating in the joint kingdoms of Castile and León and largely authored by the law doctors of the University of Salamanca, could not be promulgated until 1348. Even then, initially it acquired the force of law as an appendix to another code, the *Ordenamiento de Alcalá*. That is, it was a subsidiary statute, one having effect only where the *Ordenamiento* was silent.[13]

The *Siete Partidas* were organized as seven books, or parts (*partidas*), that in turn were broken into titles (*títulos*), each denominating a category of juridical principles and rules. They incorporated the *Decretum* of Gratian and the *Decretals* of Pope Gregory IX, texts from the Glossators on civil law, especially Accursius, or those on canon law. The third and fifth *partidas* were taken almost verbatim from Justinian's *Corpus Juris Civilis*. The *Siete Partidas* nevertheless represented a compromise between the customary laws of Castile and León, known as the *fueros*, especially the codified *Fuero Juzgo*, and Roman-canonical sources. The books of the *Siete Partidas* and their respective titles served as a rough template for the Portuguese codifiers who appropriated them in the fifteenth century, when they drew up their first national law code. What was also the earliest code in vernacular Spanish was inspired by Alfonso El Sabio—King Alfonso X of Castile and León. His grandson Dinis first introduced it in Portugal. D. Dinis (1279–1325) founded the University of Lisbon (1290) and ordered the *Siete Partidas* to be assimilated within Portuguese law. Reception of Roman law, however, did not follow, given the absence of a Portuguese code that articulated systematic principles and rules derived from the *Corpus Juris*. A genuine assimilation of the latter further awaited the institutional development of the embryonic university founded by D. Denis. More to the point, the strength of both canon and feudal law in Portugal effectively impeded any major impact by Roman civil law in the fourteenth century.[14]

The importance of the *Siete Partidas* for Portugal's juridical evolution lay in the greater prominence they gave to Roman civil law, as opposed to canon law. Novel reliance on Justinian's Digest and Italian juridical commentary meant that the *Siete Partidas* innovatively drew on Justinian's legacy. Equally significant, however, the jurists of Alfonso El Sabio determined that canon law, together with the customs of Castile and León, be incorporated in their royal code.[15] Although the heaviest borrowing in the *Siete Partidas* came from the *Corpus Juris*, weighing that code in favor of *ratio scripta*—the written reason of Roman law tantamount to a rational system—it nonetheless represented a compromise between the latter and Iberian customary law. This circumstance of juridical hybridization would recommend the *Siete Partidas* to the Portuguese jurists who subsequently authored the *Ordenações Afonsinas*. It accounts for why Portugal's early national code would be the one to retain the greatest amount of Visigothic law.[16]

Contrary to scholarly assertions, evidence suggests that the *Siete Partidas* were translated into Portuguese only in the fourteenth century, during the era of D. Dinis' successors.[17] Initially, therefore, the influence of the *Siete Partidas* on a Portuguese legal tradition remained very restricted, largely being limited to aspects of procedural law in the royal courts—precisely the place where canon law enjoyed a strong position. When the First Statutes were drawn up for Coimbra University, in 1347, for instance, no chair in Roman law was created. Instead, one was established in the canonical *Decretals* of Gratian, a circumstance that would oblige Portuguese scholars to travel to the universities of Paris in order to study Roman law. Only in the fifteenth century, after D. Manuel I brought Coimbra University under direct royal authority and assumed the right to make law for that institution, was the study of Roman law firmly established in a university faculty separate from canon law.[18]

Not until the Aviz dynasty (1383–1580) did Roman law begin to exercise an important role in Portugal's royal legislation and law courts. The aptly named Dr. João das Regras (1324–1404) brought Roman law directly from Bologna to Lisbon, during the final years of the reign of D. Fernando I (1367–1383), whom he served as juridical advisor.[19] Under the pivotal influence of Bartolus' disciple, the reception of Roman law in Portugal gained a foothold only when the founder of the House of Aviz, D. João I (1383–1433), ascended the throne. Candido Mendes deemed Regras Portugal's "first notable juris-consult," given that his appointment defined one feature of what was known as the 1383 revolution. The latter witnessed a disputed crown passing to D. João I, establishing the House of Aviz as the founding dynasty of Portugal's modern state. João das Regras is thus credited with "absorbing or suppress-ing many, many norms lacking scientific content, largely those of civil law that [had] followed canonical or ecclesiastical values." Erroneously, Regras was popularly credited with authoring the first Portuguese vernacular edition of the *Siete Partidas* and, also erroneously, the translation into Portuguese of the *Corpus Juris Civilis*.[20] Careful scrutiny of Portugal's legal evolution none-theless indicates that Roman law continued to be imperfectly received at the time of his death in 1404.

João das Regras rose to prominence in an era when scholars trained in Roman law, known as *legistas*, were few in Portugal. His fame as the arriviste jurist from Bologna speaks implicitly to the inseparable role the university would play in the evolutionary impact of Roman law on Portuguese positive law. Yet his reputation as the scholar-counselor to kings, and the man who masterminded "the true artifice of the reception of Roman law," more prop-erly deserves to be postponed to forty years after his death. Roman law gained central prominence only with the promulgation of the *Ordenações Afonsinas* in 1446.[21] Although D. João I usually is credited as the prime mover for the code project, it was the name of his grandson, D. Afonso, that the code bore. In fact, compilation of the *Ordenações Afonsinas* began during the reign of D. João's son Duarte (1438–1446). Work was largely completed dur-ing the stormy regency of Duarte's younger brother, D. Pedro, Duke of Coimbra (1438–1446), and it is he who deserves most of the credit for achieving the task of producing the code that bears the name of Afonso V (1446–1481). As Pedro's nephew and son-in-law, Afonso attained his legal majority and ascended the throne in the same year that the new *Ordenações* were promulgated, explaining why they received his name.

The *Ordenações Afonsinas*, like its successor codes, synthesized multiple strands of diverse and competing law derived from a mélange of sources, in-cluding both conciliar and canon law; Visigothic law; local customary law, especially what was often enshrined in the *foros* that stipulated the privileges of the nobility and the church; the *forais* that pertained to the rights of municipalities and guilds, usually derived from charters; the statutory determinations of the Cortes Gerais, Portugal's equivalent of the Estates General; and, last but not least, royal law. This circumstance, that the Afonsine Code retained a great deal of customary and local, as well as canon law, can be easily overlooked, especially where the rules of the inheritance system mattered, in Book 4. For instance, Justinian's revision of Roman rules of heirship, imposing equal shares for forced heirs, regardless of sex or age, was assimilated within the *Ordenações Afonsinas*. However, the Germanic preference for rights in primogeniture also found its way into that code, by virtue of the privilege of entailment. Similarly, Germanic rules defining representation for the inheritance rights of more distant collateral heirs overrode Roman rules.[22] As we shall see, in treating marriage and concubinage, the *Ordenações* again assimilated customary law along with Romanized canon law. With each successive codification, where marriage mattered, the contradictory rules that derived from the clash between customary and Roman law become more glaring.

Moreover, the Roman law that provided the analytical structure and juridical precepts for the *Ordenações Afonsinas* was subject to diverse origins. Although it derived largely from Justinian's *Corpus Juris*, some of it was traceable to the pre-Justinian heritage as distant as the second-century Institutes of Gaius. The talent of the royal *legistas*, and the triumph of codification, lay in uniting heterodox and even contradictory sources of law to give prominence to extant but previously scattered royal "legislation." The latter was authored by the sovereign, his royal ministers, jurists, and high crown judges. Additionally, the *legistas* provided a complementary updating that reconciled more recent positive law with older Portuguese sources reaching to the late medieval *Ordenações de D. Duarte* and the *Livro das Leis e Posturas* (The Book of Laws and Precepts).[23]

The systematically compiled, but not always doctrinally reconciled, "*Ordenações do Reino*" literally translated as "the laws of the kingdom." The latter, as a designation originally applying to the *Ordenações Afonsinas*, eventually connoted either a specific successor code of the latter or the generic "three codes" promulgated in Portugal by 1603: those of Afonso V, Manuel I, and Philip III of Spain (Felipe II of Portugal). The *Ordenações* signified the plurality of individual provisions categorically arranged in titles and divided into books. Parsed as either a title or one of its sections, a singular "*ordenação*," or law, would be glossed and interpreted by legal commentators who were almost always royal jurisconsults or Coimbra University professors. The word derived from the Latin "*ordinatio*," meaning what legally was ordered to have the force of law, regardless of whether the *ordenação* in question had originated in a royal law or decree known as an *alvará*, or a resolution or regulation of the king's minister, or the *estilos* that constituted the body of rulings produced by each of several high crown courts. Significantly, custom also explained the origin of a given *ordenação*. In the plural, the *Ordenações* were divided into four principal books reflecting divisions of public and private law inspired by the Justinian legacy of the *Corpus Juris*. In fact, the principal divisions were rudimentarily traceable to Gaius' Institutes. Thus Book 4 followed the classical Roman category of the law of things— ownership, inheritance, and obligations or contracts, including matrimony. A fifth book, similarly modeled on Roman divisions, contained a criminal code that would endure in Brazil until 1830.

Although the historical significance of the *Ordenações Afonsinas* lay in the instrument they offered for systematizing law for a national monarchy founded on the House of Aviz, they equally proclaimed the growing influence of a new breed of royal jurist who wove Roman law into Portugal's national positive law. A direct line would run, consequently, from João das Regras in the 1380s to the *legistas* under Duarte and Pedro in the 1430s and 1440s, and culminate in the late eighteenth-century jurisconsults who revised law on behalf of an absolutist state, above all, the law professor whose name became synonymous with legal nationalism: Paschoal José de Mello Freire dos Reys—"Mello Freire of the Kings." Although promulgation of the *Ordenações Afonsinas* predated the arrival of Gutenberg's printing press by only a few years, the Portuguese crown never ordered them published while they were in force. Publication came only in 1792, nearly two centuries after the promulgation of the *Ordenações Filipinas*. Presumably, their publication complemented the draft civil and criminal code projects produced under Mello Freire's direction in the late 1780s.[24]

The novelty of redaction in the *Ordenações Afonsinas* lay not only in how they drew directly on Roman civil law but also in the new reliance they placed on Roman law as a "subsidiary," or secondary, source for national positive law. Following the *Siete Partidas*, Book 2, Title 2, of the *Ordenações Afonsinas* ordained that the opinions of Bartolus or the glosses of Accursius be consulted as a source for law, whenever the *Ordenações* or other royal sources were silent or contradictory on a point of law. Accursius, the most celebrated Glossator of the first half of the thirteenth century, had his commentaries written into all subsequent manuscript editions of the *Corpus Juris Civilis* that were copied at Bologna. They were known as the *Glossa Ordinaria*, or *Magna Glossa*. From 1446 onward, in other words, Roman law was used to "fill in the gaps" in Portugal's positive law. The *Ordenações Afonsinas* specifically provided that Roman law would be consulted when cases could not be decided by either the laws of the realm or the rulings issued by the high crown courts, known as the *estilos*, or by custom. In matters of sin, where the sacred canons were silent, then Roman law similarly would be a subsidiary source for canon law.[25]

Until the second half of the eighteenth century, when excessive reliance on Roman law produced an abrupt juridical reaction, Portugal's kings, ministers, and jurists applied Roman law as the principal subsidiary source for articulating national positive law. Therefore, Roman law offered the Portuguese monarchy a means for organizing and resolving a legal heritage resting on an array of sources. Politically, Roman law mattered as a means for reducing the force of local custom and feudal law, including what was written into municipal charters as the *forais*. Alternatively, it served the same utility vis-à-vis ecclesiastical law.

Between 1512 and 1521, the *Ordenações Afonsinas* were gradually replaced by the *Ordenações Manuelinas*. Although the Manueline Code was promulgated as a revision of the Afonsine Code, and it updated the latter, it brought no big changes. Consistent with the demands of a Renaissance state, the *Ordenações Manuelinas* imposed greater centralization by incorporating reliance on juridico-administrative tribunals dating to the fifteenth century, such as those of the Casa da Suplicação and the Desembargo do Paço, whose presiding magistrates were close to the king, often his relatives. The code of D. Manuel I (1495–1521) retained the original five books, a simplification of the *Siete Partidas*, but generally reinforced to a greater degree the tendency of its predecessor to rely on Justinian's *Corpus Juris*. In one important respect, however, it restricted how the *Ordenações* previously had depended on Roman law as a secondary, or subsidiary source, due to the fact that legal humanists had begun to discover limitations in the scholarship of the celebrated Glossators. No longer would the opinions of Bartolus and the glosses of Accursius be dogmatically followed when positive law failed to decide a case.[26]

The Manueline Code articulated for the first time what the late eighteenth century would celebrate as the rule of "*boa razão*"—right reason—as a guide for addressing the gaps in national positive law. Roman rules of law would still be followed as a subsidiary source, but only when they could be found to be based on "right reason," that is, on the rational inquiry of jurists. The *Ordenações Manuelinas* thus offered a different solution than their predecessor code, the *Ordenações Afonsinas*, reflecting a shift of juridical authority from the Glossators to the Commentators who were associated with sounder, humanistic study of the law.[27] Subsequently, the notion of "right reason" would be used to elaborate the cornerstone of an eighteenth-century juridical reaction to an overreliance on Roman law, and find embodiment in the celebrated 1769 Law of Right Reason (*Lei da Boa Razão*) that finally spelled out the notion's meaning in great detail.[28] The *Ordenações Manuelinas* further enhanced crown authority by suppressing important features of feudal law, curbing the power of church and nobility. They relied directly on sources for royal law absent in the *Ordenações Afonsinas*, such as the *Decisões da Corte* and the *assentos* of the high crown courts known as the *Casa da Suplicação* and the *Casa do Porto*. The timing of their promulgation coincided with the initial decline of the political influence exerted by the Cortes Gerais, Portugal's Estates General, due to the irreversible centralization of monarchical power. Finally, D. Manuel's code complemented the expansion of crown prestige due to the acquisition of a trans-Atlantic empire. The code of Manoel I thus applied to a Lusophone world that for the first time stretched from Lisbon to Africa to Brazil and the East Indies.[29]

Canon Law

The central importance of canon law, as part of the *jus commune*, derived from the movement that proceeded pari passu with the eleventh-century revival of Roman civil law. Originally, as the law of the Roman Catholic church, canon law drew directly on Roman law, given that Christianity became the religion of the Roman empire in the fourth century. In the early Christian era and the Middle Ages, however, canon law also reflected the determinations of general church councils that ordinarily received papal confirmation. In contrast to those general councils of the church, which met rarely and drew on all of western Christendom, episcopal councils convened in Portugal defined a complementary source of conciliar law for that Iberian nation. Dependent on royal validation, the latter became an important source of positive national law that encouraged the evolution of what both crown and episcopacy regarded as a "Lusitanian church." Nearly one hundred of the canons in Gratian's *Decretals*, for instance, were promulgated as positive national law by the Visigothic rulers of the Iberian peninsula, following the adoption of those canons by church councils in Spain and Portugal.

Nevertheless, the strands of canon law reached into Iberia's Germanic law as well as into the Justinian corpus of *ratio scripta*.[30] A good example was the church's method of reckoning prohibited degrees of kinship for contracting holy matrimony, a formula received in Portuguese national law by virtue of the *Ordenações do Reino*. Eventually, the formula rested on a Germanic system of reckoning. Formally initiated in 1076 under Pope Alexander II and finalized at the Fourth Lateran Council of 1215, the Germanic method replaced

Isidore of Seville's Roman system of reckoning degrees of kinship formerly used by the church. As a result, Germanic reckoning roughly doubled the number of relatives with whom marriage was prohibited. Unless the church granted the couple a dispensation, the partners could not be declared in the "free state" to marry.[31] The *Ordenações* thus implicitly endorsed what was a canonical definition of incest derived from Germanic customary law, notwithstanding that otherwise they relied on the Roman formula of reckoning degrees of kinship that were purely civil.

Beginning with the *Siete Partidas*, royal codifiers in Iberia adopted the sacred canons as moral norms, giving them effect in national positive law. Equally important, they also adopted canon law's judicial procedures. Wherever "sin" was equated with crime, such as in the fifth and final book of the *Ordenações do Reino*, then canon law exerted a major impact. Furthermore, because the twelfth-century reception of canon law in Portugal preceded the reception of Roman civil law by two centuries, the *Ordenações Afonsinas* exerted only a limited restraint on the effect of canon law. Although the *Ordenações Manuelinas* pushed those limits further, they, too, basically validated canon law, above all, in the private law of the family.

By the sixteenth century, however, canon law's impact on Portuguese positive law involved a great deal more than the *Decretals* of Gratian or even the assimilation of discrete canons into the *Ordenações*, for the law of the church had been reduced to a single compilation known as the *Corpus Juris Canonici*. The latter thus became a parallel source of law analogous to the *Corpus Juris Civilis* and was widely received throughout western Europe.[32] In other words, as a full fledged component of the *jus commune*, canon law conveyed important juridical effects in positive national law. It evolved within the civil law tradition, determining features in the law of things treated in Book Four of the *Ordenações*, such as the inheritance rights of both legitimate and non-legitimate children. The convocation of a general council of the church at Trent, between 1545 and 1563, brought into high relief the impact that canon law would exert on Portugal's codification efforts. The Articles of the Council of Trent became incorporated throughout Catholic Europe as the canon law of a reinvigorated Roman Catholic Church synonymous with the Counter Reformation. Once adopted by the Vatican as official church dogma—the official teachings of the church—the pope then proposed that the canons of Trent be promulgated by the Catholic monarchs. Depending on the national monarchy, they were received, in the whole or in part, as positive national law. With important exceptions, the canons of Trent continued to be positive law in the constitutional monarchies of nineteenth-century Europe. On the other hand, from the sixteenth century onward, adoption of those Tridentine canons was widely perceived by Europe's Catholic monarchies as part of the Vatican's efforts to expand papal power at their expense.

The Council of Trent interrupted what had been a cumulative incorporation of Roman civil law in Portugal's royal codification efforts. The princes and prelates of the Catholic Church concluded their great conclave at Trent in the same year that Cardinal Henrique (1563–1568) became regent of Portugal. As Manuel's last surviving son, he was determined to bring the Counter Reformation to Portugal while acting as regent for his great-nephew Sebastian (1554–1578), a nine-year-old boy. Presiding over a juridical reaction against the code bearing his father's name, Cardinal Henrique lost no time in heeding Pope Pius IV, who called for the sovereigns of Europe to execute *Benedictus Dei*, the bull containing the papal decrees confirming the Articles of the Council of Trent. Henrique immediately recommended their observance in 1564. A year later, he promulgated the Tridentine canons in their entirety throughout the Portuguese realms, entrusting their enforcement to the Jesuit Order. Then he promoted a new codification of Portuguese national law that became the short-lived *Código Sebastianico* in 1569, the year when D. Sebastião's majority was proclaimed.[33]

Political historians frequently ignore the *Ordenações Sebastianicas*, for, officially, they were not counted as one of "the three codes." Their promulgation largely explained why the *Ordenações Filipinas* would be drafted to replace them. The new code not only incorporated all of the canons on marriage adopted by the Council of Trent but it also retired a great deal of the *Ordenações Manuelinas*. Furthermore, Cardinal Henrique's code restored ecclesiastical law that the latter had deliberately set aside, giving legal effect to the decisions of certain church councils that Manuel's code ignored. The *Código Sebastianico* updated the Manueline Code, by incorporating post-1521 legislation, including the *estilos*, or decisions, of the Casa da Suplicação, Portugal's high court of crown appeal. Nevertheless, its promulgation produced "great confusion in the royal courts," because it overturned how the preceding code defined the relationship between civil and canon law.[34]

Left in place, Cardinal Henrique's code would have returned to canon law the preeminence it enjoyed during the reign of D. Afonso II (1211–1223), that is, prior to promulgation of the *Ordenações Afonsinas*. The standard used in the thirteenth century for judging whether civil law deserved to be in force had turned on whether it conflicted with canon law. Unless the crown explicitly declared it to be in force, civil law had to yield to canon law.[35] When the throne of Portugal passed to Philip II of Spain, in 1580, it may have initiated sixty years of "Babylonian Captivity," but it certainly liberated Portugal from a legal tradition that in the 1560s had been rededicated to canon law. Although Philip's jurists retired Cardinal Henrique's code, they did not directly tamper with his promulgation in 1564 and 1565 of the articles on marriage adopted at the Council of Trent. Those canons would therefore endure in Brazil until 1890. Prior to Trent, beginning in the late fifteenth century, the Portuguese crown had embarked on a policy of acquiring legal prerogatives vis-à-vis the Vatican, known as the *regalias* of the crown. Elaborated in a series of concordats with the Holy See, the *regalias* originally limited the power of the papacy to promulgate bulls and decretals within the Portuguese realms. They required the monarch's prior permission. Although the Articles of Trent had been given immediate effect in Portugal, the crown enjoyed the right to limit or deny the pontiff subsequent opportunity to employ bulls or decretals for disseminating canon law in Portugal.

The Ordenações Filipinas

The Philippine Code that the Spanish *legistas* of Philip II bestowed on Portugal in 1603 applied exclusively to the Portuguese realms. Contrary to Portuguese propaganda, the Philippine Code was neither the work of Jesuits nor exclusively Spanish jurists. Two high crown judges and two jurists who were Portuguese collaborated with the latter. Despite the blandishments of Philip's jurists, who expressed the Spanish motive of gaining the esteem of his newly incorporated subjects, the *Ordenações Filipinas* responded fundamentally to Philip's goal of replacing the reactionary *Código Sebastianico*. That is, he was determined, for reasons of state—*imperium*—to undo the dangerous effect given to canon law by Cardinal Henrique's code. In order to do so, his jurists regrounded Portuguese national law on a firmer foundation of Roman law than the Manueline Code had provided. Thanks to Philip's influence, canon law would be permanently restricted. His father, Charles V, when faced with the papal bull *Bendictus Dei*, had sagaciously promulgated the Tridentine canons on marriage on a selective basis in the Spanish realms. In keeping with a less dogmatic position, one that Charles had personally defended at Trent against the canonists loyal to the Holy See, Philip's jurists prevented canon law from being restored to late medieval preeminence in Portugal. His "Romanist" jurists produced the most enduring and final codification of Portugal's national law, the *Ordenações Filipinas* bearing his son's name. They also consulted Spanish sources extraneous to the *Ordenações Manuelinas*, such as the *Fuero Real*, *the Fuero de León*, and the more recent Laws of Toro (1502), in addition to the older sources of the *Fuero Juzgo* and Roman and canon law. The *Código Filipino* nevertheless retained a great deal of Portugal's local and customary law within an overarching structure that drew directly on Roman law. Although the *legistas* perpetuated almost all of the Manueline Code, with both its consuetudinary and Roman law, they expanded and reinforced the latter.[36]

Thus it was no accident, but the deliberate design of Philip's team of jurists, that Portugal's code of 1603 treated marriage and concubinage very ambiguously. As much for Spanish reasons of state as for the bias of Portuguese jurists, consuetudinary law on marriage was perpetuated from the Manueline to the Philippine Code. Much to the consternation of Portuguese jurists in the late eighteenth century, Philip's *legistas* gave equal validity in national law to sacramental marriage defined at Trent and to medieval definitions of marriage rooted in Portuguese custom—what popular speech in Portugal already consecrated as "marriage according to the *Ordenações*." We will return to this dissonance in the legal definitions of marriage, especially in the volume that follows, where a chapter is devoted to marriage.

The second half of Book 4 of the Philippine Code, beginning at Title 80, contained the rules pertaining to the inheritance system, those treating wills, *ab intestato* succession, and entail, as well as the guardianship of minor heirs. The second half of Book 4, in tandem with Book 5, drew on conflicting definitions of valid marriage, due to how Book 4 differentiated rights to patrimony in terms of individual quality of birth—as either legitimate, legitimized, natural, or spurious. Thus a discrete *qualidade* defined the essence of a person's legal and social identity, deriving directly from canon and Roman law as received national law in Portugal. Vis-à-vis the preceding Manueline Code, the greatest change the *Ordenações Filipinas* imposed on marriage pertained to the incorporation of a definition deriving from the Tridentine canons, one adopted by the church forty years after promulgation of the D. Manuel's code. The rules of heirship were little altered by the Philippine Code, however, except to give greater prominence to patrimony constituted as entail, a feature that reflected the late medieval importance of entail and its rising importance in Spanish positive law. Otherwise, the Philippine Code continued to reflect the mélange of legal sources, often contradictory, that originally were articulated in the Afonsine Code.

To conclude, the main features of Luso-Brazilian succession law derived from the *jus commune*, with its dual strands of civil and canon law, as well as from Iberian local custom. That legacy deserves to be kept in mind, given how positive law and juridical doctrine would be reworked after 1750. During the reign of D. José I (1750–1777), Portugal's civil law tradition reflected deliberate revision, as a new emphasis was placed on discarding or restricting legal precepts that originated in Roman civil law or canon law. Although the movement of legal nationalism never rejected outright the firm foundation of Roman law reaching to João das Regras and the fifteenth-century reception of Roman law, it established that national positive law in the eighteenth century should privilege the central role of the monarch as the nation's "Legislator." His or her power to make national law by statute extended to the royal courts, where, by 1769, the writs issued by a crown judiciary would be expected to reflect determinations consistent with the national law emanating from an absolutist state.

Where the private law of the family and inheritance mattered after 1750, a new generation of Portuguese jurists loyal to the legal nationalism and the regalism of the king's first minister, the marquis of Pombal (Sebastião José de Carvalho e Mello), would privilege the centrality of "our customs" as the source for national law. Their juridical arguments rendered Roman civil law less significant as a subsidiary source for national law and purged positive law of much of the force of canon law, above all, in the courtroom where law was applied. As Candido Mendes observed about the civil law in the *Ordenações Filipinas*, it contained two elements: "*national* legislation, the product of ideas, opinions, and customs of the population in different eras; and *Roman* law, considered the common law to the extent it was incorporated, what the Legislator viewed as subsidiary."[37]

However, the impact of what jurists referred to as "*direito pátrio*," national positive law, proved piecemeal and cumulative after 1750, for the Portuguese monarchy failed to replace the *Ordenações Filipinas* with the innovative civil and criminal code projects that were drafted in the late 1780s. Similarly, the consolidation of legal nationalism had to await not one, but two, royal reforms of the law faculties at Coimbra University, given the indispensable role that royal institution played in training the crown jurists who were now expected to impose national law in the courts. Although the detailed story of this juridical transformation has been left for the final chapter of this book, where relevant to the position of illegitimate individuals in succession law or juridical interpretation, the major features of *direito pátrio* are identified throughout the intervening chapters. Notwithstanding the substantial delay that accompanied the institutionalization of Portugal's reformulated legal tradition, one that did not jell until the first decade of the nineteenth century, the incremental changes imposed by new national laws on a Luso-Brazilian inheritance system began to matter as early as the 1750s. Those laws would cumulatively transform rules of heirship and their juridical interpretation by the time the Portuguese monarchy found safe exile from Napoleon's invading armies in the vice-regal capital of Brazil.

CHAPTER 1

Inheritance As a Legal System

And if law students find stronger systematization and a clearer exposition in my book than in what they find in that of Gouvêa Pinto, when, as now, they go about collecting the elements of succession law, then I will not have written a useless work.

Clovis Bevilaqua, *Direito das successões* (1899)[1]

The position of individuals who were illegitimate in Brazilian inheritance law can be apprehended only by acquiring familiarity with a set of key concepts. Those concepts, however, need to be appreciated within a historical context, due to the considerable change imposed on family and inheritance law after 1750. Together with a set of terms articulating the language of the inheritance system, the concepts demonstrate the admirable logic on which Brazil's inheritance system rested. Before approaching the special position that several categories of illegitimate individuals occupied in Luso-Brazilian inheritance, the broad features of that system deserve explanation. In this respect, Jack Goody's notion of "diverging devolution" is very helpful. He has emphasized that inheritance deserves to be seen as a system of devolution by which "rights are transferred to the heir over the life-span of the holder, whether at birth, marriage, or the holder's death." Rights to goods—property—"diverge" because they are grounded in a European system of kinship that is bilateral or cognatic, meaning that ordinarily property devolves to descendants of both sexes and from female as well as male relatives, in accordance with the rule of "equal shares for all." In restricted contexts, such as dowry and dower, engendered rules can apply. Moreover, patrimony often devolves prior to the parent's death. Succession and bequests therefore must be considered as part of a more comprehensive set of property transfers from older to younger generations that encompasses matrimonial property as well as gifts inter vivos.[2] Inheritance mechanisms per se, consequently, comprise only one of several ways that property is transferred through generations.

Heirs Necessary and Collateral

Portugal's modern system of succession, succinctly articulated in the *alvará* of November 9, 1754, offers no better starting point for apprehending how illegitimate individuals were treated in Brazilian inheritance law. First, this basic law of legitimate succession defined a new precept and derivative rules, thanks to the deliberate effort of the Pombaline state to ground the inheritance system in positive national law. The *alvará* of 1754 initiated a new era because Coimbra law professors and royal jurisconsults redefined the meaning of succession vis-à-vis a preceding reliance on both Roman and canon law. Second, positive law after 1754 curbed the *forais*, what were local rights reaching to medieval times, granted by crown or nobility, by means of charters conceded to municipalities. Finally, the watchword of *"direito pátrio"*—national law—implied a gradually reorganized inheritance system that unfolded piecemeal after 1754. In concert with the Portuguese state's emphasis on legal nationalism, *direito pátrio* represented a new juridical direction, one proclaiming the preeminence of statutory law made by the crown and applied in royal law courts. As a result, Roman and canon law became restricted and supplanted, while substantial portions of the *Ordenações Filipinas* were rendered null.

The *alvará* of November 9, 1754, which was not substantially revised until 1907, defined a system of legitimate succession in tandem with provisions already embedded in the *Ordenações Filipinas*. The latter had prescribed a fixed order of *ab intestato*, or intestate, succession, synonymous with legitimate succession and largely derived from Roman law. It spelled out in rank order what amounted to a ladder of heirship that was left unchallenged by the 1754 law.[3] First, legitimate descendants, and, in their absence, ascendants, were called to succeed *ab intestato* as "necessary heirs." They inherited equal portions, irrespective of gender or age, given that the system was partitive. In the absence of necessary heirs, law next called collateral heirs, starting with the decedent's siblings and moving to uncles and aunts, then to nephews and nieces, and, finally, to cousins as distant as the tenth civil degree of collateral kinship—the descendants of a common great-great-great grandparent. In the absence of the latter, the surviving spouse succeeded. Otherwise, the royal treasury fell heir to the decedent's estate.[4]

During Brazil's existence as a colony, from the 1530s to 1822, law excluded ipso facto various classes of persons from being called to succession. All were denied the right to succeed because they were not legal persons: foreigners, individuals stripped of nationality or declared outlaws by a bill of attainder, heretics and apostates, slaves, criminals who committed crimes of lesé majesty (divine or human), together with their sons and grandsons (but not their daughters and granddaughters); those civilly dead; members of religious orders who professed in a community life in which goods were held in common, as well as those who, after so professing, abandoned monastery or convent; and spurious offspring.[5] Women who married according to a community property regulation could succeed only if their husbands authorized them to accept their inheritance portions. In practice, husbands signed the documents on their wives' behalf, explaining why historians have not found signatures of married women appended to inheritance documents that transferred property.[6] After independence, the list of those excluded from succession shrank markedly. The 1824 Constitution "imposed more liberal features on civil law," rendering null the former status in heirship enjoyed by foreigners and unnaturalized citizens, heretics and apostates, as well as stateless persons and outlaws, including the "*degredados*" who were penalized with foreign exile.[7] The 1830 Criminal Code eliminated the intergenerational punishment of criminals.

Although slaves continued to be the most important class of persons denied succession rights in imperial Brazil, great ambivalence existed over their legal situation. Law denied them the right of acquisition, explaining why historians have not found many wills written by slaves. An important appellate decision, delivered in 1832, sealed the slave's legal inability to acquire property and set the course of law for the next forty years. The court ruled against the succession rights of a natural offspring whose mother was a slave and whose father was her owner. Although the father had recognized his son in his will, and declared him his *ab intestato* successor, he neglected to provide for his son's posthumous manumission in the will. Consequently, his natural offspring remained part of his estate, merely property to be transmitted to heirs. The high court, or Relação, of Rio de Janeiro, ruled that the paternally recognized natural son could not succeed his father because, at the moment of his death, the son had remained a slave.[8]

Challenges continued to be filed in the courts, contesting a slave's legal incapacity to succeed because social practice diverged considerably from law. Until 1871, when law was modified, legal appeals seeking inheritance rights for slaves were uniformly denied. In 1850, for instance, the director of Brazil's national treasury issued a clarification to a treasury inspector in the Province of Piauí, ruling that the possessions of slaves who had died "belonged to the nation, as mistress of the same," and not to the relatives of the deceased slaves. "For inasmuch as among us law regulates the succession of property, it does not apply to slaves, given that they are incapable of acquisition, according to the *Ordenações* (Book 4, Title 92, principally), nor are they able to make a will (Book 4, Title 81, Section 4)."[9]

Only in 1871, with adoption of the Law of the Free Womb, did legislators alter the precept borrowed from Roman law that slaves could not acquire *peculium*, or property. Consequently, for the last seventeen years of slavery's existence, Brazilian slaves possessed the right to *peculium* (property) and, therefore, to succeed to property as forced heirs or to be the beneficiaries of a bequest. Nevertheless, they could not make wills.[10]

The *alvará* of November 9, 1754, carefully distinguished inheritance by succession (*successões*) from inheritance by virtue of a bequest, or legacy (*legado*).[11] It introduced novelty and a key change by explicitly deeming succession to follow from natural law. During the last quarter of the eighteenth century, jurisconsults authored, and crown officials issued, directives known as *assentos* that responded to conflicts between specific laws. The *assento* of February 16, 1776, for instance, elaborated on the 1754 *alvará*'s sparse text in key respects. It spelled out the prior rights of the favored "necessary heirs"— descendants and ascendants—vis-à-vis both collateral heirs and legitimized individuals of all types. If no legitimate or legally equipped illegitimate offspring outlived the parent, then the children of the former—the decedent's grandchildren—would succeed *per stirpes* (per stock), or *por cabeça*. Otherwise, parents and grandparents would be called as the second group of necessary heirs. Despite a range of legal heirship extending to ten civil degrees, an important trend emerged in the 1760s that eroded the rights of all collateral heirs, for law carefully discriminated the latter from both groups of necessary heirs. The winners in a protracted battle for legal rights, however, would not be the necessary heirs, but appropriately equipped illegitimate offspring.

The Portuguese crown paid great and deliberate attention to succession and family law during the administration of the marquis of Pombal (1750–1777). Issues of political power and the crown's aspiration to regulate the private sphere of the family, encouraged additionally by rising demands of the royal fisc, explained why rules of heirship were redefined or clarified as Portugal entered the modern era. The utility of *direito pátrio*—as legal nationalism—for a centralizing, absolutist state lay in the overriding motive of supplanting the church as prime arbiter in all matters touching on inheritance. In this respect, the state assumed more direct responsibility for directing the transmission of patrimony after 1754. One powerful goal presumed that the state would redirect capital accumulation into commercial activity, encouraging the expansion of a middle class. By redefining the system of succession, positive law not only diminished the ability of both church and nobility to

accumulate capital—and withhold it from investment in commercial enter-
prise—but it also imposed rules that vested in the apparatus of royal bureaucracy greater responsibility for overseeing the transmission of inherited
wealth. By regrounding succession in natural law, the eighteenth-century jurisconsults who reshaped Portugal's inheritance system insured that the
crown would have wider latitude to intervene directly in all matters affecting
transmission of patrimony.

In the rewriting of private law that occurred between 1754 and the 1790s,
certain doctrines and rules deriving from Roman law became supplanted by
those identified as local customary law. The latter, however, were enacted in
Portuguese positive law as statutes that often reflected borrowing from other
European nations. For instance, Portuguese succession law abandoned the
Roman definition of a necessary heir, wherein the latter was legally obliged
to accept an inheritance, including the decedent's financial liabilities, and
when liabilities were in excess of the value of the inheritance portion. Hence,
necessary heirs in a Luso-Brazilian inheritance system enjoyed the right to
refuse an inheritance portion. A daughter who had received a dowry prior to
marriage, for instance, routinely refused her inheritance portion, or *quinhão*,
whenever the dowry exceeded the value of the *quinhão*. Of course, she did
not do so directly unless she was a widow, for husbands acted on their wives'
behalf, acceepting or refusing the *quinhão*. The motive for refusal derived
from a procedure known as the *colação*, which required her to return the
amount of dowry in excess of her inheritance portion for redistribution
among the other *ab intestato* heirs.

Even prior to 1754, Portuguese law never accorded necessary heirs the
same exclusive responsibility over the decedent's estate that Roman law had
imposed. Nor did the administrator and executor of the will have to be a
forced heir, as in Roman law.[12] The individual known by the end of the
nineteenth century as the *inventariante* was the administrator of the division
of the estate, tantamount to executor, but with much more legal discretion.
In the colonial period, the term preferred over "*inventariante*" in both colloquial speech and inheritance documents was "*testamenteiro*," a designation
that persisted for most of the imperial period. Although the designated *testamenteiro* often turned out to be a necessary heir, Luso-Brazilian law did
not require a forced heir to serve in this capacity. The *inventariante* drew up
an inventory listing the decedent's goods, both movable and real property,
and then individually assigned each a monetary value. He or she next decided the specific content of each heir's inheritance portion, according to the
"*partilha*," a division of the estate into equal shares, colloquially termed the
"*legítimas*," but referred to as "*quinhões*" in legal commentaries. Frequently

the oldest male descendant, the *testamenteiro* often reflected the decedent's hand-picked choice prior to death. Customarily, widows, the eldest son, or brothers and even sisters of the deceased would discharge this responsibility.

Historians of Brazil have often failed to distinguish succession, the major form of devolution in Brazil's inheritance system, from the volitional act of making bequests, known as *legados*. They have even focused primary scrutiny on the latter, due to the instrumentality of a will, notwithstanding that bequests represented a secondary form of transmitting patrimony. In a partitive system of inheritance, where forced heirship determined the predominant disposition of property, wills usually disposed of only a fraction of the estate, meaning that the *partilha*, read in conjunction with the inventory, defined the key document. Until the twentieth century, no more than one-third of a decedent's estate could be assigned as a bequest. Known as the *terça*, this third was what wills customarily termed the "*remanescente da terça*," what remained of the third after deduction of debts, burial expenses, masses for the soul of the deceased, and taxes. Consequently, the minimum portion of an estate passing in succession under forced heirship amounted to two-thirds of the decedent's property. If no will had been drawn, then the entirety of the decedent's estate passed in *ab intestato* succession as the *legítima*, minus the above-mentioned deductions.

The portion passing in forced heirship is still known today as the "*legítima*," or legitim, although now it amounts to a minimum of one-half the decedent's estate. Legal commentaries in the nineteenth century referred to an inheritance portion derived from the *legítima* as the "*quinhão*," but wills often followed colloquial usage, preferring to speak of portions as "*legítimas*." The *legítima* passed in forced heirship according to a legally defined ladder of "legitimate" succession synonymous with both "*ab intestato*" and "natural" succession. By the close of the eighteenth century, the legitimate heirs were starkly differentiated as either "necessary" or "collateral."

Intestate or legitimate succession was synonymous with natural succession because, following the 1754 law, legal doctrine grounded succession in notions drawn from natural law. "Legitimate" succession reflected the nuance of legitimate marriage. However, church and state agreed that sacramental marriage was grounded in not only divine but also natural law. The ladder of succession was identical, whether natural or legitimate, because intestacy was always assumed for the sake of forced heirship. Juridical commentary routinely spoke of legitimate succession as "*ab intestato* succession" and legitimate heirs (*herdeiros legítimos*) as "*ab intestato* heirs." Technically, legitimate heirs were also natural heirs, because their succession rights derived from natural law; however, "natural heir" (*herdeiro natural*) was a term reserved for natural offspring, the subject of the next chapter. They were the offspring of unmarried parents who might have married; therefore, law could convey more of the civil effects associated with "legitimate marriage" to the children.

What mattered most about *ab intestato* succession, to heirs as well as to readers of inheritance documents, was that no will had to be drawn up in order for devolution to be effected. Instead, a ladder of *ab intestato* succession already existed in law, specifying the rank order for members of the decedent's blood kindred to succeed to the *legítima*. Where Anglo-American law has assumed the centrality of a will in matters of succession, Luso-Brazilian law has taken intestacy, the natural order of succession, as the normal course of events. Wills nevertheless became advisable in many individual contexts in Luso-Brazilian inheritance, above all, where patrimony for illegitimate offspring was at issue. Yet the overriding point remains that a ladder of intestacy automatically vested succession rights in either the necessary or collateral heirs. In contrast, probate proceedings in Anglo-American law had to verify the identity of the heirs. To the extent that, until very recently, the North American historiography on Brazil has emphasized wills, at the expense of *ab intestato* succession, scholars have stood the logic of the Brazilian inheritance system on its head. Succession according to the rules of intestacy, and not bequests by virtue of a will, should have assumed major significance for those attempting to trace either the devolution of property or the fundamental aspects of any decedent's testamentary dispositions.

Many scholars have not understood that *ab intestato* succession must be distinguished in a Luso-Brazilian legal context from both intestate and testamentary succession in Anglo-American law. However, virtually no one has distinguished *ab intestato* succession from testamentary succession in Brazilian law. The latter is easily and frequently confused with bequests, because both required a will. Testamentary succession, known as either "*sucessão testamentária*" or "*sucessão por testamento*," derived from civil, not natural, law. It was a device artificially created, so to speak, for modifying the ladder of heirship dictated by natural, or *ab intestato*, succession. Testamentary succession, to put a fine point on the confusion it continues to generate, applied almost exclusively to illegitimate offspring. Otherwise, the special features in law permitting the testator to institute a "universal heir" constituted a variant form of testamentary succession. We will return to both situations in this and following chapters.

Clovis Bevilaqua's declaration that "Roman doctrine received profound alteration in national law with the *alvará* of November 9, 1754," implied why probate would be foreign to the meaning of *ab intestato* succession in a

Luso-Brazilian inheritance system. According to that basic *alvará*, succession implied the automatic transmission of the decedent's effects to his or her legitimate heirs, instantaneous with death. This immediate passage of goods was said to "open succession." By the same token, unfungible and unconditional bequests were said to pass instantaneously with the death of juridical personality, automatically transmitting possession, or *posse*, of the decedent's patrimony.[13] Hence, a will was unnecessary for *ab intestato* succession, even irrelevant, given that the necessary heirs were already known and the passage of the decedent's goods became instantaneous with death.

In Anglo-American legal tradition, on the other hand, transmission of the decedent's property was not automatic, for legally it had to be preceded by probate proceedings. The latter amounted to the judicial act of "proving" that the instrument nominating the heirs had been executed in conformity with the required legal procedures. Confirmation of the will's validity, which also authenticated the heirs, necessitated demonstration before a judge in order for the decedent's goods to pass in succession. Where succession was intestate, a judge's oversight was also required to rule on the appropriate identity of the legal heirs. In a Luso-Brazilian legal context, wills performed a different function when succession was *ab intestato*. Ordinarily they identified heirs who already occupied a place on the ladder of intestacy but were not "commonly known," such as a father's natural offspring whose paternity had been concealed. Alternatively, wills rendered unequivocal the rights of forced heirs who might be challenged. For instance, they might specifically disallow any claim made by someone purporting to be the testator's offspring. More to the point, a judge was not needed for succession to occur in a Luso-Brazilian context. Beginning in 1754, the fundamental concept of *posse civil*, civil possession or ownership, that had resided in the decedent, was conveyed instantaneously at death to the *ab intestato* heirs "without need for physical apprehension."[14]

The law of 1754 drew on the Germanic concept of *seisen*, derived from feudal law, for positing a succession that opened at the exact moment of the decedent's death. As a feature of medieval customary law, *seisen* had been applied in early modern French legal commentaries before Pombaline jurists appropriated it.[15] In 1776, the 1754 basic *alvará* on succession received complementary reinterpretation. The *assento* of February 16, elaborating and refining the latter, would stand as the other pillar of the inheritance system throughout Brazil's imperial period.[16] Together, the laws of 1754 and 1776 illustrated how statutory and administrative law inexorably modified and supplanted the *Ordenações Filipinas*. The *assento* of 1776 addressed misgivings over a range of kinship extending to ten collateral degrees, due to the likelihood that law could call collateral heirs to succession who were so distant as to be virtually unknown. Henceforth, the range of kinship inscribing *ab intestato* heirs within ten collateral degrees admitted a limitation on the instantaneity of *posse*; that is, on the immediate transmission of patrimony at juridical death. *Posse* would apply only to those heirs who had "a certain and indubitable right of succession," meaning juridically that more distant collateral heirs, where they were unknown, would not automatically enjoy instantaneous *posse*. Now those *ab intestato* heirs might be obliged "to justify" before a judge the right to be called to succession.

Such a limitation implied common sense more than any systematic restriction of rights, for it threw open to question the *ab intestato* rights of only those heirs who were not "publicly known" in the community. For the first time, however, *posse* had been made conditional, albeit in a limited context. Over the long run, the 1776 *assento* offered opportunity for further restriction. Brazilian legislators in the 1850s, for instance, would use it to tie the rights of distant collaterals to a judge's prior approval, privileging only those who were siblings, uncles and aunts, or nephews and nieces as *ab intestato* heirs who were bona fide.[17]

After Brazilian independence, as before, the state was unable to enforce uniformly the legal requirements for filing the inventory and *partilha*. Legally stipulated time periods for filing both those documents with a judge of the first instance, once a notary prepared them, often were deliberately ignored. Delays occurred due to deliberate family strategies that militated against the mandatory fragmentation of patrimony, but they took into account the instantaneous nature of *posse civil* through informal divisions acknowledging lawful heirs. This circumstance also encouraged informal negotiations among the co-heirs, leading some to buy the shares of others, once a judge concluded the *partilha*. It accounted for why those shares might be called "*tornas*" in certain inheritance documents.[18] In a majority of cases, consequently, *partilhas* would be informally transacted as de facto arrangements, leaving de jure documentation for much later. Not uncommonly, years could pass before the necessary heirs assembled in the presence of a judge to commit the division of an estate to formal resolution.

An expanding central state gradually imposed the presence of a judge, due to progressive taxation of inheritance after 1808. Pombaline law had stipulated that the *partilha* be drawn up within ninety days after death, but Brazilian law shortened that period to thirty days by 1842, only because some heirs became liable for taxes.[19] The fact that necessary heirs were tax-exempt offered yet another reason why families delayed filing a *partilha*. In perhaps a majority of cases, the need to bring the division of an estate before a judge

was not urgent. His presence would be indispensable only when minor children were heirs, or a surviving parent had married too soon after the death of
a deceased spouse, or the necessary heirs could not be located.

Routine delay in filing *partilhas* is another feature of Luso-Brazilian inheritance that contrasts markedly with Anglo-American procedures, wherein probate was indispensable for conferring each heir's inheritance portion. In Brazil, normally a judge's presence merely confirmed the instantaneous transmission of property that already had taken place. Otherwise, the collection of a tax
from heirs who were not necessary gradually made his presence mandatory.
The Luso-Brazilian state began to reassess the inheritance system—both succession and testamentary bequests—as an important, new source of revenue
as soon as the Lisbon Court was established in Rio de Janeiro. It made the
rights of collateral heirs a logical starting point. The *alvará* of June 17, 1809
(Section 8), first broke new ground by taxing all testamentary heirs in succession, as well as beneficiaries of bequests from the *terça*, at the rate of ten percent. Then it imposed the same tax for the first time on *ab intestato* heirs who
were collaterals within the second canonical degree—that is, on all who were
descended from a common grandparent—meaning all collaterals within four
civil degrees (uncles and aunts, nephews and nieces, and first and double
cousins). Collaterals beyond the second canonical degree, that is, beyond first
cousin, or cousins at least once removed, were taxed at the steeper rate of
twenty percent of the value of their inheritance portion (Section 9).[20]

By scrupulously exempting the *ab intestato* successors favored as necessary heirs, the *alvará* of 1809 rendered collateral heirs increasingly more marginal in inheritance. More to the point, this law transformed the role of first
crown, and then imperial, judge, by making them significant collectors of
royal revenue. The 1809 *alvará* stipulated the judge himself would be indispensable for affixing revenue stamps to inventory and *partilha*, attesting to
payment of the tax. It also implied that all but necessary heirs would have to
proceed with a formal inventory and *partilha* in order to pay the inheritance
tax, thus compromising the notion of instantaneous *posse* for collateral heirs.

By independence, consequently, tax liability corresponded to a hierarchy
of heirs, inscribing those who were necessary as the exempt group among *ab
intestato* successors. Otherwise, revenue collection was predicated on the existence of testamentary heirs. To the other reasons accounting for why heirs
delayed completion of a *partilha*, now could be added the motive of postponing payment of a tax. Payment might require sale of the patrimony in
order to raise the necessary cash. In 1819, D. João VI clarified application of
the 1809 *alvará* and determined that a new group was now eligible to pay the
ten-percent tax formerly required of only testamentary heirs. Natural off-

spring whose fathers had used only wills for the purpose of declaring them their *ab intestato* heirs would no longer be exempt from taxation. They, too, became subject to the ten-percent tax imposed by the 1809 *alvará*, unless their declaration of paternity had been made before a notary.[21]

Consequently, this law twisted juridical definition by construing as "testamentary" heirs, for purely fiscal ends, natural offspring who were recognized in a will, but not a notarial affidavit. A glance at any contemporary legal commentary revealed that recognized natural offspring constituted a population of *ab intestato* heirs synonymous with necessary heirs. On the other hand, now only natural offspring who were formally recognized by notarial affidavit were placed on an equal footing with legitimate offspring, as tax-exempt.[22] This step, privileging natural offspring recognized before a notary, amounted to the first taken to delineate paternally recognized natural offspring from legitimate offspring. It anticipated a future revision of the rules of evidence for establishing paternity by devaluing evidence from wills. The latter would become less trustworthy by mid-century, given that they could depend on the hearsay of five witnesses supportive of the testator.

To sum up, the logic of the system of legitimate succession, redefined between 1754 and 1776, confirmed the automatic rights of the legitimate heirs, but favored those who were necessary over all others. It followed that the most comforting position for parents who were joined in legitimate marriage was the secure knowledge that their children were ideally protected when they died without a will. The rules of *ab intestato* succession guaranteed their legitimate offspring instantaneous transmission of each parent's property and exemption from taxes. Stated differently, one-half of the matrimonial community would pass to the legitimate children *in toto* as the *legítima* at the death of each parent.

Universal Community Property

How matrimonial property was regulated by law directly affected outcomes in intestate succession. For that reason, the legal distinction between a surviving spouse, on the one hand, and the necessary or legitimate successors, on the other, must be kept in mind. The Luso-Brazilian community property regulation, known as *communhão de bens*, in tandem with forced heirship, complicated diverging devolution. By calling collaterals to the tenth degree, the ladder of intestate succession intended not to favor a surviving spouse, but to reward cognates—members of the blood kindred.[23] For that matter, illegitimate offspring of varying sub-categories might supersede collateral relatives and, therefore, surviving spouses. One frequently reads that a surviving spouse in a community property regulation is a "successor" or an "heir" of the deceased spouse; in fact, he or she succeeded to nothing. Instead, the surviving spouse continued to hold title to one-half of the couple's community property—called the *metade, meia,* or *meiação.* Inheritance documents always identified him or her as the *"meeiro"* or *"meeira"*—the holder of the half.

The *Ordenações Filipinas* also referred to the community property regulation as *"casamento pela carta de metade"*—marriage according to half-shares—because of the presumption that each spouse held one-half of the matrimonial community. Like the maxim "equal shares for all" characteristic of a partitive system of heirship, the *"carta de metade"* proclaimed equal shares in martrimonial property for both spouses. Almost always, however, the *carta de metade* was a legal figment, implying that a hypothetical "certificate" had established the community. In most marriages, the document discriminating matrimonial property as two equal halves came into existence only after the death of one of the spouses. Thus the inventory listing the decedent's property began by describing the one-half of the community, the *"meiação,"* or *"meia,"* that belonged to the surviving partner, and deducted it from the community, leaving the other half to pass in succession as the decedent's estate.

Clovis Bevilaqua succinctly dispelled the impression perpetuated by many twentieth-century historians that the widow or widower was an "heir": "Regarding the surviving spouse, in his quality as heir, the transmission of *posse* [ownership] does not happen, because it is in the quality of *meeiro* that he is guaranteed his property, until the [two halves] are divided."[24] The scholarly slip construing *meeiras* as "heirs" undoubtedly can be traced to the inferior position that, by comparison, married women enjoyed in law, especially for scholars coming from an Anglo-American legal tradition. Furthermore, it followed from the nature of community property that where Brazilian widows were heirs, they did not inherit according to any "customary right"—that is, analogously to the "widow's share" in Anglo-American legal tradition. They succeeded to the entirety of a husband's *legítima* only when he lacked collateral heirs—or the wives themselves were his cousin or niece. Normally, they remained in possession of their half of the community, a situation contrasting them very favorably vis-à-vis widows in Anglo-American inheritance law.[25]

Brazilian widows perhaps could be said to enjoy a "customary right" to their husbands' "third," or *terça,* but it depended always on a husband's contractual assignment. Either it was assigned by a prenuptial assignment—as dower (*árras*)—or as a bequest from the *terça* via a will.[26] In neither case did it pass in *ab intestato* succession. That a married woman could transmit her own property, via diverging devolution, to the couple's legitimate successors further set her legal position apart from what Anglo-American law historically prescribed.[27] At a widow's death, her dower and dowry usually passed as part of her *legítima* to her children, if they had not already been given as dowry at an older daughter's marriage. During her lifetime, a widow's ownership of one-half the matrimonial community gave her not only a prior and independent legal claim to matrimonial property, but it also conferred considerable prestige and leverage over her adult children.

Community property also implied "universal goods," or *bens universais*, meaning that all property acquired at the moment of marriage and afterward, with the exception of the wife's dowry, belonged to the couple. Where partners wished to keep the property they brought to marriage separate, or to keep separate what was acquired following marriage, then a separate property regulation (*separação de bens*) had to be executed as a prenuptial contract officiated by a notary. The major change brought by the death of a spouse redounded more to widows than widowers, because wives lacked the right as married women to administer their half of the community, as well as related dowry, unless the husband executed notarized permission. *Meeiras*, like *meeiros*, enjoyed the right to alienate their property, given that it no longer constituted part of the matrimonial community. A husband's death thus freed a wife to sell, mortgage, or bestow as a gift what formerly had been her property in the community.

The community property regulation provides one of the best illustrations of how customary arrangements in Portugal gained the force of law over centuries, prior to being incorporated in the *Ordenações do Reino*. In this respect, the importance of customary law that was Germanic mattered to eighteenth-century Portuguese jurists, because, in their efforts to diminish the authority of Roman law, "our customs" represented what they construed as national law. The Visigothic Code (Código or Lei Wisigotho) remained in force until the fourteenth century, having been introduced before the Muslim conquest. It explained why universal community property continued to flourish in Portugal, and why it always enjoyed greater acceptance there than in Spain. Thanks to *Las Siete Partidas*, Spanish law placed greater limitations on universal property in the community, restricting its size and discriminating property acquired by each spouse following marriage, such that it tended to favor separate property more than did Portuguese law. Community property was so rooted in local custom that Portugal's first national law code, the *Ordenações Afonsinas* (1446), incorporated it for being "a usage throughout the population, which made it in force either by the simple fact that it entered conjugal life in some places, or, elsewhere, it was a [written] device."[28]

In 1521, the *Ordenações Manuelinas* imposed universal community property as the legal norm, explicitly describing it for the first time as *"por carta de metade."* Unlike the preceding Afonsine Code, the *Ordenações Manuelinas* presumed the existence of community property wherever couples did not legally execute a written agreement for separate property. In Brazil, that assumption endured until the 1960s. In both colonial and imperial Brazil, consequently, universal community property became the regulation synonymous with marriage, in the absence of a prenuptial agreement to the contrary. This is why law also deemed community property intrinsic to "marriage according to the custom of the realm" (*casamento segundo o costume do Reino*), that is, inherent even in non-sacramental forms of marriage. The Portuguese jurist Coelho da Rocha pointed to what he called the dual face of the community property regulation in the *Ordenações Filipinas*, because they used both terms interchangeably. One face resided in written law, although it implied only a hypothetical document: the carta de *metade*. The other face rested explicitly on Portugal's customary law, by sanctioning marriage "according to the custom of the realm."[29]

TESTAMENTARY SUCCESSION

"Sucessão Por Testamento"

Finally, succession proceeded according to two parallel ladders that positive law careful distinguished. Where individuals were not legitimately born, some could still succeed, not *ab intestato*, but according to testamentary succession. Like *ab intestato* succession, testamentary succession transmitted the *legítima* from one generation to the next. Jurists explained that, in contrast to intestate succession, which followed natural law and occurred instantaneously with the parent's death, testamentary succession had to be effected by a will. Because a testator "instituted" a testamentary heir to the *legítima*, testamentary succession, rather than being "natural," was an artificial creation in civil law. It constituted "the result of human will."[30]

The circumstance of two, parallel ladders of succession has eluded historians today, both North American and Brazilian. One reason is that legal commentaries left a great deal tacit. "Testamentary succession" was deemed *"sucessão por testamento"*—succession by means of a will. The technical language has caused researchers to confound the latter with testamentary bequests that assigned dispositions from the *terça*. Likewise, *"herdeiros por testamento"*—heirs by virtue of a will—has been confounded with heirs to a bequest. Otherwise, legal reform in imperial Brazil definitively eroded testamentary succession for illegitimate offspring, a development the volume that follows will explain. The 1916 Civil Code definitively extinguished it where illegitimate children mattered. It is not surprising, therefore, that historians have neglected to identify testamentary succession as a distinct form of succession, or that they have failed to apprehend that it pertained precisely to legitimized individuals. The concept of testamentary succession, however, survives to the present in the legal option of universal heirship, one available exclusively to individuals who lack necessary heirs.

Testamentary succession derived fundamentally from Book 4, Title 92, Section 1, of the Philippine Code, which provided that, in the absence of legitimate descendants and ascendants, a father could use a will "to dispose of all of his goods as he wished."[31] How it operated with respect to several subcategories of illegitimate children, all of whom needed legitimization by the crown in order to become testamentary successors, is addressed in the following chapters.

The other group benefiting from testamentary succession was "universal heirs," individuals similarly instituted by testators who lacked both ascendants and descendants. If one remembers that testamentary succession remained an option for individuals lacking necessary heirs and applied in only two situations, either to legitimized individuals or to universal heirs, then its logic is readily apprehended. Because the *Ordenações Filipinas* permitted a select group of testators, those lacking necessary heirs, to dispose "of all of their goods as they wished," they could nominate testamentary heirs who were kin, non-kin, or ecclesiastical corporations. Universal heirship thus permitted those without any lineal relatives to "opt out" of forced heirship—to evade the ladder of *ab intestato* succession altogether—by using a will to institute an heir to the *legítima*. Childless couples might use this option to write wills in favor of the other partner, creating a device that enabled the widowed spouse to supersede all collateral relatives within the tenth civil degree. Alternatively, childless individuals might institute a favored sibling or a niece or nephew as their testamentary heir, at the expense of all other collateral relatives or even a spurious child.

Prior to 1750, the most common use of the option of testamentary succession favored the church. The latter's charitable corporations, as well as its regular orders, cathedral chapters, seminaries, dioceses, and parish churches, in addition to the lay sodalities known as *cofradias*, could all be indirectly nominated a universal heir. The fact that Portugal lacked a law of mortmain encouraged the use of this form of testamentary succession as a surrogate, one dictated by customary practice and deliberately encouraged by the church. Nominations in testamentary succession might also operate in tandem with ecclesiastical entail, especially the arrangements known as *capelas*, that generated income for clerical stipends (*côngruas*) or a specific endeavor of the church. Testamentary succession, consequently, acquired great political significance during Pombal's era, when crown law substantially modified the *Ordenações Filipinas* in order to curb severely the right to use universal heirship. Although testators regained the freedom to nominate a universal heir of their choice by the end of the eighteenth century, the manner in which positive national law encumbered nominations during the 1760s, 1770s, and 1780s produced lasting effect by encouraging a wider range of identities among those instituted as universal heirs.

Universal Heirship

Because testamentary succession contravened legitimate, or *ab intestato*, succession, its legal evolution after 1750 proved complex and contradictory. Pombaline regulation of universal heirship, which dated to the Law of September 9, 1769, severely restricted the right to nominate a universal heir as well as the nature of patrimony that could pass in testamentary succession. Initially, the 1769 law represented an attempt to deprive the church of patrimony by a strategy that restricted the testator's freedom of choice to nominate a universal heir from among his or her *ab intestato* heirs. For instance, childless testators could nominate one or more universal heirs only from among their living "legitimate heirs." The law of 1769 defined the latter as relatives within the fourth canonical degree (Paragraph 1). In contrast to heirs reckoned by civil degrees of kinship, those reckoned within four canonical degrees often comprised a huge population: everyone descended from a common great-great-grandparent. However, testators were permitted to leave the universal heir only property "acquired by their own labor, industry, or service" (*bens adquiridos*). That is, the 1769 law excluded patrimony testators had acquired by inheritance from being transmitted in universal heirship. What a testator possessed from a parent's *legítima*, consequently, had to be transmitted according to the basic, 1754 ladder of *ab intestato* succession (Paragraph 1). If no collateral heirs or surviving spouse existed, then the inherited patrimony passed to the royal fisc, not to a universal heir.

When no necessary heirs were living, the Law of September 9 permitted a childless testator to institute a universal heir from among "strangers"—those beyond the fourth canonical degree—but for only fifty percent of his or her inherited goods (Paragraph 3). The other half passed in *ab intestato* succession, to the royal fisc (Paragraph 3), in the absence of either collateral heirs within the tenth civil degree or a surviving spouse. The 1769 law also restricted the use of the *terça* for bequests, again in an attempt to deny patrimony to the church. By stipulating that all property comprising the *terça*, acquired through inheritance, had to be bequeathed in favor of either children or other *ab intestato* successors, the law (Paragraph 2) curtailed the plenary rights to nominate a universal heir, countermanding the *Ordenações Filipinas*. An exception was made for surviving spouses in marriages that were childless, but only where the couple were "reputed to be relatives." Then the *terça* could be bequeathed (Paragraph 4) to the widowed survivor.

In 1775, the crown imposed direct bureaucratic control over all nominations in universal heirship and the transfer of patrimony via gifts inter vivos. In both cases, the Law of January 31, 1775, reiterated the requirement that the customary consent of collateral heirs, even beyond the fourth civil degree, would be needed before a universal heir could succeed. It made explicit that the Tribunal of the Desembargo do Paço, Portugal's high court of crown appeal, would have to confirm all nominations in universal heirship. The main thrust of the 1775 law, nevertheless, attempted to undo the damage ascribed to the Law of September 9, 1769, by restoring the childless testator's opportunity to leave patrimony to a limited number of charities operated by the church. It encouraged charitable giving, due to a drastic decline of resources within the benevolent institutions of the church. However, childless testators lacking collaterals within the fourth degree remained under the previous restriction of 1769: They could nominate a universal heir for only one-half of their inherited wealth, although all the wealth they had personally acquired could be transmitted to the universal heir who met the eligibility qualifications.[32]

The failure of the 1775 law to identify canonical degrees in multiple references to "relatives beyond the fourth degree" provided a deliberate signal. It paved the way for later elimination of legal restrictions on how much of the *legítima* could be disposed in favor of testamentary successors who were close collateral heirs. "Civil degrees" was not specified in the law, but omission of "canonical degrees" implied use of the former, drastically reducing the range of kinship that testators had to take into account when they nominated a universal heir. In fact, the law proved pivotal for issuing the directive that collateral relatives beyond the fourth degree "should be considered strangers (*estranhos*)," wherever the alternative existed to dispose in favor of a charity from a short list of benevolent entities operated by the church. By shrinking the relevant collateral heirs, the law permitted more testators to avail themselves of universal heirship.

Legal commentaries usually discussed testamentary succession exclusively in regard to illegitimate offspring, declining to elaborate the variant of universal heirship. For the first half of the nineteenth century, their authors said little or nothing explicitly about the important option of universal heirship, merely implying its existence when they discussed testamentary succession.[33] Universal heirship nevertheless represented an important inheritance strategy in late colonial Brazil, although it proved even more important after independence. Late colonial law returned to childless testators the unrestricted power they had enjoyed by virtue of the *Ordenações Filipinas* to nominate universal heirs, including "strangers," or non-kin. Stipulations on the nature of property, as either derived from inheritance or acquired during the owner's life, for devolution to a universal heir via the *legítima* were also rescinded by the 1790s. In 1828, approval of the Tribunal of the Desembargo do Paço ceased to operate as the key constraint on this very special strategy of heirship. Consequently, universal heirship became a popular device in imperial Brazil for transmitting patrimony, above all, to preferred siblings or spurious children. It was particularly useful where the latter were informally adopted, in the absence of legitimate issue, because adoption did not begin to enjoy a firm position in positive national law until the 1870s.[34]

Universal heirship deserves greater scrutiny from historians analyzing the transmission of wealth over the long run. Its operation illustrated not only the decline of ecclesiastical power but also the inexorable marginalization of collateral heirs in a Luso-Brazilian inheritance system. Moreover, the emergence of individualism as a construct of nineteenth-century liberalism can be clearly detected in the changing preferences testators demonstrated in nominating universal heirs. Historians undertaking research in Brazilian notarial archives will eventually plot out the ingenious ways that a select group of childless testators, lacking ascendants, imaginatively employed the option of universal heirship. Undoubtedly, both the century and the place in Brazil, not to mention demographic and economic factors, will account for distinct patterns in how universal heirship was employed.

Kathleen Higgins, for instance, found that in the eighteenth-century mining center of Sabará, Minas Gerais, a significant proportion of individuals electing to write wills did so in order to nominate universal heirs. Furthermore, universal heirship consistently demonstrated a singular propensity stretching from 1716 to 1806, in a province known for its high proportion of resident Portuguese immigrants. Namely, the Sabará testators who opted for universal heirship in all but one instance favored the institution of their "*Alma*"—or "Soul"—as the universal heir to the *legítima*.[35] Francisco Gonçalves Pinheiro, an immigrant from the Isle of Madeira, began his 1719 will by declaring his legal eligibility to institute a universal heir: "I am not, nor have I ever been married; I have no forced heir, [either] ascendant or descendant." He then nominated his testamentary successor: "I declare and institute for my universal heir of everything, what remains of my estate, after . . . my debts are paid and my bequests fulfilled, my *Alma*."[36]

Testators tersely instituted their "*Alma*" a universal heir, leaving moot the end to which the *legítima* would be applied. Their intentions nevertheless can be inferred with certainty, given that, beginning in 1769, Pombaline legislation explicitly prohibited the practice of instituting one's *Alma* a universal heir.[37] The *Alma* destined the testator's *legítima* as patrimony for the church, making this variant of universal heirship tantamount to a Portuguese device of mortmain. In Minas Gerais, where the wealth of the gold fields produced innumerable churches, chapels, convents, lay brotherhoods, and many more ecclesiastical entities, the *Alma* was dedicated to those ends. Future research, however, will have to confirm the precise significance of the *Alma* as a patrimonial mechanism for transferring real and movable property to the church.

What is striking about the pattern uncovered by Higgins is the absence of wills that instituted either a collateral relative or a friend as a universal heir. Only one testator, a Portuguese bachelor, instituted a sibling as a universal heir, dividing his *legítima* among a brother, a sister, an executor, and "the souls in purgatory." His 1790 testament also disposed of a modest *terça* in favor of collateral relatives in distant Portugal.[38] Higgins found only one testator who instituted a personal friend as his sole universal heir. Caetano Fernandes da Silva's identity as a former slave, whose self-ascribed origin was the Mina coast of West Africa, undoubtedly accounts for why his 1771 will did not institute his *Alma* as his universal heir. Furthermore, his failure to assign any of his *terça* for masses for his soul confirms his tacit preference for maintaining allegiance to the religion of his birth. Fernandes da Silva left his substantial estate, including twelve slaves, to a universal heir who was his friend and his *testamenteiro*.[39]

In Minas Gerais, unmarried Portuguese men amounted to a substantial population. Those who were childless often construed collateral relatives in Portugal as "lost" kin, or "strangers," preferring to write wills that nominated their *Alma* as the universal heir to the *legítima*. Donald Ramos' research confirmed such a propensity. In eighteenth-century Vila Rica de Ouro Preto, also in Minas Gerais, Ramos' findings contrasted with those of Higgins. His data revealed that 79 percent of the testators who used universal heirship employed it to nominate a universal heir who was not their *Alma*.[40] The widespread practice in Minas Gerais for Portuguese bachelor immigrants to manumit their offspring born to a slave mother, equipping them for heirship as free and therefore *ab intestato* successors, confirmed a special strategy in heirship. Such children, often identified as "*libertos da pia*," freed at the baptismal font, represented a popular alternative beneficiary in universal heirship to the *Alma*.[41] On the other hand, Ramos' data revealed that virtually every testator who chose to institute the *Alma* as universal heir, a total of 21 percent, was an immigrant, either Portuguese or African.

The practice of instituting a universal heir who was a blood relative, but not an illegitimate child, although encouraged under Pombaline law, appears to have become common only after Brazilian independence. Bernardo Pereira de Vasconcellos, the consummate liberal politician of the First Empire and Regency, followed what became a modern convention when he drew up his final will and testament in 1847. He began with a formulaic introduction dating to colonial times, whose purpose had been to remove any ground for declaring the will null, on the ground the testator possessed "infamy" as either an apostate or heretic:

I, Bernardo Pereira de Vasconcellos, legitimate son of Diogo Ribeiro de Vasconcellos and D. Maria do Carmo Barradas, have determined to make—and do make—the declarations and dispositions of my last will in the following manner: I am an Apostolic and Roman Catholic Christian; as such I affirm I will continue to live and die with the help of Divine Grace and, as such, when I will have given up my soul to the Creator . . .'[42]

Next, Vasconcellos asserted his legal right to nominate a universal heir, designating one of his sisters:

I am a bachelor. I do not have children nor any descendants; and because my above named parents already are dead, I have full liberty to dispose of all of my goods . . . . I institute for my universal heir my sister, D. Deoguina Maria de Vasconcellos, in order that all my remaining property belong to her, after the fulfillment of bequests and dispositions enumerated in this testament.

Then he disposed a bequest on behalf of his other sister, what amounted to an income from an endowment:

I leave to my sister Dona Jacinta Carolina de Vasconcellos the sum of 600 mil-réis annually, as long as she is living; and my *testamenteiro* will establish and ascertain the effective and prompt payment, whatever will be most suitable and legal with authorization by the appropriate judge.

Despite a formulaic profession of Catholic faith, Vasconcellos' will paid homage to the modernity of his century, striking a resoundingly secular accent throughout. He stipulated that the *remanescente da terça* bequeathed to his other sister, Jacinta, be used to establish a charity hospital, in the event that she predeceased him. The hospital was to be an uncharacteristically secular charity, a family creation named the "Casa de Caridade Barradas," after his mother. The anti-clerical Vasconcellos left nothing for the church. He meticulously restricted to a bare minimum the amounts his sisters could pay for masses for his soul. As if to put the finishing touch of a liberal credo on his will, he made no mention of God or Divine Providence in the conclusion, avoiding the formulaic conventions standard in the early nineteenth century. Instead, he spoke of the law and the courts, institutions that Vasconcellos had personally done so much to promote and shape throughout his political career. He called on his witnesses to fulfill his dispositions, "begging the respective courts to safeguard and execute them to the fullest, in conformity with the law."

Universal heirship grew in popularity in imperial Brazil as a mechanism for transmitting patrimony to non-kin as well as to close relatives. The will of Francisca da Silva Costa, executed in the 1860s, epitomizes the distance testators had traversed in their nominations of universal heirs by the second half of the nineteenth century. Francisca resorted to universal heirship in order to endow a friend, Esméria Maria Pereira, "for treating me with utmost charity" during her presumably final illness. What made the nomination singular was Esméria's identity. She was Francisca's slave. Therefore, her will first freed Esméria and four other slaves, equipping all of them for heirship, although freedom carried the qualification of "the burden that they serve me while I live." However, Francisca protected their future freedom by declaring that her will would "ratify" the manumission papers she had already filed with the local notary. She used the will to institute Esméria as her universal heir for the two-thirds of her property. What remained as the *terça* she disposed as bequests. Francisca justified the generous act of leaving her *legítima* to Esméria merely "for the sake of the good she deserves from me."[43]

THE INHERITANCE SYSTEM ON THE EVE OF BRAZILIAN INDEPENDENCE

Vasconcellos' will mirrored a broader shift in a Luso-Brazilian inheritance system evident by the independence decade of the 1820s. The trend it demonstrated, toward instituting a universal heir drawn from among the testator's blood relatives, frequently siblings, became common. It was another piece of evidence for concluding that the boundaries of family in the Empire would narrow in the aftermath of Pombaline legal change. Law gradually withdrew rights in heirship from members of the wider kindred—the collateral relatives who reached to the tenth degree. The means for restricting the range of those heirs drew on social and economic change as much as on legal reform. Recognized natural offspring, or those who were legitimized by the crown and spurious, increasingly preempted collateral heirs. Even close collaterals, like siblings, uncles/aunts or nephews/nieces, and double or first cousins, who retained a legal position on the ladder of intestate succession, would find themselves preempted, thanks to universal heirship or, more likely, as we shall see, testamentary succession on behalf of non-legitimate issue. Both arrangements reflected demographic features easily forgotten if the legitimate family is taken to be the sole focus. Many couples were childless, but at least one-third of all births by independence occurred outside legitimate marriage. After independence, therefore, greater opportunity would exist for illegitimate children who were either natural or spurious to gain rights in heirship, further reason why they would be so prominently featured in wills as heirs.

After independence, what changed even more dramatically than the legal position of collateral heirs was the legal position of the church. The church ceased to be as privileged by universal heirship as it had been in the eighteenth century. The 1769 prohibition on instituting the *Alma* as a universal heir was only one law that dramatized the change. It was not rescinded. Yet Higgins' research established that in Sabará testators continued to write wills in universal heirship that, until the early 1800s, contradicted an express Pombaline prohibition. The disregard of law in social practice offered one reason why the crown made repeated efforts to stamp out use of the *Alma*, incorporating the prohibition into crown legislation through the 1790s.[44] On the other hand, the 1769 law prohibiting testators from instituting the *Alma* as a universal heir also restricted the use of the *terça* for endowing the church by means of the *capela*, an entailment. It prohibited real property from being used to constitute the latter.[45]

Parliamentary debate over the abolition of entail, a subject treated in the volume that follows, confirmed that by the 1820s ecclesiastical entails tended to reflect the 1769 law's prohibition of real property. Doubtlessly, the arrival of the Lisbon court, which reestablished the Desembargo do Paço on Brazilian soil in 1808, signaled more effective enforcement of the 1769 prohibition pertaining to *capelas*. Such arrangements had to be committed to contracts approved by the Desembargo do Paço. However, the wishes of individual testators proved more tenacious, a circumstance that future research ought to reveal and clarify. As Teixeira de Freitas later observed, the Law of May 20, 1796, also prohibited the evasive device of instituting "uncertain persons" as universal heirs, a practice that since 1769 had replaced the *Alma*.[46] It would take a liberal government to end endowments to the church that relied on manipulation of devices deriving from the inheritance system. Consequently, Bernardo de Vasconcellos' last will and testament struck the new ideological note, even intimating that after independence Brazil's historical liberalism had fulfilled an important piece of what had been an unfinished agenda of Pombaline reform.

Unlike Vasconcellos, most Brazilians employed wills in conjunction with provisions turning on *ab intestato* succession. Universal heirship addressed very special circumstances that operated in the absence of legitimate children. In contrast to Vasconcellos, most parents drew up wills on behalf of heirs who were their own children, their *ab intestato* successors. Frequently, however, they were not their legitimate heirs. In writing wills, those parents had in mind children born of illicit sexual relationships, whom law regarded as natural offspring (*filhos naturais*). Their right to be called to succession often required parental recognition or testamentary confirmation that recognition had already occurred. Consequently, the other side of *ab intestato*, or legitimate, succession applied precisely to the population that would occupy the explicit attention of liberal legislators in imperial Brazil: natural offspring. It was one from whom the "surprise heir" would emerge as a stock figure during the Regency and Second Empire.

CHAPTER 2

A Forgotten Population of Heirs

Natural Offspring

I certify that in the year 1780 I baptized and placed the holy oil on the child Joaquim, the illegitimate son of Francisca das Chagas, a free, unmarried mulatto woman, herself illegitimate and baptized in the parish of São João of an unknown father, then a servant in the house of the Rev. Joaquim Gonçalves de Figueiredo . . .

Pe. Alberto Caetano Alves,
Bairro da Caturra, Minas Gerais[1]

When the Rev. Robert Walsh, an Anglican clergyman who resided in Brazil during 1828 and 1829, found the birth certificate of Col. Joaquim Francisco das Chagas Catete published in a Rio de Janeiro daily newspaper, he was astounded. As a candidate aspiring to be an elector in the Province of Minas Gerais, Col. Chagas Catete had used the press to respond to the slander that he was an emancipated slave. Since freedmen were ineligible to vote under Brazil's 1824 Constitution, the accusation of slave birth had been an attempt to disqualify him from acquiring status as a prestigious player in the national system of indirect elections. Walsh was nonetheless shocked by a politician's public confession in the press, identifying himself as a matrilineally natural offspring, not to mention the inference that the would-be legislator had been fathered by a country priest. He could not resist drawing a cultural contrast: "I doubt if there could be found, amongst the humblest class in England, a man who would establish his right to vote by such an exposure." Col. Chagas Catete's use of a newspaper to publish the parish registry's verbatim record of his baptism produced the desired effect. It scotched any rumor his mother had been a slave at the time of his birth, verifying that he was born free. Furthermore, as even Walsh was obliged to concede, the act of divulging one's individual *qualidade* as maternally natural—in this case, of acknowledging that one was of unknown father—carried little consequence: "In Brazil, where so many in high station are themselves the founders of their own families," he acknowledged, "respectable descent is but little regarded, except by the few who have a claim to it."[2]

Natural offspring, a distinct and sizable population, have not been as frankly acknowledged by historians and demographers of Brazil with anywhere near the frequency that their contemporaries in late colonial and imperial times routinely remarked on their existence. Usually, they have been ignored or mislabeled in the scholarly literature. A historiographical sin of omission—the failure to acknowledge the existence of natural offspring, either juridically or socially—accounts for why this important population has not received the attention it deserves. By rendering "natural child" as "illegitimate child," scholars have obliterated a central category in Brazilian heirship. Natural offspring enjoyed a socio-legal identity that past generations of Brazilians from all walks of life took for granted when they carefully discriminated between natural and spurious offspring in colloquial speech and inheritance documents. Both were illegitimate, born outside legal wedlock, but natural offspring, whenever recognized by a parent, hardly bore the stigma of illegitimacy.[3] Because many couples fell under canonical prohibitions to marry, or simply lacked the resources to ask the church to declare them in "the free state" to marry, they lived as husband and wife without the sacrament of marriage. In these situations, their natural children would often be taken as tantamount to legitimate offspring.

Brazil's historically high rate of non-legitimate births in colony and Empire derived substantially from the canonical impediments to marriage, coupled with the considerable expense of having them dispensed. The significance of natural offspring in family life, consequently, can be traced to low rates of marriage or, conversely, to a cultural toleration for consensual unions, or *mancebia*, that endured throughout the Empire. Of course, reluctance by whites to marry across racial lines, and, otherwise, to contract matrimony with persons deemed "unequal," amounted to the most fundamental reason why Brazilians did not marry. Many other features of social life encouraged transitory and random sexual unions that also contributed to a high proportion of natural offspring in late colonial Brazil: migration, slavery, poverty, and even small community size—implying an imbalance in prospective partners due to sex or age ratios. Value systems viewed legal marriage, which, until 1890, was synonymous with sacramental marriage in the Roman Catholic Church, as an institution appropriate for only property-owning groups. Even within propertied families, certain siblings would be selected for "celibacy," further accounting for why many Brazilians, perhaps a majority, held little or no expectation of marrying. Lowered expectations of marriage helped to account for why recognized natural offspring frequently were accorded a social evaluation on a par with legitimate offspring.

For North American scholars, natural offspring have often been viewed as

anomalies, given the perspective of Anglo-American legal tradition. Some
have assumed that Brazilians employed "natural child," *filho natural,* merely
as a colloquialism intended to soften the meaning of "bastard" in linguistic
usage. They have been unaware that explicit emphasis on "natural" children
was intended as an emphatic, precisely to distinguish them from spurious
children, the authentic bastards in Luso-Brazilian inheritance law. Explicit
references by testators to their "natural offspring" have sometimes been dismissed by North American historical researchers who interpret wills, leading
them to substitute the adjective "illegitimate" for "natural." As a result, they
have destroyed a key category in heirship that might have unlocked a chain
of logical inferences about social behavior and values in documents. For Brazilians, legal change introduced by the 1916 Civil Code obliterated the special
status natural offspring historically enjoyed in law. Consequently, many of
them have been pushed in the direction of a North American perspective
that conflates "natural" with "spurious" offspring. Nevertheless, Brazilians
are still more inclined to respect *"filho natural"* as an important social
marker than scholars hailing from an Anglo-American legal tradition.[4]

A FAVORED STATUS IN HEIRSHIP

Offspring of "Merely Illicit" Unions

A single linguistic stroke has thus obliterated both a clear legal distinction
in heirship and a subtle boundary in the family's socially constructed nexus,
one stretching to medieval times. In point of fact, scholars have overlooked
the basic circumstance that "natural offspring" pertained fundamentally to a
legal category of heirship. Any social connotation the term conveyed derives
from this fact. Why were natural offspring distinct in law? Rules of heirship
drew a sharp line between two principal categories of illegitimacy, singling
out natural offspring as favored heirs in *ab intestato* succession, while excluding altogether from succession those who were "spurious." In the words
of the Philippine Code, Book 4, Title 93, spurious offspring were born of
sexual unions that were "damnable and punishable," accounting for why
they were deemed the true bastards in Luso-Brazilian legal tradition. Although canon law construed them as "damnable and punishable," Roman
law provided the precedent for denying spurious offspring rights in *ab intestato* succession.[5] Born of unions "prohibited" in canon law, spurious offspring admitted three sub-categories carefully discriminated in both positive
law and popular speech: incestuous, adulterine, and sacrilegious. Their parents' sexual union had broken a dire matrimonial impediment. Given the
complexity of their position in inheritance law, and their more varied social

identities as bastards, discussion of spurious offspring has been left for the chapter that follows.

In contrast to how the *Ordenações* punished spurious offspring, Title 92 of Book 4 departed from Roman law to follow canon law, by permitting natural offspring to be equipped as *ab intestato* successors.[6] Those whose quality of birth was natural escaped punishing condemnation because they were born of sexual unions that canon law regarded as "illicit." Stated most simply, natural offspring received special consideration because they were the children of individuals who might have married—but did not. That is, canon law imposed no grave, or "dire," impediment prohibiting their parents' sexual union or hypothetical marriage. Either the absence of impediments, or sometimes the existence of only minor, dispensable ones, explained why the parents' sexual union was illicit, as opposed to prohibited.[7] Most commonly, the parents of natural offspring declined to marry for reasons of social differences, wherever their union was not ephemeral. Following the canons on marriage, a hypothetical opportunity—the absence of impediments prohibiting their marriage—determined that the offspring would be "natural" in positive law. Furthermore, the latter regarded the parents' sexual union as occurring in a state of nature, illicit, but lacking only the construct of matrimony that derived from a civil society.

The fact that the Portuguese crown could not effectively enforce sacramental marriage after the Council of Trent (1545–1563) helped to explain why recognized natural offspring would enjoy a favorable social status vis-à-vis their spurious counterparts. Prior to Trent, most marriages were rooted in customary arrangements unsanctified by the church, but socially validated. After Trent, natural offspring born of stable, de facto unions frequently continued to be taken as socially equivalent to those born of legitimate, or sacramental, marriage. Furthermore, a common understanding that the Philippine Code endorsed several variants of marriage, deemed "marriage according to the *Ordenações*," in addition to Tridentine marriage, reinforced the weight of preceding custom and perpetuated a favorable evaluation of natural offspring over centuries.

The legal status of natural offspring favored them with a unique position in the rules of Luso-Brazilian heirship only when the parent was a commoner. In the words of Book 4, Title 92, of the *Ordenações Filipinas*, natural offspring would be called to succession "equally" with a father's legitimate children. In the absence of the latter, natural offspring would "inherit all of his goods," even "if the mother was a slave."[8] As "natural successors," wherever recognized by the father, they were called to *ab intestato* succession as forced heirs, on a par with legitimate children.[9] This circumstance set natural offspring completely apart from their counterparts in Anglo-American legal tradition. For that matter, even Spanish law, which also granted natural offspring rights to patrimony, stopped short of according them the equality of position they enjoyed in a Luso-Brazilian legal tradition.[10] On the other hand, rules of heirship in Spain, which still varied considerably by region, similarly underscored that illegitimacy was neither immutable nor generic.[11] "Bastardy" in Spain, as in Portugal, little resembled what the term connoted in either England, the United States, or Protestant North Europe. For these reasons, it is impossible to exaggerate the importance of recognized natural offspring as a key category in Luso-Brazilian heirship. Until 1916, whenever appropriately recognized, they possessed the same legal rights in succession as legitimate children; furthermore, they preempted ascendants on the ladder of intestacy whenever legitimate offspring did not exist.

Scholars must take into account the precise rules that over time determined succession rights for natural offspring, because they began to change subtly by the late eighteenth century. Fundamentally, that two important populations of illegitimate individuals existed—one often only technically illegitimate and freely admitted to *ab intestato* succession as recognized natural offspring, the other excluded altogether as spurious offspring—pivoted on procedures of paternal recognition.

What difference should it make to historians whether an individual was merely natural or "illegitimate"? First, important subtleties in inheritance documents revealing the patrimonial intentions of testators can be overlooked, given how birth status defined legal opportunities or constraints. Second, important features of social mobility can be clearly deduced from the same documents, particularly when attached to racial markers, once the precise rules of heirship are known. Third, strategies of heirship resting on testamentary provisions that were null, though nonetheless adopted by testators as a deliberate means for circumventing law, can be identified only when the precise rules of succession are firmly in mind. Finally, and above all, the paternal recognition clauses in wills that have attracted so much scholarly attention can be accurately interpreted only by keeping in mind that "recognition" implied enjoyment of equal succession rights for any natural offspring born of a commoner parent. A parent's testamentary recognition alone was sufficient to convey those succession rights in *ab intestato* heirship, thus implying the fundamental difference between paternal recognition and legitimization.

Although parental recognition could be accomplished as a legal procedure, via either notarial affidavit or testamentary clause, it could also be conferred informally, simply by virtue of the father's customary behavior in the community. Until 1847, paternal recognition needed no written documentation to be valid, except where previously denied by a testator or disputed by the necessary or collateral heirs. Indeed, where an estate was divided amicably, the legitimate heirs often concurred that their natural half-siblings be called to succession. By comparison, legitimization was a procedure reserved for those whom law excluded from *ab intestato* succession, either because they were of spurious birth or, as a natural offspring, born of a parent who was noble.

Eighteenth-Century Legal Change

Natural offspring became more prominent as a class of *ab intestato* heirs by the close of the eighteenth century, in no small part due to evolving legal interpretation. Jurisconsults and law professors during the 1770s and 1780s argued heatedly over the definition of natural offspring, because many found the 1603 Philippine Code anachronistic for failing to keep pace with changing juridical notions arriving from northern Europe. In fact, legal debate responded to changing social behavior. The key criterion associated with Book 4, Title 92, of the *Ordenações Filipinas*—that natural offspring were the result of merely "illicit" sexual unions—dated to late medieval times, when canon law had figured strongly in the incipient codification efforts of Portugal's fifteenth-century monarchy. The important assumption in Roman law, that the natural offspring's mother had to be the father's concubine, initially supplied the key definitional element that received incorporation in Portugal's Afonsine Code (1446). Following Roman law, however, the *Ordenações Afonsinas* explicitly construed the concubine as "maintained as a wife by an unmarried man."[12] Although, subsequently, Book 4, Title 92, of the Philippine Code omitted emphasis on the quasi-wife status, it reiterated the preceding assumption that natural offspring resulted from the union of "a man with any single woman or his only concubine, there being no kinship or impediment [to marriage] between them." After nearly two centuries, however, the mother's restrictive identity proved indefensible.

In the final quarter of the eighteenth century, Portuguese jurists discarded older presumptions about the mother's identity. No longer would a natural offspring have to be born of the father's concubine. The mother could be a casual partner, even a prostitute. Borges Carneiro reiterated this change for the 1820s, giving it a very modern ring: "Among us and in Spain the [precept of] Roman law has been abolished, according to which a natural offspring must be born of only one concubine (that the father not have another) or an honest woman in order to be natural and capable of succeeding."[13] Jurists, construing social practice as "custom," had modified this particular *ordena-*

ção in the eighteenth century. Reinterpretation of the royal code of 1603 on this important point amounted to a dismissal of Roman law and its replacement by "custom." The mother of the natural child no longer had to be—in the words of the *Ordenações Filipinas'* immortal cliché, "*teúda e manteúda*" by the child's father—"taken to be and supported as his [the father's] own." She might be of questionable reputation, even a prostitute.

Despite a changing juridical definition, not all notaries, even after Brazil's independence, would abandon the outdated formula derived from the *Ordenações Filipinas*. Especially where fathers denied paternity, historians can be led astray by nineteenth-century documents. For instance, the notary whom Capt. Manoel Alves da Costa, engaged to draw up his will in 1826 inserted the legal argument that a natural offspring was born only to a woman maintained in a relationship of concubinage by the father. The will's principal purpose was to disavow paternity of two boys whom Capt. Alves da Costa had raised in his home from the ages of six and eight. Their mother, Josefa da Fonseca, believing him the father, had sent her sons to him twenty years earlier. Subsequently, Capt. Alves da Costa acquired a wife and three legitimate children. Although he confessed to "years" of "illicit sexual relations" with Josefa, he denied paternity of her children and accused her of "attributing these two to me" despite her "coming to understand they were not my sons." Josefa, who was deceased when her former lover drew up his testamentary denial of paternity, could not contradict him.[14]

For good measure, Capt. Alves da Costa slurred Josefa's public reputation, by insisting that "I did not live in the same house [with her]. Due to her freedom of intercourse, her bad habits and bad customs, I never had her for my *manceba* and *barregã*." The will thus explicitly repudiated Josefa as a cohabiting partner, by employing the contemporary term for both concubine and consensual partner—"*manceba*." The notary also threw in the outdated term, "*barregã*," a synonym for "*manceba*," because it derived from the Philippine Code. Finally, Capt. Alves da Costa destroyed whatever remained of Josefa da Fonseca's good name, by ambiguously referring to her as "a woman, lady, *and* a prostitute." He moved to firmer ground, however, when he insinuated that she had had many sexual partners. His will argued that in order "for law to recognize natural offspring on the paternal side, it is necessary that the concubine keep her womb under guard." In insisting that "she be carefully watched, honest, and live with her *mancebo* [consensual partner] in the same house and not give access to another [man]," he invoked the code of behavior sanctioned by the *Ordenações Filipinas*.

By fundamentally resting his denial of paternity on a point of law still in force in the 1820s, he clinched his denial of paternity: "[I] should not call mine some offspring of uncertain and dubious sexual intercourse [*cópula incerta e duvidosa*]."[15] According to him, Josefa had "lived in a house giving access to as many who had intentions for her." Given that he had been unable "to watch her zealously," his will invoked the definitional standard "of an isolated concubine" prescribed by Book 4, Title 92 of the *Ordenações*. "Vague and uncertain sexual intercourse" therefore made it impossible to determine who had fathered Josefa's children. Basically, however, Capt. Alves da Costa's winning argument triumphed because the mother was dead and could not rebut his testimony.

Judicially Determined Paternity

Natural offspring enjoyed a favorable position in Luso-Brazilian inheritance law for yet another reason, one directly relevant to their growing significance after 1800. They possessed ample right to petition the court for a judicial determination of paternity, known as an *ação de filiação por sentença*. Furthermore, the evidence they could introduce in court was extremely diverse. A natural child, either as an adult or, where a minor, through the intermediary of the mother, could initiate court proceedings for legally establishing the blood tie between offspring and father. Once judicially established, the child's legal filiation to the father equipped him or her as an *ab intestato* successor. When the father failed to recognize his natural offspring through his personal behavior, or where he had not declared paternity in a will or the notarized affidavit known as an *escritura pública*, then the child or the mother could petition the court to establish the father's paternity. Similarly, when legitimate half-siblings denied the natural offspring's claim to a full share of paternal patrimony, the excluded child could demand a judicial determination of paternity.

The range of evidence admissible in court made the right to a judicial determination of paternity exceptionally attractive. Although written evidence most commonly consisted of either notarial affidavits of paternal recognition or testamentary clauses declaring paternity, common knowledge in the community that a man had fathered a child could also be introduced as decisive evidence. Judges could take into consideration a number of conjectural circumstances depending on hearsay for establishing paternity, including the father's "public declarations made to neighbors attributing the child's paternity to himself." Public knowledge of the sexual relationship between the parents mattered in court, for the concept of "*fama pública*"—public reputation—ascribing paternity to him counted as fundamental. Otherwise, even the child's physical resemblance to the father, or to another child whom the father had previously recognized, was admissible evidence. If the father raised

the child himself, placed it in the care of a wetnurse, or by reputation provided food, shelter, or a dowry for the child, then those observable acts of
paternal responsibility also counted as evidence. Finally, his reputation for
economically supporting the mother, or his established sexual relationship
with her, including neighbors' testimony about the regularity of his noctur-
nal visits, could be introduced in court as evidence.[16]

Stuart Schwartz cites a fascinating 1766 petition brought before the *ouvidor*, or crown judge, in Santo Amaro, Bahia, that conveyed how the crucial
contrast between "natural" and "spurious" turned on eligibility for *ab intestato* succession rights. An action for a judicial determination of paternity, the
petition illustrated a situation where the *ab intestato* heir, or heirs, had denied succession rights to a natural offspring, probably because she would
have displaced those heirs. A *liberta*, or manumitted slave, who had been
born at Engenho Mombaça, she sought to be called to succession as her deceased father's heir. Testifying that she had been "freed in the womb" by her
father, who was formerly an overseer on that sugar estate, the *liberta* established her eligibility for succession. Simultaneously, his manumission of her
ipso facto signified paternal recognition.[17] She further implied her eligibility
to be his *ab intestato* successor by testifying that her father "was an ordinary
man," meaning that he lacked noble rank. In stating that she was of "illicit"
birth, the *liberta* explicitly confirmed that "no impediment to marry" had
existed between her parents. "If he had wished," her father could have married her mother.[18]

The *liberta*'s petition illustrated two important points about how law mediated rights in heirship for natural offspring.[19] First, that the complainant
was of low social status, a woman manumitted from slavery, is a striking re-
minder of the access ordinary individuals might have to a crown judge. Second, the *liberta* had not been called to succession as a matter of course, but
excluded. That her filiation to her father had to be judicially determined implied her rights in heirship had been denied, by either her father's legitimate
offspring, his parents, collateral relatives, or surviving spouse. Complaints
similar to this found their way into Brazil's law courts usually when *ab intestato* heirs excluded their father's natural offspring from succession. By the
same token, a father's bequest from the *terça* on behalf of a natural offspring
who was not called to succession suggested that he was complicit in a strategy for reserving his *legítima* for his legitimate children. Not surprisingly, ex-
slaves turned up as plaintiffs in such courtroom dramas because the owners
who freed them frequently had fathered them.[20]

Paternal recognition determined by a judge constituted the exception.
Ordinarily, recognition was said to be "spontaneous." That is, fathers volun-

tarily recognized their natural children by freely acknowledging their blood bond within the community, even when they did not live in consensual unions with the mothers. Publicly recognized, natural offspring did not have to be concerned about their succession rights as long as the father's legitimate heirs concurred. Even when they did not, *ab intestato* succession rules insured those rights, placing the burden of denying paternity on the legitimate heirs. Some fathers nevertheless were well advised to execute written declarations of paternity, where they feared a natural offspring's claim to *ab intestato* succession would be unclear or subject to dispute. Posthumous declarations of paternity, written as guarantees of rights, have led many historians to conclude that parents were legally required to "recognize" natural offspring in a will. Worse, they have assumed those declarations of recognition constituted "legal" legitimization. Yet such clauses were merely safeguards as long as the decedent had not denied paternity.

Declaring Paternity: Recognition, Not Legitimization

Fathers and mothers could not randomly use wills or notarial declarations for "legally" legitimizing natural offspring, as a number of historians have assumed. Instead, testamentary legitimization pertained only to natural offspring of a noble parent. Alternatively, it applied to all spurious offspring. When the parent was a commoner, the natural offspring was "recognized" by the father, or he "declared" his paternity, implying the legal notion of "*perfilhação*," the father's declaration of a blood tie to the child. *Ab intestato* succession rights followed. However, when the parent was noble, legitimization by the crown was necessary for conferring those succession rights. Legal commentaries approached recognition as a procedural question. They applied it only to fathers, given the juridical presumption that maternity was "obvious," unless the mother had concealed it. "Regarding maternity, filiation can easily be proven and with certainty," asserted Borges Carneiro in the 1820s.[21] Or, as Lafayette Rodrigues Pereira, Brazil's famous jurist of the late Empire, pronounced with considerably less inhibition: "Maternity reveals itself by unequivocal external signs: pregnancy and childbirth."[22] Hence mothers of natural offspring normally did not "declare" maternity. Baptismal registers, however, amounted to the same thing, for, customarily, unwed mothers presented themselves at the font in confirmation of the child's maternal filiation, and in the company of witnesses. That circumstance accounted for why positive law defined parish registries as civil registries.

The sole context for legitimization to apply to a natural offspring was when the parent possessed any degree of noble rank. Those situations will be considered very briefly here, but explored more extensively in Chapter 4.

Historians need to appreciate that testators who used wills to declare they were "legitimizing" a natural offspring deserve special attention as parents who possessed at least a minimal degree of nobility. Otherwise, there was no legal reason for a commoner parent to resort to a will for "legitimizing" a natural offspring.

Parents used wills and notarial declarations to bestow formal recognition, commonly, paternal recognition, on behalf of a natural offspring for many reasons. Above all, when they had previously concealed or denied paternity. The motive almost always admitted inheritance rights, but desire to give the child a name and an identity also counted a great deal. Otherwise, where competing legitimate heirs might later exclude a natural offspring from the *legítima*, then the father or mother was well advised to document paternity or maternity in a will.[23] Manuel Garcia, for instance, recognized his natural children in his 1750 testament in order to insure they would be the successors to his *legítima*, in company with his two legitimate children. The daughters he had fathered before marriage had been baptized "of unknown father," meaning that he had concealed paternity. Hence his will served to declare or reveal his paternity posthumously, and, by conferring paternal recognition, guaranteed that his natural daughters would be called as his forced heirs.[24]

Alternatively, complex property arrangements might prompt a notarial declaration of paternal recognition, in anticipation of marriage. The well-known founder of the Paulista family bearing his name, Dr. William Ellis, formally recognized his two natural daughters, Maria and Sofia, in the pre-nuptial contract that he signed with his future wife in 1839.[25] Prior to marriage with Maria do Carmo da Cunha Bueno, a widow with two legitimate children, Ellis clarified and confirmed the inheritance status of his natural daughters, intending that they would share his *legítima* equally with any children born of his marriage to Maria do Carmo. Ellis' caution doubtlessly pertained to his identity as an English immigrant, but his use of a prenuptial contract was a device protecting the patrimonial rights of natural children. The arrangement simultaneously safeguarded his future wife's dowral wealth as maternal patrimony reserved exclusively for her legitimate children by her first husband. In fact, her family, rather than Ellis', may have insisted on such a contract.

Sen. Francisco de Paula Pessôa, patriarch of a powerful political family in the Province of Rio Grande do Norte, used a different device to guarantee the same objective that motivated Ellis. Although his example is drawn from the imperial period, it illustrates the extent that some testators were willing to go in order to execute strategies of heirship that were invalid. In the 1878 will he executed shortly before his death, on behalf of his seven legitimate offspring, he referred to a prior will, on deposit with a notary in the provincial capital. Drawn in 1858, the first will had recognized and disposed in favor of Leocadio d'Andrade Pessôa, his natural son. Leaving nothing to chance, Sen. Paula Pessôa left the instruction in his last will and testament that the earlier will retain its validity, giving it simultaneous effect. Because Leocadio was himself a prestigious imperial judge, doubtlessly his father's wishes prevailed over any point of law.[26]

Disavowing Paternity: A Strategy of Parental Concern

As the above-mentioned example of Capt. Manoel Alves da Costa illustrated, testators wrote wills for the deliberate purpose of denying paternity of a child who was illegitimate, sometimes even withdrawing paternal recognition they had previously declared before the community. Their wills nevertheless provide clues to motives that as testators they left implicit. Yet rules of heirship usually make it possible to deduce those motives, as in the case of Capt. Alves da Costa, whose will nevertheless obliged him to record his paternity of several legitimate children, the very beneficiaries of his denial of illicit paternity. On the other hand, rules of heirship sometimes forced fathers to devise ingenious strategies, usually with the assistance of a notary, when they wanted to favor the natural children they cherished most. Their motives were not always reprehensible, for sometimes they sought to bestow patrimony on natural offspring whom law denied succession rights.

Sargento-Mór Custodio Gomes de Almeida left such a will in 1820. Initially enigmatic, the document stood as the most convoluted and bizarre last will and testament encountered in the research for this book. Eventually, however, it emerged as a master text for unlocking one of the strategies devised by testators whose natural offspring were barred from succession. In the case of Sgt°-Mór Custodio Gomes de Almeida, the pivotal rule of heirship was unstated, but otherwise assumed in the text of his will: As a militia officer, he enjoyed minimal nobility, making any natural offspring born after he acquired his officer's patent ineligible to succeed him as his *ab intestato* heir.[27] In that respect, the birth order of the two children his will disavowed as his natural offspring fundamentally mattered. Unfortunately, he stated only his son's approximate age, but referred to the daughter in terms suggesting she may well have been older. Either she was born before her father acquired his minimally noble rank or, by virtue of the latter, she, too, was excluded from succession. In any case, familiarity with the rule of heirship excluding the natural offspring of a father possessing any rank of nobility permits the testator's otherwise puzzling statements about his paternity of both natural children to be decoded.

Sgt°-Mór Custodio Gomes de Almeida began his will with the admission that he was "fearful death would take me unexpectedly and leave me intestate." Ordinarily, fear of succession would be followed by the declaration of paternity on behalf of a natural child, but his concern focused on the person he used his will to nominate as his universal heir. Although a universal heir implied the testator was childless and his parents had predeceased him, in this case, the nominee was none other than the child to whom the testator had given his family name and recognized in the community as his natural son: Joaquim Manoel de Almeida. Born around 1801, Joaquim Manoel was nearly twenty, and mentally disabled, leading the testator to foresee the day when his own death would necessitate special financial arrangements for the young man's custodial care.[28]

This Bahian militia officer nevertheless used his will for a dual purpose. After nominating Joaquim Manoel as his universal heir, Sgt°-Mór Custodio then denied paternity of a young woman named Maria Custodia. Like Joaquim Manoel, he acknowledged, she was taken by reputation in the community to be his natural child. Maria Custodia had been "born of illicit relations with a *parda* by the name of Leandra, now deceased," the testator explained. Leandra, he claimed, "knew how to persuade me that I was the father." More to the point, Sgt°-Mór Custodio knew that Maria Custodia could have recourse to the court and would be on firm ground in bringing an action against him either for a judicial determination of paternity or child support. He stated he had accepted her into his home when she was around four years old and raised her "with the attentions appropriate to a true father." To wit, he had recognized his paternity of the young woman before the community.

The second purpose for the will turned on the testator's contradictory declaration. Although Sgt°-Mór Custodio flatly denied paternity of the young woman, he also disinherited her—reinforcing the suspicion that she was his biological daughter. He used the standard ground sanctioned by the *Ordenações Filipinas* for daughters, "moral turpitude." He recounted that he had turned Maria Custodia out of his home at age sixteen or seventeen, when she "let herself be seduced, deflowered, and [became] pregnant in my own house." His rejection of her was absolute: "She no longer belonged to my family, due to her unnatural deflowering." The imputation of "unnatural" connoted incest, but he did not identify the seducer. Perhaps the man was a close relative, his brother, or even Joaquim Manoel. "Soon after this event," he continued, "I came for a very precise reason to be persuaded that this girl was not my daughter and never had belonged to me." He therefore named another man as her father.

He offered no explanation for why this remarkably timely disclosure occurred, but leapt straight to the main point. Maria Custodia "cannot demand of my heir the right of [child] support, as [my] natural daughter," he pronounced, "nor could she be either his [*ab intestato*] successor or extract support [from Joaquim Manoel]." The notary inserted explicit reference in the will to the Law of June 19, 1775, and the earlier *assento* of April 9, 1772, both of which stipulated that natural and spurious offspring enjoyed the right of paternal child support. Curiously, he cited the very laws Maria Custodia hypothetically could invoke for claiming child support, but only on the ground she was the testator's natural daughter. Sgt°-Mór Custodio feared her claim to child support, one the court could uphold even if confirming disinheritance of his daughter, because it would deplete his estate of the resources he wanted to reserve exclusively for Joaquim Manoel.

The enigmatic and contradictory facets of Sgt°-Mór Custodio's will did not stop with his repudiation of Maria Custodia as his natural daughter—or his disinheritance of her as his *ab intestato* heir. They also pertained to how he construed his tie to the individual whom he instituted as his universal heir at the will's outset, the man he had informally recognized for two decades as his natural son, Joaquim Manoel. Throughout the will, Sgt°-Mór Custodio avoided identifying him as his natural son, even though he eliminated Maria Custodia as his heir. The formulaic introductory statement in wills routinely offered by fathers of natural children, when declaring paternity, was missing. Instead, he called into question the presumption of his paternity and resorted to the strategy of nominating as his universal heir the natural son he had repudiated. Nor did he offer any details of his own relationship with the child's mother. The reason must be deduced from rules of heirship. Joaquim Manoel could not be his *ab intestato* successor, because, as Sgt°-Mór Custodio's younger natural child, he had been born after his father received his patent as a militia officer. His minimally noble rank, intrinsic in the patent, prohibited his natural son from being called to succession as his heir.

Maria Custodia threatened the son's welfare, presumably because she was the older natural child, meaning she probably had been born before her father acquired his officer's patent. In that event, she would have been his sole *ab intestato* successor. If her rights in heirship were upheld in court, then her half-brother, Joaquim Manoel, would have been ineligible to succeed, either as a universal heir or a natural offspring. He would even have been ineligible for a bequest from his father's *terça*, due to the existence of a half-sibling who was natural, given his father's minimal nobility. In an alternative scenario, where Maria Custodia was born after Joaquim Manoel, like him, she could not succeed. In that case, the father merely disinherited her as preemptive protection for his mentally disabled son, although the effect was null. Even if disinherited, she could petition the court for child support for herself and young child until she turned 25, the age of legal majority.

Yet the father's tie to his son was so strong that, even after initially nominating Joaquim Manoel his universal heir, and disavowing the paternity everyone believed existed, he made a unique reference to their blood tie. After several pages, the will recorded an angry paragraph devoted to the testator's repudiation of the young woman he had accepted as his natural daughter until she was sixteen: "I declare that I have no other natural child to share my inheritance with than the one I nominate as my [universal] heir." The father's anguish over the fate of his son could not prevent this admission from falling into the text of his will. Otherwise, the words that Sgt°-Mór Custodio used to deny his paternity of Joaquim Manoel strikingly resembled the very words he used to construe Maria Custodia as the daughter of another man. Acknowledging only that he had had "illicit relations with Antonia Fernandes da Costa," the mother of Joaquim Manoel, Sgt°-Mór Custodio carefully left his own relationship to her moot. He stopped just short of saying he was the father: "She gave birth to a son whom she named Joaquim Manoel de Almeida, whom I have taken and recognized as my son and who can be found [living] in my company, for whom I institute and nominate and call my universal heir to the two parts [thirds] of my goods." He placed on the mother even the responsibility for giving the boy his father's family name, a privilege that law awarded only to him.

The contradictions in how this testator acknowledged Joaquim Manoel as his natural son became clearer where the will's main preoccupation, eliminating Maria Custodia's potential claim to her father's *legítima*, mattered. He feared that child support for Maria Custodia and her child could leave destitute the boy he had "taken to be my natural son." Concern was compounded by his admission that Joaquim Manoel "did not enjoy perfect common sense." If that stated motive also explained Maria Custodia's pregnancy, then it would have meant that her daughter was also the testator's granddaughter. In such a circumstance, where paternity of Joaquim Manoel was disavowed and his older, natural daughter disinherited, the rules of heirship would have indicated his granddaughter as his sole heir *per stirpes*. That outcome, leaving Maria Custodia her daughter's guardian, was equally unacceptable to the testator.

The will's strategy of heirship became perfectly transparent only in the testator's final disposition. When Sgt°-Mór Custodio exercised his right to dispose of bequests from the *terça*, he left the meaningful sum of 200 *mil-réis* to "Leandra's daughter"—to Maria Custodia—"in the state of poverty and disgrace in which she lives." Nevertheless, he encumbered the bequest, further corroborating that he feared Maria Custodia could go to court to undo his will. He stipulated that if she made any legal claim, either to his *legítima* or for child support, then the bequest from the *terça* would be revoked. The purchase of her silence doubtlessly guaranteed not only that she would not make any claim to his estate but also that the knowledge she possessed of the paternity of her own child would never come to the attention of a judge. Sgt°-Mór Custodio named his brother the executor of his will, and, together with his nephew, the guardians for the disabled Joaquim Manoel.

When he died, within a month of making the will, the invalidity of Sgt°-Mór Custodio's strategy of universal heirship did not matter. Presumably, his will was not challenged, because he made his brother and his nephew the *testamenteiros*. More to the point, the approval of the Tribunal of the Desembargo do Paço that law required after 1775 was not sought. After his death, Sgt°-Mór Custodio's *legítima* was mortgaged as he had arranged, in order to provide income for the custodial care of the disabled Joaquim Manoel during the twelve remaining years of his life. When he died in 1833, the account records on the estate suggest it was not well managed, but that he alone enjoyed the benefit of the income it had provided.

LEGITIMIZATION

The common assumption that recognition and legitimization were one and the same has arisen because the types of legitimization, and what rights each conveyed, not to mention the specific procedures they required, have gone unapprehended in the scholarly literature. Legitimization had nothing to do with the legal situation of natural offspring, as long as the parent was a commoner. Indeed, legitimization was a legal impossibility for the latter. Legitimization pertained exclusively to either the natural offspring of a noble parent or to all spurious offspring regardless of the parent's legal estate. Fundamentally, the purpose of legitimization was to "break" bastardy, another reason it did not apply to natural children of commoner parents. Furthermore, legitimization always occurred at the parent's initiative, never because the child obtained it by judicial determination.

Paternal or maternal recognition, consequently, must always be distinguished as legal constructs separate from legitimization in reading inheritance documents, however much they were prerequisites for either spurious offspring or the natural offspring of a noble parent to obtain legitimization. Whereas a commoner parent could recognize a natural offspring as an act of personal volition, or his child could petition for a judicial determination of paternity, legitimization was an act, whether accomplished by the parent or confirmed in court, that depended solely on the parent's initiative. Neither a spurious offspring nor the natural child of a noble parent could initiate a judicial determination of paternity, except to obtain child support.

The *Ordenações Filipinas* stipulated three distinct modes by which legitimization could be accomplished: 1) by the parents' subsequent marriage; 2) by means of a will or affidavit, making it simple legitimization; and 3) by royal authorization, making it crown legitimization, known as "*per Rescriptum Principis.*"[29] The following chapters will elaborate considerably on the second and third modes, but they will also receive brief attention below in order to clarify why legitimization and recognition were not necessarily synonymous.

Legitimization by Subsequent Marriage

Declarations of paternity—and, rarely, maternity—in wills and notarial affidavits did not convey legitimization for natural offspring, where the parent was a commoner. Yet there was a form of legitimization that did apply to all natural offspring, whether the parent was commoner or noble. Gouvêa Pinto alluded to it in emphasizing the legal parity of legitimate and natural offspring in succession law: "Legitimate children and natural children of a commoner father, and even children who have been legitimized through subsequent marriage, individually share equal-sized portions of the *legítima*, without distinctions due to sex, age, or family affiliations . . . ."[30] In other words, the subsequent marriage of either the commoner or noble parents of the natural offspring automatically legitimized the latter. Derived from canon law, legitimization by subsequent marriage (*legitimação por matrimônio seguinte*) merely had to follow conception. It could occur many years after the child's birth. In imperial Brazil, the parents' marriage sometimes took place on the eve of the natural child's marriage, or in the context of a double wedding celebrating both marriages, simultaneously equipping the child as a legitimized spouse. Although individuals legitimized by subsequent marriage were identified as "*filhos legitimados*," that is, identically to those legitimized by the crown, inheritance documents still carefully discriminated them from the latter. The reason was that those legitimized by the parents' marriage automatically enjoyed *ab intestato* rights in succession and, in every other legal respect, were equal to legitimate offspring. However, the beneficiaries of crown legitimization might differ, especially if they enjoyed only testamentary succession rights.

Legitimization by subsequent marriage contributed significantly to Brazil's low rate of marriage, because couples who were not canonically prohibited from marrying could postpone marriage until after the birth of their children and still confer all the effects of legitimacy on the offspring. Indeed, postponing marriage until the birth of a child remained a common feature of family formation in both Portugal and Brazil into the twentieth century. Parish and civil marriage registries recorded the names of simultaneously legitimized children together with those of their parents. Succession law thus worked to favor postponement of marriage, but not to delay starting a family. Of course, legitimization by subsequent marriage was not necessary in order to convey succession rights to children when the parent was a commoner, for only the parent's recognition was required. However, when parents belatedly married, following several children, then legitimization by subsequent marriage often guaranteed that older, natural children would be placed on the same social footing with younger children born in legitimate marriage.

Simple Legitimization

The second means of legitimization can be construed as "simple" because it was executed by a declaratory clause in either a will or a private or public—notarized—affidavit. Simple legitimization pertained to both spurious offspring and the natural offspring of noble parent. It consisted of merely the parent's written declaration that the blood tie existed with the child and, technically, the explicit affirmation that he or she "legitimized" the offspring. Therefore, in reading wills or notarial affidavits, the historian's discovery that a parent "legitimized" a child offers a key clue, especially when accompanied by information that the child was natural. Then the unstated assumption should be that the parent was not a commoner, but possessed minimal nobility, like the example of the above-mentioned Sgt°-Mór Custodio. Jurists frequently distinguished this simple form of legitimization from the parental "recognition" a commoner parent conferred, by referring to it as "*perfilhação*"—what hypothetically translates awkwardly in English as "perfiliation." Unlike filiation, "perfiliation" meant that the parent established his or her blood tie to the child, not vice-versa. Of course, *perfilhação* amounted to recognition, and occasionally the word was applied to a commoner father's recognition of a natural offspring, especially in contexts where he executed a notarial affidavit to that effect. Jurists considered "*perfilhação*" synonymous with simple "legitimization" deriving from the parent's recognition and distinguished it from the "solemn legitimization" by the crown, known as "*perfilhação solemne.*"

The key point about simple legitimization, especially when conferred in wills, was that it never conveyed succession rights.[31] From Pombaline times onward, simple legitimization conferred few legal effects, for its value lay in "breaking" bastardy in an elementary fashion. It signified the parent acknowledged his or her blood tie to the child, enabling the latter to use the family names. Usually, for spurious offspring, it was bestowed posthumously, by a will, due to their "damnable and punishable" birth. Where the child was a natural offspring of a noble parent, the tie was more often revealed and a notarial affidavit frequently the means for conferring simple legitimization. In the latter context, simple legitimization gave the child a restricted right to enjoy some of the parent's "honors," or legal privileges, in addition to family names. The offspring was entitled to use the parent's coat-of-arms, a prerogative tantamount to "breaking" bastardy among the children of the nobility.[32]

Yet simple legitimization never conveyed succession rights to those children, a circumstance historians reading wills usually have not apprehended. Its utility lay solely in removing the stigma of bastardy, permitting the child to be received in the society of the parent's peers.

Crown Legitimization

Crown legitimization was carefully distinguished as "solemn legitimization," what jurists underscored as *perfilhação solemne*. Unlike simple legitimization, it fulfilled formal procedures required by positive law that culminated in a legitimization certificate issued by the high crown Tribunal of the Desembargo do Paço. In breaking bastardy, crown legitimization implied a list of legal effects that more closely equated the beneficiary with legitimate offspring than did simple legitimization. Above all, solemn legitimization was intended to confer succession rights, the most common motive leading Brazilians to petition the Tribunal of the Desembargo do Paço after 1808.

Two groups were eligible for crown legitimization, both of whom the *Ordenações Filipinas* excluded from *ab intestato* succession: all spurious individuals—those who were incestuous, adulterine, and sacrilegious—and the natural offspring of noble parents. Only the former, whom the *Ordenações*, Book 4, Title 93, stigmatized as of "damnable and punishable" birth, were true bastards in Luso-Brazilian legal tradition, for the natural offspring of noble parents were treated rather ambiguously. Jurists appreciated their legal position as anomalous. The fact that they were of illicit birth considerably mitigated their social standing; yet for purposes of succession, they had to be regarded as bastards, because Book 4, Title 92 (Sections 2, 3), of the *Ordenações* clearly denied them *ab intestato* succession rights.

The act of *perfilhação*—the parent's declaration of the biological link to the child—was an indispensable prerequisite for crown legitimization. Ordinarily, notarial or testamentary declaration served to establish simple legitimization. Equally necessary, however, was the parent's explicit declaration that he or she wanted a child to be legitimized by the crown. Because crown legitimization was often conferred after the parent's death, a petition for legitimization might be initiated by either the child or the surviving parent. Evidence for the deceased parent's prior intent to legitimize the child, however, had to be introduced in preliminary judicial proceedings.[33] Thus *perfilhação* implied an exclusive parental prerogative to recognize a child who was a legal bastard. When rendered "solemn" by the crown, then *perfilhação* amounted to crown legitimization—*perfilhação solemne*. Solemn legitimization was always an expensive and protracted judicial proceeding conducted before the Tribunal of the Mesa do Desembargo do Paço, as Portugal's highest court of royal appeal, and it was awarded "by the mercy and grace of the sovereign."

Writing around 1805, royal jurisconsult Lobão reiterated the emphasis that his predecessor, Mello Freire, had placed on the key element of parental intent in petitions for crown legitimization. He scrupulously enumerated the prescribed procedures to follow for obtaining succession rights concurrent with crown legitimization. His instructions are worth quoting at length, for they were reproduced verbatim in all the authoritative legal commentaries consulted after Brazilian independence:

In this kingdom, customarily fathers make . . . a will in which they recognize as being their offspring those whom they intend be legitimized. They declare the persons [mothers] of whom they were born, the qualities of the spuriousness and vices [from which the union sprang] . . . and in the same affidavit (or in the will), [the father] beseeches the crown that it be for the best to legitimize and to dispense this offspring in order to be his heir, according to the custom of the realm. . . . One can also institute the spurious offspring an heir in a will with the qualification, "If the monarch would legitimize" [*si a principe legitimetur*] . . . in order to prove the father's intent and to enter a plea for legitimization for [the offspring] to succeed to the father's inheritance.[34]

The key point about crown legitimization, underscored Lobão, was that it could never be conferred when the parent had deliberately withheld or neglected to bestow the simple legitimization of recognition—*perfilhação*—as a preliminary act. Nor could solemn legitimization be awarded without evidence for the parent's prior intent to seek crown legitimization for the child. These circumstances caused crown, or solemn, legitimization to differ from the judicial determinations of paternity that natural offspring could routinely obtain in court. When spurious children petitioned a crown judge to rule on their parent's *perfilhação*, almost always they did so in anticipation of petitioning the Tribunal of the Desembargo do Paço for solemn legitimization.

However, they did not ask the judge to determine their paternity, but to rule on evidence left by a parent whom they alleged established a future intent to legitimize them before the crown.

Without the presumption of parental intent to legitimize before the crown, the door to a legitimization petition was shut. Thus the distinction between filiation, on the one hand, and "perfiliation" on the other, turned on the natural offspring's right to demand paternal recognition from a judge, and the spurious offspring's total dependence on the parent's volition for conferring simple legitimization. Finally, crown legitimization, like simple legitimization, merely broke bastardy. It, too, bestowed the right to use the parent's honors and names. What made it so coveted, on the other hand, was that it opened the door to gaining concurrently awarded succession rights.

Lobão, then, offered the standard notarial formula written into wills, wherever the testator had in mind the future crown legitimization of either a spurious offspring or a natural offspring whose parent was noble: "if the monarch legitimizes." Alternatively, the formulaic "if legitimization is obtained," was written into wills to signify the testator's intent that the child be legitimized by the crown.[35] This clause of intent then equipped the child to petition the Tribunal of the Mesa do Desembargo do Paço. The formula fulfilled procedures prescribed by the *Ordenações*, in Book 2, Title 35, Section 12.[36] Notaries well versed in testamentary procedures advised their clients to insert the requisite clause, "if legitimization is obtained," into their wills as explicit confirmation of their intent the child should receive solemn legitimization. Where they were less expert, or absent, testators' colloquial language could nonetheless convey intent. For that matter, the children themselves sometimes petitioned for crown legitimization, relying on the simple legitimization in a parent's will or notarial affidavit, but complementing it with a wide array of supplemental evidence to substantiate parental intent.

The Tribunal of the Desembargo do Paço

Crown legitimization, the legal remedy for all offspring who were spurious, as well as the natural offspring of a noble parent, was bestowed by the Tribunal of the Desembargo do Paço. This direct organ of the sovereign's "mercy and grace" dated to the reign of D. João II (1481–1495), although Mello Freire located the official year of its creation as 1477, toward the end of D. Afonso V's long reign. Only in 1574, however, did Portugal's uncrowned monarch, D. Sebastião, delegate responsibility for crown legitimization to the Desembargo do Paço.[37] Until then, the sovereign personally bestowed his royal "mercy and grace" in an act that dispensed positive law for the purpose of conveying crown legitimization. In his capacity as "the Legislator," the monarch possessed the power to "suspend" law that barred two categories of illegitimate offspring from succeeding *ab intestato*. That is, legitimization certificates issued *"per Rescriptum Principis,"* by writ of the prince, dispensed, or "suspended," Titles 92 and 93 of Book 4 of the Philippine Code, denying *ab intestato* succession rights to spurious children and the natural children of noble parents—to bastards.[38] Legal commentaries in imperial Brazil reiterated the monarch's prerogative as a precept of law: "Precisely to the monarch belongs the power to expand or to restrict the rights of [legally distinct] offspring."[39] Even after authority to legitimize was transferred to Brazil's imperial judiciary, in 1828, jurists continued to refer to solemn legitimization as originating *"por provisão régia"*: by royal determination.

As "the central organ in the bureaucratic structure of the Portuguese empire," the Mesa do Desembargo do Paço operated as both an administrative board and a tribunal. It functioned as "a council and advisory board [*mesa*] on all matters of justice and legal administration."[40] A complex bureaucracy that oversaw royal authority in the courts and related administrative bodies, the Mesa do Desembargo do Paço also functioned as a royal court of final judicial appeal. It reviewed cases referred from Portugal's high court of appeals, the Casa da Suplicação. Where the sovereign's Brazilian subjects mattered, the Desembargo do Paço coordinated judicial determinations and administration with the Overseas Council. It was analogous to what in Spain was the Camara de Justicia e Gracias, which made similar judicial determinations for Spanish American subjects in tandem with the Council of the Indies.[41] In its capacity as a tribunal, the Desembargo do Paço was deemed one of "royal privilege," meaning it was a court empowered to grant petitions by dispensing law in force, even to overrule the Casa da Suplicação. Practically speaking, from the Pombaline era until Brazil's independence decade of the 1820s, it functioned as a court of royal appeal relying on the sovereign's "mercy and grace" to issue not only legitimization certificates but also to authorize the creation of entails, approve adoptions, and confirm nominations in universal heirship. Each of those arrangements contravened the rules of *ab intestato* succession, explaining why they needed the monarch's dispensation of law. As a high court, the Tribunal of the Desembargo do Paço also appointed the judges who staffed the royal magistracy and otherwise enjoyed broad powers to review all judicial decisions.[42]

Only very recently have the legitimization decisions issued by Portugal's Tribunal of the Mesa do Desembargo do Paço attracted attention from Brazil's social historians. Beginning in the 1960s, historians of Spanish America accorded important significance to analogous *"cédulas de gracias al sacar,"* royal certificates "dispensing law by the grace of the crown." They paid them

important attention for removing the notorious "defect" of color associated
with both indigenous and African ancestry.[43] Yet the historical literature for
Brazil remained silent until the 1980s on what were analogous certificates issued by the Tribunal of the Desembargo do Paço, for removing a different
"defect": illegitimate birth. Ann Twinam's comprehensive study of the eighteenth-century policies of Spain's Camara de Justicia e Gracias has recently
revised the earlier assumption about the centrality of color in those royal
dispensations. Her research has shown that Spanish American petitioners,
like their Brazilian counterparts, almost always sought crown legitimization
for a different motive: the removal of the "defect" of illegitimate birth. Color,
despite the great attention social historians of colonial Spanish America have
paid it, played a marginal role in such crown dispensations.[44]

Unfortunately, the Lisbon archive of Portugal's Tribunal of the Mesa do
Desembargo do Paço has not been located. Consequently, no analogous set
of records related to crown legitimization in the eighteenth century, such as
Twinam found for Bourbon Spain, has been discovered for Pombaline Portugal. That future researchers may yet locate the archive should not be discounted.[45] When the Portuguese court took refuge in Rio de Janeiro, in 1808,
a new Mesa do Desembargo do Paço was immediately created on Brazilian
soil.[46] Until its abolition in 1828, it performed functions identical to those
undertaken in Portugal, including the issuance of legitimization certificates.[47]
The key principle prevailing in decisions to bestow succession rights concurrent with legitimization was that they should not prejudice the existing rights
of either necessary or collateral heirs. The Law of September 9, 1769 (Article
1), prohibited anyone with *ab intestato* relatives within the fourth canonical
degree from using a will for disposing of all of his inherited property "in
prejudice to and without the consent of those relatives." The prohibition anticipated a testator's nomination of either a legitimized offspring or a universal heir. *Ab intestato* relatives defined the "third parties" that legal commentaries frequently mentioned enjoyed protection vis-à-vis the "two parties" of
legitimizing parent and legitimized offspring. Possessing prior rights on the
ladder of *ab intestato* succession, those third parties of forced heirs could not
be displaced by legitimized offspring unless a judicial hearing was held in
which the former first agreed to waive their rights to the latter.

Two important points followed from this legal rule. First, the crown judge
known as the *ouvidor* was obliged to conduct a hearing with the *ab intestato*
heirs in order to determine whether the latter agreed to waive their succession rights in favor of the illegitimate candidate for crown legitimization. The
classic statement on this important procedure, quoted in virtually every
nineteenth-century legal commentary, again belonged to Lobão. As a royal

jurisconsult appointed by D. João in 1798, he probably wrote the crown's two responses to a famous case appealed in the late 1790s directly to the prince regent. Lobão's dissertation on entail made direct reference to the case, explaining why subsequently his exegesis found its way into all of imperial Brazil's authoritative legal commentaries.[48]

The complainant, Leonor Mayor da Gama, was a noblewoman who contested the posthumous legitimization with concurrent *ab intestato* succession rights that the Tribunal of the Desembargo do Paço awarded to the spurious offspring of her brother, Luiz Lobo da Gama. A titled nobleman, he had inherited their father's entail. On behalf of her children, Leonor asked that her dead brother's patrimony be restored to his legitimate collateral heirs—to herself and her daughters—on the ground that she ought to have been consulted before the high court conferred *ab intestato* rights on her brother's spurious offspring. Portugal's prince regent ruled favorably on D. Leonor's appeal, first in 1798, by means of a resolution clarifying law that concluded that the Tribunal of the Desembargo do Paço had not followed its own procedures. Then, two months later, on January 18, 1799, a royal *provisão*, or directive, rescinded the legitimization certificates and pronounced a blistering condemnation of the Paço's presiding high judges, accusing them of malfeasance and corruption. The *provisão* restored rights in *ab intestato* succession to D. Leonor, on behalf of her legitimate children.[49]

Lobão incorporated the language of the Resolution of November 16, 1798, within what became his much-quoted warning in legal commentaries: "It is not the custom in these realms to concede legitimization in prejudice to the legitimate heirs." Thus the succession rights bestowed on D. Leonor's brother's spurious offspring by the Paço lacked validity because a preliminary hearing had not been held with his closest heir, namely, his sister, Leonor da Gama. The failure to follow procedures had preempted her and her children from the line of legitimate succession to her brother's estate. The *Provisão* of January 18, 1799, elaborated the key juridical principle: Legitimization certificates "do not have the characteristics of a plenary restitution [of rights], but of a mere dispensation [of law]." In other words, legitimization alone did not preempt the prior rights of existing legitimate heirs, because crown legitimization merely broke bastardy. It did not follow from legitimization that the beneficiaries were automatically equipped with succession rights.[50] The latter had to be concurrently conferred according to specific procedures, including consultation with the legitimate heirs.

A second point followed from the first. Because legitimization certificates did not confer plenary rights in succession, petitioners were obliged to construct ad hoc cases for those rights. Besides the consent of the existing *ab in-*

testato heirs, petitioners had to present evidence establishing the deceased parent's prior intent to legitimize the offspring as a successor. Although hearsay evidence might be accepted by the high judges known as *desembargadores* of the Tribunal of the Mesa do Desembargo do Paço, ordinarily it was supported by private (unnotarized) or notarized affidavits.[51] Once authorized, concurrent succession rights had to be written into the certificate of legitimization.

Despite formal reiteration of the procedural requirement to consult with the *ab intestato,* or legitimate, heirs, and the oft-cited Resolution of November 16, 1798, that affirmed the succession rights of the latter, a marked erosion in the rights of collateral heirs was perceptible by Brazilian independence. Maria Beatriz Nizza da Silva's pathbreaking investigation of the Rio de Janeiro archives of the Desembargo do Paço, from 1808 to 1828, has confirmed that the Desembargo do Paço's high judges "in principal" imposed the requirement to consult with the *ab intestato* heirs, a procedure that was part of the Mesa do Desembargo do Paço's *Novo Regimento* (Paragraph 18). She also noted that the inquiries could not always be done, possibly due to the difficulty of contacting relatives scattered throughout Brazil and Portugal. At least written consultations with the necessary heirs were conducted, although when opposition from the latter was encountered, the *desembargadores* issued divergent instructions. The consultative hearings constituted for that purpose were conducted by an *ouvidor,* or royal judge of the first instance, and they conformed with what legal commentators such as Gouvêa Pinto, Lobão, and Borges Carneiro stated were the requirements of solemn legitimization. The *ouvidor*'s official recommendation, for or against succession rights concurrent with legitimization, following the consultative hearing, was then forwarded to the Tribunal of the Desembargo do Paço as part of the legitimization petition.[52]

Change appears to have emanated from the pinnacle of the system, from the high judges of the Desembargo do Paço in Rio de Janeiro and, presumably earlier, in Lisbon. Given the right of injured third parties, the *ab intestato* heirs who objected to waiving their position in succession, to litigate in court, Nizza da Silva suggests that the high crown judges "more prudently" declined to involve themselves directly in those disputes. Instead, they directed the *ouvidor,* as the royal judge of the first instance, to settle those disputes before passing on legitimization awarding concurrent succession rights.[53] Little is known about the precise reasons why the high judges acted as they did, but even when, in the absence of litigation, the heirs' objections to ceding their rights were attached to the *ouvidor*'s recommendations, then legitimization certificates ordinarily were issued conferring the succession rights.[54] The high judges' preference for letting the *ouvidor* settle conflicts and make the crucial determination over whether succession rights should accompany crown legitimization, must have responded to a rising number of conflicts after 1808. Although Nizza da Silva reported a total of 114 petitions of legitimization filed before the Desembargo do Paço in Rio de Janeiro, between 1808 and 1828, most of them appear to have been filed prior to independence.[55] Once the Tribunal of the Mesa do Desembargo do Paço was abolished, in 1828, the echo of those challenges would continue to offer a counterpoint to reform efforts by liberal legislators.

A decade after he wrote his dissertation on the 1798 landmark decision that ruled on behalf of Leonor Mayor da Gama, Lobão would offer the observation that legitimate heirs were one and the same with necessary heirs.[56] In other words, he confirmed that "legitimate heirs" had ceased to inscribe even the closest collateral heirs. No longer did jurists distinguish necessary heirs from the "legitimate" heirs who were collateral relatives of the deceased. Instead, the latter became increasingly secondary vis-à-vis the class of preferred legitimate heirs who were necessary. Legal commentators restricted application of "legitimate heirs" to the decedent's lineal relatives—legitimate children and grandchildren—or, where the latter were deceased, to parents or grandparents. Terminology, consequently, registered an important marginalization of all collateral heirs in favor of the necessary heirs. By Brazilian independence, "legitimate heirs" had become congruent with a narrowly inscribed family of lineal kin—the necessary heirs. In the courtroom, of course, the *ouvidor* continued to consult with the collateral heirs, as well as the legitimate, or necessary, heirs. Collateral heirs retained their *ab intestato* rights in succession and possessed the right to go to court in order to contest legitimization proceedings that attempted to undo succession rights concurrently awarded by the Tribunal of the Desembargo do Paço.[57] Yet the *ouvidor*'s recommendations, even when doing harm to third parties—the *ab intestato* heirs—simultaneously acquired greater authority. In a few cases from the archive of the Desembargo do Paço examined by Maria Beatriz Nizza da Silva, the *ouvidor* set aside even the objections of necessary heirs and recommended succession rights concurrent with legitimization when they deprived the latter of patrimony.[58] Yet necessary heirs, as well as collateral heirs, were not necessarily dissuaded. They would plead their rights in court as Brazil moved from colony to empire.

LAW VERSUS SOCIAL PRACTICE

Pombaline reform of a Luso-Brazilian inheritance system proved remarkably enduring, laying the basis for changes proposed by Brazil's first generation of liberal legislators. The standing of legitimized individuals in Luso-Brazilian inheritance, or for that matter, arrangements of universal heirship, was fundamentally derived from the new attention that the Portuguese crown paid to a plethora of arrangements falling under diverging devolution. Eighteenth-century assaults on both ecclesiastical power and the titled nobility went hand-in-hand with sustained and largely successful attempts to weaken the society of estates, implying important changes in inheritance law. The Tribunal of the Desembargo do Paço was charged with central responsibility for enforcing legislation that curtailed the power of church and nobility by eliminating the inheritance system as an institutional mechanism for acquiring or transmitting corporate wealth. By the nineteenth century, consequently, the capacity of the inheritance system for channeling economic resources to the church had been substantially reduced. Although ecclesiastical entails had not been prohibited, laws forbidding the church as an ecclesiastical corporation from acquiring real property in entailment, or prohibiting large amounts of monetary income devoted to the latter, had taken effect by Brazilian independence. Furthermore, individual religious who professed as members of corporate communities—the regular clergy—lost all individual inheritance rights as *ab intestato* successors.[59]

The new spirit of absolutism that opposed corporate privilege regarded the church's role as a property holder with hostility and instead endorsed the economic aspirations of the third estate, in order to promote deliberately the wider circulation of property. The antagonism toward the church reflected a policy favoring the rules of *ab intestato* succession that, in turn, favored fragmenting patrimony on behalf of legitmate heirs. In the words of the Law of September 9, 1769 (Paragraph 21): "Real property—houses, lands and landed estates—is created to sustain the living, and therefore cannot belong to the dead . . . there is no reason for any human being, after death, to keep dominion over property he owned when alive—until the Day of Judgment." Property now was expected to circulate in an economy manifesting a reinvigorated commercial capitalism, one progressively unrestrained by corporate privilege. Rules of heirship needed policing in order to insure that a partitive system of inheritance operated optimally on behalf of fragmenting patrimony and preventing its concentration.

On the one hand, invigilation by the crown extended to arrangements made by wealthy lay propertyholders that still depended directly on the inheritance system. The very nature of diverging devolution, especially among the higher nobility, began to change as the absolutist state imposed new criteria, by limiting the size of entails. Secular entail became a salient example, suggesting why the Tribunal of the Mesa do Desembargo do Paço would play a more important and authoritative role in the establishment of the family entail known as the *morgado* in Brazil. The same tendency toward royal oversight accounted for the new crown scrutiny that accompanied proceedings for crown legitimization, because they usually involved succession rights that required suspending the rules of *ab intestato* heirship. Wherever arrangements for diverging devolution ran counter to the rules of natural succession, then the role of the Tribunal Mesa do Desembargo do Paço had to be confirmatory. Hence crown legitimization, because it almost always involved succession rights, demonstrated a new vigilence during the era of Pombal. After the Lisbon court moved to Rio de Janeiro in 1808, the royal judiciary also exerted a greater presence in the colony, by expanding the regional appellate courts known as *Relações* to five.

On the eve of independence, crown permission was a key factor in all exceptional arrangements that disposed of substantial family patrimony, whether the latter amounted to ecclesiastical or secular entail or they found their raison d'être in petitions that proposed to substitute legitimized offspring for those who already enjoyed firm footing on the ladder of *ab intestato* succession. The decision to tax certain heirs who had not been born in legitimate matrimony, or all but the closest collaterals mentioned in the preceding chapter, amounted to another instance of policing the inheritance system.

On the other hand, where patrimony failed to be of impressive size, and the heirs merely nondescript individuals, *partilhas* were drawn up and wills could be written in ignorance or deliberate contravention of law. As long as necessary heirs concurred on dividing a parent's *legítima*, even null wills would stand, given the cursory oversight of local magistrates. In this respect, the customary practice of delaying preparation of inventories and *partilhas*— often for years—continued to deflect a judge's gaze until children married or the surviving parent died. Even in wealthy families, co-heirs would advantageously defer settling the *partilha*. Parallel to more restrictive de jure rules of paternal devolution that channeled patrimony within families and away from corporations, de facto strategies of devolution proceeded in divergent directions, thanks to family-defined approaches that ignored or circumvented the rules of heirship.

Wills, in conjunction with inventories and *partilhas*, often revealed ingenious applications of rules of heirship wherever families incorporated illegitimate members. Even when they served as devices to deny patrimony, wills testified to the integration of both natural and spurious children within the legitimate family's most intimate private space. Unlike natural offspring, who frequently figured as *ab intestato* heirs whenever their parents recognized them, those who were spurious enjoyed a more marginal position in succession law. The same was true for those who were natural, when a parent, usually the father, enjoyed any rank of nobility. Above all, wills testified to the growing size of the population born outside wedlock, as parents resorted to wills as instruments for redressing the inferiority of their children's position in inheritance law. They often did so extra-legally, by writing wills that, although technically null, proved enforceable. Where crown legitimization frequently implied a will's valid use for instituting an otherwise ineligible offspring as an heir and successor, parents still tried to do the same thing by making declarations of simple legitimization on behalf of children excluded from succession rights. Alternatively, they disposed on behalf of offspring who were of "damnable and punishable" birth by making bequests from the *terça*.

Despite the assault on a society of estates, rules of heirship defined in terms of birth, gender, and estate remained in force in late colonial Brazil. A growing and variegated population of non-legitimate offspring was excluded from succession regardless of a parent's respectable social station. Furthermore, parents found their children consigned to legal bastardy thanks to their own upward mobility. In a society where minimal nobility had become widely diffused, where matrimonial impediments could be insuperable, and vows of clerical celibacy both unenforceable and increasingly contested, parents became more determined to resort to crown legitimization, or to evade the consequences of birth, gender, and estate inherent in the rules of Luso-Brazilian inheritance.

CHAPTER 3

Birth and Gender in Succession Law

Spurious Offspring

———◆◆◆———

> Spurious offspring, commonly called *quaesitos*, as they do not have
> a definite father, succeed their mothers. . . . It is just the opposite
> for offspring of damnable sexual unions, because the latter succeed
> neither the mother nor the father, even when no legitimate or
> natural offspring exist, according to . . . the *Ordenações*, Book 4,
> Titles 92 and 93. However, it must be noted that what it says in this
> respect is relative to legitimate succession, not to testamentary suc-
> cession, for all these offspring can succeed by testamentary succes-
> sion.
> Antonio de Gouvêa Pinto, *Tratado dos testamentos* (1813)[1]

> *Direito pátrio* makes distinctions among illegitimate offspring in
> order to call them to succession. In the first place, once succession
> is opened, the same rights do not exist in the death of the father
> [as] in the mother. . . not all illegitimate individuals are favored
> with equality in the bestowal of inheritance portions.
> Clovis Bevilaqua, *Direito das successões* (1899)[2]

When Candido Mendes looked back on the legal position of children who
were born of either incestuous, adulterous, or *sacrilegious* sexual unions, he
stressed the severity of the law. From the vantage point of the 1860s, he offered a bleak pronouncement that captured how the *Ordenações Filipinas* had
treated spurious offspring. Underscoring the deprivation of *ab intestato* succession rights they imposed on those of damnable and punishable birth, he
pointed out that "nothing could be patrimonially disposed in favor of such
offspring, it being permissible only to leave them bequests or to give them
child support."[3] Law might prove even more punishing where legitimate
half-siblings existed, for certain parents were then prohibited from disposing
from the *terça*.

On the other hand, Candido Mendes spoke only of the rules applying to
ab intestato succession. He did not introduce the important consideration

that, by virtue of the monarch's "mercy and grace," law could be dispensed, permitting exceptions to the exclusionary provisions dictated by the Philippine Code. Crown legitimization proved the key means for remedying the stain of spurious birth, the stepping stone to acquiring succession rights. Furthermore, Candido Mendes neglected to mention that the Philippine Code did not deprive spurious offspring of all *ab intestato* succession rights. They were entitled to succeed their legitimate or natural half-siblings in the maternal line, as well as all of the mother's relatives; they could also be collateral successors for each other.[4]

Brazilians of all social classes understood that the "loophole" of crown legitimization could equip spurious offspring for full rights in succession, and, by the same token, the natural offspring of a noble parent. The vagaries of "suspending the rules" penetrated popular conceptions about illegitimacy so thoroughly that a "defect" of birth was taken to be mutable, perhaps temporary, but always potentially reversible. Although the full complexity of the rules of heirship, especially as they were mediated by individual circumstances of birth, gender, and estate, could be apprehended only by those with some training in the law, at a popular level those intricate rules were perceived as opportunities for negotiation and manipulation. In the second half of the eighteenth century, removal of the "defect" of spurious birth mattered a great deal more, as new groups began to emerge within what was still an inchoate middle class. Crown legitimization, consequently, promised the prize of upward social mobility for many of bastard birth and was coveted for the advantages it conferred in pursuing a career or achieving a good marriage.

The precise ways that the *Ordenações Filipinas* and other positive law defined gradations of spurious illegitimacy, or, alternatively, differentiated natural offspring according to whether the parent was a noble or a commoner, held direct implications for inheritance rights. For instance, individuals might be called to succeed either according to testamentary succession or to *ab intestato* succession, a circumstance always specified in a legitimization certificate. Concomitantly, an individual's gender and estate— noble or commoner—further mediated rights in heirship. These variables, either individually or in tandem, defined the position in inheritance law occupied by individuals who were spurious, much as they did for the natural offspring of a noble parent.

How individuals in both legal categories of illegitimacy could take advantage of the "loophole" of legitimization, largely for acquiring rights in succession, describes the focus of this and the following chapter in two respects. First, discussion attempts to remove the confusion over how procedures worked and when and why they were modified in highly significant

ways. Second, by paying attention to how individual social identities intrinsically projected specific positions in heirship, both chapters underscore why
legitimization mattered enormously as part of an individual's quality of
birth. Quality of birth, as an individual's primordial identity, fused birth to
gender and estate. Nevertheless, it proved mutable and would raise new issues after Brazilian independence, in a society where all citizens were "equal
before the law."

Although law offered precise, technical terms implying a refined array of
distinctions that specifically applied to inheritance rights, colloquial speech
approached those gradations from a different perspective. Distinctions of
birth tied directly to heirship became implicit in ordinary speech whenever
individual identity was assessed as legitimate, legitimized, illicit, or spurious.
Colloquially, those four identitites registered an individual's "*qualidade*," or
"quality." They took as a starting point the fact or absence of legitimate
birth. As a synonym for "birth," *qualidade* encapsulated an ascribed identity,
implying the answer to the unstated question of whether an individual was
legitimate. The term proved much more complex, by creatively joining imputations of legitimate or illegitimate birth to a second element, family af-
filiation. Thus "*qualidade*" also registered either the prestige of a lineage embodied in a family name or the lack thereof.

Color was another feature implicit in *qualidade*. When an individual was
not white, color frequently was construed to imply a more fundamental identity of being either a slave or a freed man or woman. The association of color
with lack of legitimate birth, even connoting identity as a slave, reinforced the
essence of "*qualidade*" as a construct turning on legitimate birth. Alternatively, individual *qualidade* implied identity as a noble or a commoner, especially whether or not someone possessed nobility by descent—the rule of
three generations. Then it defined an individual's estate. Where individual
status mattered as either noble or commoner—or free or slave—sometimes
"condition" (*condição*) replaced *qualidade* as the preferred term. The essence
of *qualidade* nonetheless pertained to an identity assigned by birth, whereas
"condition" usually projected an identity bestowed by civil society. Colloquial
speech used "condition" to describe servile or free status as well as an individual's occupation, especially when the latter denoted a trade. The linguistic
distinction between "*qualidade*" and "condition" sometimes got blurred, for,
as even Borges Carneiro conceded, it was "always arbitrary."[5]

As Brazil moved in the direction of a class society after independence,
"*qualidade*" continued to capture the key element for determining social position in a society of rank. Although admitting a subjective accent, "*qualidade*" still proved less ambivalent and better understood than "class." Its

starting point, legitimate birth, would endure as the fundamental social marker in imperial Brazil, permitting separation of those of "good" family from the majority who were largely slaves or the free poor. Legitimacy, consequently, defined an implicit threshold for incipient class identity, although historians usually discuss the slippery notion of class in imperial Brazil without much reference to legitimate birth. By the independence era, how *qualidade* was embedded in colloquial speech contrasted starkly with liberalism's new stress on "equality before the law." Appropriate to a society of rank, *qualidade* nonetheless operated in tandem with an emerging consciousness about class and testified to the survival after independence of a criterion derived from an eighteenth-century status society.

Not surprisingly, "*qualidade*" remained so ingrained in speech at all levels of imperial society that it survived well into the twentieth century, where it continued to operate as a significant marker for denoting individual identity. It persisted long after its historical utility disappeared, because, for an older generation, the term connoted subtle gradations of non-legitimate birth that repaired individual identity. Reaching to the preceding century, when rights in heirship corresponded to a given quality of birth, the term registered the remedies of paternal recognition or legitimization. "*Qualidade*" thus signified that natural offspring who enjoyed recognition were *ab intestato* heirs, equal to legitimate offspring. Alternatively, it identified those whose bastardy had been broken by legitimization, implying rights in heirship ranging from a bequest to either testamentary or *ab intestato* succession.

"DAMNABLE" BIRTH AND RIGHTS IN HEIRSHIP

Spurious Offspring

Recognized natural offspring, as we have seen, were the result of merely illicit sexual relations between the parents. They enjoyed *ab intestato* succession rights because no canonical impediment prohibited their parents from marrying. In contrast, where unmarried parents possessed a diriment impediment, one that prohibited marriage and was not dispensed, then canon law determined that offspring would be spuriously illegitimate. Luso-Brazilian succession law, it has already been suggested, did not leave spurious offspring generically undiscriminated. They were sorted in terms of three discrete sub-categories, corresponding to the precise canonical impediment that prohibited their parents from marrying: 1) canonically incestuous by virtue of a prohibited degree of consanguinity or affinity between parents; or 2) adulterine by virtue of one or both parents' marriages to other partners; or 3) sacrilegious by virtue of a parent's broken vow of clerical celibacy.

The church offered remedy only to certain parents in the first group. It came in the form of a dispensation suspending canonical rules for couples who possessed prohibited degrees of kinship. The ecclesiastical dispensation, however, had to precede the birth or conception of an incestuous child. Timing was the key, for even if a dispensation followed the child's birth and parents then married, canon law remained clear. Legitimization by subsequent marriage could not apply to an incestuous or adulterine offspring. Of course, the church offered papal legitimization directly to a rare number of children in all three sub-categories of spurious birth, just as it does today. By the late eighteenth century, however, papal legitimization conveyed no civil effects in Portuguese positive law.[6] Beginning in the second half of the eighteenth century, certain Portuguese jurists began to voice dissent over the failure to apply legitimization by subsequent marriage to spurious children. They raised a new juridical issue, one that was fundamentally political, because they sought to expand national positive law at the expense of canon law.

Canon law deemed all three sub-categories of spurious birth "punishable," because the sexual unions in which the offspring had been conceived were "damnable." By receiving the canons of the Council of Trent on marriage in the 1560s, Portuguese positive law had echoed this notion. Although the *Ordenações Filipinas* directly incorporated the canonical definition of "damnable and punishable," how they treated those of spurious birth, by excluding them altogether from *ab intestato* succession, derived from Roman law.[7] As legal commentaries never tired of repeating, their spuriousness made them "the fruit of a crime," accounting for why they were "punishable" in positive law. Yet, by the end of the eighteenth century, the harsh punishment meted to the offspring contrasted starkly with the remarkable toleration that statutory law displayed toward the parents' behavior.

Although ecclesiastical law regarded adultery and canonical incest as "crimes," positive law did not pronounce the same, unequivocal condemnation. Reform of law in the era of Pombal substantially revised how adultery or concubinage would be prosecuted, with the result that cases were rarely brought into the royal courts. The standard adopted from 1769 onward sought to protect the legitimate family's honor, basically, to shield its public reputation. Crown law therefore confined judicial investigation of adultery to only those situations where public scandal ensued and in the specific situation where the husband "took as his own and supported" another woman as a concubine. The celebrated yardstick deriving from the *Ordenações*—"*teúda e manteúda*"—endured into the twentieth century.[8]

Although the *Ordenações Filipinas* permitted commoner parents to leave bequests from the *terça* for their spurious offspring when legitimate children existed, they treated the spurious offspring of a noble parent less generously. A noble parent could not leave a bequest for spurious children, even in the absence of legitimate offspring. However, when neither natural nor legitimate children existed, gender further mediated the possibilities for endowing a spurious child. In that circumstance, a noble father could assign a bequest from his *terça* on behalf of a spurious child—but only if his parents were dead. Noble mothers, on the other hand, remained free to dispose from the *terça* on behalf of a spurious offspring if they lacked both legitimate and natural children, provided their parents consented.[9] In other words, for the spurious children of a noble parent to inherit from the *terça*, the ascendants' rights, as well as those of recognized natural offspring, were taken as preemptive. The reverse was the case for recognized natural children, whenever parents were commoners. Then the children preempted the rights of paternal and maternal ascendants, even when the parent predeceased the grandparents.

Succession law therefore explained why many parents of spurious children, as well as the noble parents of either natural or spurious offspring, resorted to wills for leaving those children patrimony. Rather than evaluating a bequest from the *terça* as evidence of parental generosity, it has to be kept in mind that bequests were all that law permitted those parents to dispose. In such cases, the *terça* served as a compensatory device, given the child's exclusion from *ab intestato* succession. Parents meticulously identified their children in testamentary dispositions as either "spurious" or "illegitimate," sometimes making very precise the offspring's identity as an "*incestuoso*," "*adulterino*," "*sacrílego*." Wills also revealed the ingenuity of parents in providing for offspring whom law excluded from *ab intestato*, or legitimate, succession. They demonstrated, for instance, how patrimony might be generously "evened up" for all offspring. In 1863, Joaquim Elias da Silva, who was a commoner, identified one of his ten children as adulterine in his will, because he left him a bequest from the remainder of his *terça*. Remarkably, the size of his legacy was exactly equal to the inheritance portions that divided his *legítima* among his nine forced heirs: seven children legitimized by subsequent marriage a year before he died, together with two natural children born prior to marriage by different mothers and properly recognized as *ab intestato* successors.[10]

Fathers who were priests possessed a different option for circumventing the exclusion of their sacrilegious offspring from *ab intestato* succession because, typically, they lacked legitimate children. They employed the device of universal heirship. Ida Lewkowicz investigated a sizable collection of wills made by priests in Mariana, Minas Gerais, between the 1770s and 1829, whose purpose was the testators' simple legitimization of the sacrilegious offspring they had fathered.[11] Such simple legitimization by means of a will removed the stain of bastard birth, what earlier in the eighteenth century was synonymous with individual "infamy" (*infame*), the absence of an honorable reputation. Legally, simple legitimization did not equip the offspring for succession, either testamentary or *ab intestato*. Yet the wills left by Mariana's priests revealed that simple legitimization was but the prologue to transmitting paternal patrimony, according to what was really a pseudo-right. Mariana's priests then used their wills to institute their children as their testamentary heirs, by nominating them universal heirs. As we have already seen, where an individual's parents were dead, and no legitimate children existed, then Book 4, Title 92 (Section 3) of the *Ordenações Filipinas* permitted them to dispose of their *legítima* "in another manner, as they deem appropriate," including disposing on behalf of any type of illegitimate offspring by means of testamentary succession.[12]

Strictly speaking, as we have also seen, there was a "catch." Wills written to nominate universal heirs needed the authorization of the Tribunal of the Mesa do Desembargo do Paço, because they contravened the rules of *ab intestato* succession, frequently displacing collateral relatives who were heirs. Only by virtue of the sovereign's "mercy and grace" could the rule of intestate succession could be suspended.[13] For precisely this reason, however, the wills archived in Mariana are very instructive. They suggest that social behavior overrode rules of heirship embedded in positive law. Although the paternal nominations instituted by Mariana's priests remained legally null without the approval of the Desembargo do Paço, their provisions were nevertheless upheld.[14] Of course, it is conceivable that some of the priests may have anticipated a future occasion when their offspring would initiate posthumous legitimization proceedings by directly petitioning the Tribunal of the Mesa do Desembargo do Paço.

A very small minority of priests applied to the Tribunal of the Mesa do Desembargo do Paço for crown legitimization of their spurious children. Usually as a posthumous act, their petitions continued to be granted after reestablishment of the Paço in Brazil, in 1808.[15] Like the parents of either adulterine or canonically incestuous children, priests petitioned in response to the *ordenação* of Book 4, Title 36 (Section 4) of the Philippine Code: "And the spurious child cannot have the same right [to succeed as the legitimate child], unless legitimized by Us in such a way that he is able to succeed *ab intestato* and in no other way." Direct appeal to the sovereign for suspending the rule excluding those of spurious birth from *ab intestato* succession anticipated not only solemn legitimization but also the bestowal of either *ab intestato* or testamentary succession rights.

Indeed, crown legitimization in both Portugal and Spain developed historically as a response largely to the initiative of priests who petitioned the king directly for removal of their children's defect of bastardy.[16] The term "bastard" was most readily understood in late medieval times as pertaining to the children of prelates and other high-ranking ecclesiastics.[17] Confirmation of the central role clerical fathers played in widening the use of crown legitimization lies in the language of the *Ordenações do Reino*. Contrary to nineteenth-century legal commentaries, which applied "spurious" to three sub-categories of damnable unions, the *Ordenações Filipinas* largely applied the term to *sacrílegos* alone, reserving "damnable birth" for those who were incestuous or adulterine. Inconsistently, they sometimes applied "damnable and punishable" to all three sub-categories of spurious birth.[18] The deviations in usage found in the Philippine Code speak to how bastardy was viewed at the close of the sixteenth century.

Priests used wills to break a public silence on concealed paternity for another reason, the expectation that their sons would follow them in holy orders. Posthumous declaration of paternity meant the child's paternal filiation would be rendered unambiguous, for, typically, priests' children were baptized as either "of unknown father" or "of unknown parents." In the latter instance, they were "*expostos,*" or legal foundlings. Even so, a *sacrílego*'s damnable *qualidade* defined a bar to ordination. It demanded a genealogical investigation prior to an ecclesiastical tribunal rendering a verdict on the candidate's suitability for having his defect of birth dispensed. Paternal declarations in wills thus facilitated the equipping of a *sacrílego* for ordination, by specifying the nature of the sexual relationship that gave birth to the candidate, and sometimes alluded to maternal *qualidade*.

A number of prominent clerics in colonial Latin America, in both Spanish and Portuguese dominions, were *sacrílegos* and began life as legal foundlings—born of unknown father and mother. Usually, the offspring of priests acquired the *qualidade* of an *exposto* due to deference to a father's vow of celibacy. The most well-known *exposto* in Brazil's First Empire and Regency was also a key political figure: Diogo Antonio Feijó. His *qualidade* masked the fact that, insofar as evidence exists, he was a *sacrílego*. The baptismal registry identifying him as an *exposto* noted he had been abandoned in the home of a priest and his widowed sister, both of whom stood as his godparents. What the registry could not note was that the two siblings lived next door to Feijó's mother, their sister.[19]

As a candidate for the priesthood, Feijó could not be ordained without first dispensing his "defect" of spurious birth. In 1808, nine witnesses who supported his ordination assembled to defend his character before an ecclesiastical tribunal. All swore that his unknown parents came from good families, but declined to identify them by name. Their testimony was important for confirming that Feijó himself had not inherited the propensity to sin after the manner of his parents. These were vital declarations due to the common belief that "blood would out." That is, that defects of character were assumed intrinsically to follow from defects of birth, because they were heritable from the sinning parents.[20] Feijó "passed" the genealogical test because the witnesses vouched for his exemplary behavior and corroborated that his unnamed mother had been white, of legitimate birth, and from a good family. The fact that her elite family—together with the family of Feijó's concealed father, a priest—included many clerics proved valuable in gaining him the dispensation.[21]

For spurious offspring who were not foundlings, gender still determined that legal recognition would be complex, differing markedly according to each parent's sex. Law presumed that unmarried mothers "testified" to their maternity as "obvious," by virtue of public knowledge of pregnancy and childbirth or of child-rearing acknowledged within the community. Even when the father was publicly unacknowledged by the unmarried mother—for being a close relative, a married man, or a priest—she usually would not conceal her own identity. Unwed mothers who concealed pregnancy and maternity were almost always from socially "respectable" families. Otherwise, they customarily appeared at the baptismal font with their infants, permitting their names to be entered into registries. They conferred recognition on their children as maternally natural offspring, leaving the father to be recorded as "unknown."

Contrary to fathers of natural offspring, the fathers of spurious children had less choice in the matter of absenting themselves at the child's baptism. Technically, confession of adulterine paternity, as well as of incest, constituted a plea of guilty to a criminal act, according to both the *Ordenações Filipinas* and Brazil's 1830 Penal Code. That is, the commitment of a declaration of paternity to a public record could amount to the creation of "public and notorious scandal." Although the Law of 1769, mentioned earlier, modified the *Ordenações* by substantially decriminalizing adultery, and imperial Brazil's criminal code followed suit, discretion was nonetheless advisable. The need to avoid "public scandal" still urged caution. The latter amounted to a legal precept, one derived from a community standard of decency. Should public knowledge about an individual's adultery be complemented by widely diffused and notorious scandal, and reflect behavior perpetuating the liaison, then the authorities could bring criminal prosecution.[22]

Fathers did not commit adulterine paternity to declarations in baptismal registers because law constituted those registers a civil, and therefore a public, registry. They did not want to cross the crucial boundary between knowledge that was private, even if tacitly understood in the community, and knowledge that was blatantly public. Hence, social conventions deemed any declaration of spurious paternity a taboo, while law would regard it as potentially self-incriminating. A man who committed adultery with a married woman also risked physical reprisal to his person from her husband or kinsmen, or criminal prosecution involving him in scandal. He might on occasion provoke wife murder, although more often the revelation of his behavior would result in the woman's confinement in what was known as "*recolhimento*," a section of a convent that functioned as a jail where husbands could imprison "disobedient" wives under the custodianship of the church.

Clerics similarly might be subject to prosecution in an episcopal court and disciplining by a bishop, where they fathered *sacrílegos*, within or without a relationship of cohabitation. Even more than married men, priests had reason not to sign the birth register. A public admission that the vow of celibacy had been broken would have labeled their children as unequivocal *sacrílegos*. The latter were better off enjoying the *qualidade* "of unknown father" or even that of a legal foundling. Given that fathers of spurious offspring of all three types customarily withheld recognition of their "damnable" paternity from baptismal registers, historians of Brazil almost never find such children discriminated in those registers as "incestuous," "sacrilegious," or "adulterine." Occasionally, however, the parish priest's marginalia identified a child as "adulterine" or "bastard." When not baptized "of unknown parents" to spare either or both parents' reputations, then spurious offspring shared the identical fate of paternally unrecognized natural offspring: They were baptized "of unknown father."

In contrast to the baptismal registers, testators were obliged to honor precision in executing wills. Inheritance rules demanded a parent identify precisely illegitimate children, those who were natural and recognized, and each type of legitimized child. The reason was that the claim to *ab intestato* rights had to be substantiated. Alternatively, children legitimized by the crown usually enjoyed rights to the *legítima* as testamentary successors; otherwise, they could be universal heirs. In the latter instance, the testator first effected simple legitimization by a testamentary declaration of his or her *perfilhação* that could serve as a prelude to legitimization by the crown. As we have already seen, where crown legitimization was intended or anticipated at a future date, the well-advised parent of a spurious child would explicitly state his or her intention for the child to become either an *ab intestato* or testamentary successor, attaching the key phrase, "if legitimization were obtained."

Although parents possessing minimal *fidalguia* were legally restricted from leaving even bequests to spurious offspring, the impression remains that some ignored the rules and disposed on their behalf from the *terça*. Parents might also nominate a spurious offspring as a universal heir even in the absence of authorization by the Desembargo do Paço. In making bequests, many parents precisely identified their spurious offspring, sometimes offering the mother's name. Although the union with the mother might simply be describe as "prohibited," avoiding explicit reference to the child as "spurious," other parents merely referred to a spurious child as "illegitimate," leaving tacit the quality of birth. The precision with which testators identified their non-legitimate children as beneficiaries of bequests often imparted the information that law prevented them from being successors to their *legítima*. Finally, posthumous declarations of *perfilhação* served the purpose of calling on the necessary heirs to provide for the spurious child's welfare and equipped the offspring to use the parent's name. By making the testator's blood tie to the child clear, simple testamentary legitimization bestowed a valuable social identity on the child. As an "*espúrio*," the child would always project the defect of birth. However, even when posthumously bestowed, simple legitimization repaired the "stain" of bastardy.

Legal Foundlings: Expostos

In rare cases, both mother and father chose to remain unknown in baptismal registers. When the mother concealed maternity, the father often collaborated in protecting her reputation by similarly withholding his identity, meaning the child would be baptized "of unknown parents." In practice, the mother's social reputation was shielded whenever she was respectably married to someone else or reputedly a virgin whose chaste behavior also projected a respectable family position. If one or both parents possessed a canonical prohibition to marry, then the child testified to transgression of a dire impediment—"the fruit of a crime." Sometimes, the father, or both parents, sought anonymity. In Feijó's case, his mother came from a good family, the Camargos of Itu, São Paulo. Yet she might have publicly acknowledged him had her sexual liaison been merely illicit. The fact that Feijó's father was a priest fundamentally accounted for why her motherhood became concealed. Consequently, an infant would be baptized as an "*enjeitado*," a rejected child, when either the mother's or both parents' identities had to be concealed. The precise nature of spuriousness, like the parents' identities, was kept private. An *enjeitado* was legally deemed an *"exposto,"* a foundling.

Deliberate strategies of fosterage, which still operate today in Brazil, suggested that the house where the baby was abandoned seldom proved random.[23] Technically "exposed," many of these children were carefully placed, with the precise home where they were abandoned noted in the baptismal register. The residents usually became the godparents and frequently doubled as foster parents, suggesting why one historian of the family has dubbed *compadrio*, or godparenthood, "popular adoption."[24] By the late eighteenth century, the proportion of *expostos* in the general population had begun to rise. Marcílio's survey of foundling wheels and baptismal registries concluded that by the turn of the eighteenth century around five percent of all baptisms were *expostos*; however, considerable geographical variation existed. Together with another thirty-five percent of births out-of-wedlock, roughly forty percent of all Brazilian children were not legitimate by the first decade of the nineteenth century.[25] Babies were being committed to foundling wheels, sometimes bearing notes averring that their unnamed parents were white and from "good families."[26] Given that legal adoption did not exist until the 1850s, and that a juridical approximation known as *adrogação* rarely was used, most individuals who were abandoned in the homes of foster parents remained legal *expostos* for life. "Foundling" advantageously rendered individual *qualidade* moot. The label mitigated spuriousness by theoretically holding out the promise of future remedy, should the offspring's parents reveal themselves and confirm that, either paternally or maternally, the child was born of merely an "illicit" union.

Beginning in 1775, Pombaline law presumed *expostos* to be freeborn, in the absence of evidence to the contrary. The law accounted for why a Brazilian slave mother might be moved to offer her newborn infant to the foundling wheel.[27] Furthermore, in the absence of evidence to the contrary, the *alvará* of January 31, 1775, determined that *expostos* were to be reputed of legitimate birth. "Where doubted, the most favorable interpretation is presumed," Borges Carneiro explained. Law now equipped them to be eligible for honors and public office, because they were presumed to be of "clean" blood and without stain "whenever this odious difference [is at issue]."[28] Reform of law on behalf of *expostos* spoke directly to new values sanctioned by the European enlightenment. Bourbon Spain enacted a similar statute in 1794.[29] The notion that children should bear the punishment for sins committed by their parents—like the assumption that national positive law should punish sin—was theoretically rejected.

The legal presumption of legitimacy served to equip *expostos* to enter the liberal professions, to serve in the highest posts of the royal bureaucracy, including the judiciary, and to marry into the best families of Portugal. Yet the law proved irrelevant to inheritance rights, because, legally, *expostos* were of unknown parents. Lacking both ascendants and collateral relatives, except in rare cases where they were exposed as siblings, they could not be forced heirs. On the other hand, wherever the parents of an *exposto* came forward and executed *perfilhação*, the motive frequently was to equip the child for heirship, including petitioning the crown for legitimization *per Rescriptum Principis* with concurrent succession rights.

Legitimization petitions filed by Brazilians proceeded apace between 1808 and 1828, given the reestablishment of the Mesa do Desembargo do Paço in Rio de Janeiro. A parent who recognized an *exposto* many years after the child's birth—the typical pattern—usually acted because the death of the other parent had released him or her from the obligation to maintain silence. Fathers, much more frequently than mothers, would initiate legitimization proceedings, underscoring the key role the category of "*exposto*" played in concealing maternal identity wherever women were of "good family." The first Brazilian novel "to cultivate maternity," Joaquim Manuel de Macedo's *Os dois amores* (1848), took an *exposto* for its central figure.[30] Ignorant of his mother's existence, Candido, the protagonist, is raised by a stepmother. Nevertheless, Macedo develops Candido's love for the biological mother as a natural feeling. When mother and son finally meet, at the conclusion of the story, Candido bows to convention and keeps her secret forever. Only his silence can insure the mother's attainment of marriage with a man she has loved for a very long time. Candido's desire to gain maternal recognition is thus sacrificed to the ideal of legitimate marriage for his mother.[31] Macedo's fictional portrayal of what legitimization petitions deemed the "urgent need to conceal"—maternal identity—captured the increasing importance of marriage within a middle-class context several decades after independence.

The convention of maternal concealment had been reinforced by statutory law in 1750, in recognition of the fact that revelation of maternity jeopardized prospects for marriage wherever women bore bastards—the "fruit of a crime"—or when it was simply impossible for the child's father to marry. Consequently, when they were canonically incestuous, adulterine, or sacrilegious, *expostos* could be legitimized before the crown, but "leaving the mother's name undeclared for the sake of decency and not bringing infamy to a woman possessing the reputation of honesty."[32]

Commonly, *expostos* themselves petitioned the crown for legitimization after one or both parents had died, explaining why many were legitimized only as adults. For instance, Col. Lourenço Maria de Almeida Portugal, an illegitimate son of the marquis of Lavradio (Luiz de Almeida Portugal), Brazil's famous viceroy from 1769 to 1779, petitioned the Tribunal of the Desembargo do Paço for legitimization in 1823, long after his father's death and when he was forty-seven years old. Baptized a foundling, Lavradio's son noted in his petition that his father had not kept his word to summon him to Portugal, in part, in order "to preserve the laws of decency." However, proof always had to be offered of the parent's intent to legitimize, either formally by notarial writ or informally. In this case, the field marshal who raised Lavradio's son in São Paulo, and subsequently became his father-in-law, testified before the *ouvidor* on behalf of his legitimization. Notwithstanding the son's affidavit confirming Lavradio's reluctance to receive him, the father-in-law offered oral testimony asserting that Lavradio had written him of his intent to summon D. Lourenço to Portugal, where he would recognize him. The crown judge accepted this evidence of the intention to bestow *perfilhação*, based purely on hearsay, for the private letters no longer existed. D. Lourenço was legitimized *per Rescriptum Principis*.[33]

GENDER AND RIGHTS IN HEIRSHIP

Offspring "of Unknown Father": The Quaesito

Although the parent's gender—the mother's precise identity as a woman to be protected from scandal—usually accounted for the *qualidade* a legal foundling enjoyed, in most cases, offspring of damnable birth were only paternally spurious. Their mothers publicly acknowledged them.[34] A father's disinclination to declare paternity proved to be the most problematic feature in Luso-Brazilian succession law, given that unequivocal proof of paternity was difficult, if not impossible, to establish. Paternal reluctance to recognize a natural offspring, however, usually explained why in baptismal registries individuals were identified as "of unknown father." What amounted to a paternal prerogative not to recognize a natural offspring became incorporated in the church's procedures for maintaining parish records. The simple notation "*de pai incógnito*"—of unknown father—was entered in the baptismal registry whenever the father failed to appear for the child's baptism.

The priest interpreted the father's absence according to procedures drawing on the 1707 *Constituições primeiras*. The latter called for recording the mother's name, but not that of the father, when it would "bring scandal."[35] This ecclesiastical rule of thumb was secularized during the late imperial era as a procedure incorporated in the new civil registry of 1881 and then perpetuated in the republic. Harsh penalties applied for any public functionary who recorded a father's name in the civil registry of birth without his personal appearance or power of attorney.[36] Although the conventional reason offered for omitting the father's name, even in the republic, turned on protecting the legitimate family's honor, it was a masculine prerogative that many fathers exercised. Unlike fathers of spurious offspring, fathers of natural offspring who withheld paternal recognition from the baptismal registry manipulated the rules of heirship for reasons of patrimony, denying their *legítima* to the child in order to reserve it for future offspring who were legitimate.

The individual labeled "*de pai incógnito*" in baptismal registries became so ubiquitous by Brazilian independence that legal commentaries paid overwhelming attention to him or her as a fourth sub-category of spuriousness. Social change explained the new prominence of the offspring of unknown father in juridical exegesis. Furthermore, they benefited from reinterpretation of their position in inheritance law. Not only were births out-of-wedlock on the rise but they also coincided with increasing opportunity for fathers to acquire anonymity. Although the label "of unknown father" generically subsumed the other three sub-categories of spuriousness, after 1800 it stood on its own. "*Espúrio*" thus functioned as a shorthand for "of unknown father," meaning also "bastard." The term's meaning was now inverted. Originally, in the Middle Ages, "*espúrio*" had been applied mostly to *sacrílegos*; only gradually did the term subsume incestuous and adulterine children.

The *Ordenações Filipinas* had perfectly captured the older construction when they spoke of "*espurios*" only in reference to the offspring of clerics. In 1813, when Gouvêa Pinto's treatise on wills was published, it emphasized a different accent, one traceable to Pombaline jurists. The latter singled out as "the *espúrio*" the individual who was of unknown father and now treated him or her as a distinct sub-category of illegitimacy. Furthermore, analytical discourse in legal commentaries implied a new interpretation. "*Espúrio*" gradually acquired meaning as an enigmatic individual who deserved to be treated merely as putatively spurious. That is, the father's silence often denied recognition to an individual who, in fact, was a natural offspring. The stigma of spurious birth therefore could be lifted simply by breaking a paternal silence. Rather than "damnable birth," the *qualidade* of an *espúrio* might derive from illicit birth.

Today researchers can easily confuse the spurious child of unknown father with those who were unambiguously spurious for being incestuous, adulterine, and *sacrilegious*. This is because after 1800 legal commentaries devoted almost exclusive attention to offspring who were "*de pai incógnito*" and treated them as synonymous with "*espúrios*."[37] By the late colonial era, they preferred another term for the offspring of unknown father, one that resolved classificatory confusion: *quaesito*. The Latin orthographic variant from which this term derived explained its aptness: "*Quoesitus?*" Of whom is he?[38] The question implied rhetorical confusion over the *quaesito*'s social space as much as the jurist's quandary over how to define his or her succession rights. This usage—that "spurious" simultaneously circumscribed the *quaesito*—in addition to those who were unambiguously incestuous, adulterine, or *sacrilegious*—is a most troublesome feature in imperial Brazil's legal commentaries. All of those offspring shared in common, at least by public reputation, that their fathers were reputed to be unknown, "because of the unconfessable nature of the sexual union from which they came, due to its condemnation either before society or before the law."[39]

Considerable analytical confusion arises because most nineteenth-century commentaries give the impression that the *quaesito* was the *only* category of *espúrio*. Ordinarily, individuals who were incestuous, adulterine, or sacrilegious were not identified in parish registries, so it helps to remember that jurists used "spurious" as a residual category. Thus "*espúrio*" denoted those who were left after bracketing "incestuous," "adulterine," and "sacrilegious" as marginal types. Because "*espúrio*" denoted both a generic (for incestuous, adulterine, *sacrilegious*) and a particular label (*quaesito*), historians must turn to the context of inheritance documents in order to decode the precise legal connotations applying to a specific "*espúrio*."

The *quaesito* was far from an esoteric figure by independence. He or she deserves evaluation as the illegitimate individual par excellence throughout Brazil's imperial decades. As the *filho espúrio* who was discretely relabeled the *quaesito*, this individual become the most problematic figure in succession law. Potentially a paternally natural offspring, but lacking legal capacity to succeed from the father, the enigmatic *quaesito* occupied a portentous position in the social landscape of post-independence Brazil. Given the ample legal right enjoyed by those of illicit birth for establishing paternal recognition in court, the *quaesito* carried great potential risk for families of substantial property. If illicit paternity was revealed or judicially established, he or she ceased to be spurious and, as a natural offspring, was called to *ab intestato* succession with the legitimate heirs.

The *quaesito*'s alternate persona—as a potentially natural offspring—gave rise to the figure who colloquially became identified as the "surprise heir."[40] The sudden appearance of such a previously undetected heir might coincide with the funeral of the family patriarch or the reading of his will. As an offspring genuinely recognized by the father, in a will or affidavit, but concealed until death—or even denied posthumously by the father—this dangerous stranger suddenly demanded a share of the *legítima* by virtue of asserting a claim to *ab intestato* rights in succession law. The appearance of the *quaesito* thus threatened to diminish the legitimate family's patrimony, beyond bringing feelings of shock and betrayal. Otherwise, as an outright impostor, appearance of the surprise heir signaled gratuitous scandal and theft of patrimony, if not extortion. Doubts about the surprise heir's true paternity could lead to court battles revealing family secrets, while acquiescence would drain legitimate patrimony.

Novels revealed the surprise heir as a Janus-headed figure: An heir who could be genuine and even welcomed, or one resented, perhaps for being deemed bogus. Machado de Assis' earliest novel, *Helena* (1876), best captured this duality, offering the twist of a patriarchal testator who himself perpetrated fraud on his legitimate son and only heir. Nevertheless, paternal solicitude, that of a widower for his dead mistress and her orphaned daughter, defined the overarching theme. In contrast, Aluizio Azevedo's *O mulato* (1881) realistically wedded the specter of a natural offspring who was genuine to the dreaded racial tare of African ancestry, driving home the point that if patrimony were not threatened by the surprise appearance of an heir, then the *quaesito* could still do irreparable damage to the legitimate family by threatening "purity of blood." Illegitimacy was the foil Azevedo used to denounce racial discrimination in the bosom of the legitimate middle-class family. Even more significantly, as the maternally adulterine son of the Portuguese consul, he indicted the neo-colonial Portuguese enclave in his native city of São Luis de Maranhão and the established church.

The important point about the *quaesito* was that inheritance law treated him or her differently from individuals who were unequivocally spurious, a gloss implying advantage. Engendered rules of heirship accounted for the *quaesito*'s unique position and contributed to why he or she defined a fourth sub-category of spuriousness, the preponderant one in nineteenth-century Brazil. Engendered rules equally rendered the *quaesito*'s mother a common figure in Brazil's nineteenth-century courtrooms, justifying for many imperial lawmakers the special hostility they reserved for her.

Matrilineal Rights in Succession

A parent's gender further refined or complicated the status of spurious offspring in succession law, rendering complex the modern historian's task of decoding inheritance documents. Legal terminology adopted a patrilineal focus because succession law assumed that maternity was self-evident. The patrilineal focus followed from a preoccupation with the complexities of ascertaining paternity. Where illegitimacy is the subject in the Philippine Code and legal commentaries, therefore, the linguistic perspective is always masculine or paternal. Thus "*pais*" refers to "fathers," never to "parents."

The *quaesito* differed from other sub-categories of spuriousness because he or she enjoyed a claim to maternal succession wherever the mother lacked legitimate children.[41] In glossing the dual identity of the *quaesito*, as a maternally natural offspring who was paternally spurious, Borges Carneiro stressed he or she could be a "true natural offspring"—were paternity only to be established.[42] Law regarded the unmarried mother generously, precisely because the father had not declared paternity. Alternatively, where the *quaesito* was revealed to be the offspring of "damnable" intercourse, because his father's transgression became known, then exclusion from maternal succession also followed, regardless of the mother's unmarried status. Thus the father's silence could guarantee patrimony from his child's maternal line.

Ambiguity over the *quaesito*'s paternity also explained why the *Ordenações Filipinas* conceded unilineal rights in matrilineal *ab intestato* succession to this individual. However, in order for those rights to follow, the *Ordenações Filipinas* required matrilineal legitimization before the Tribunal of the Mesa do Desembargo do Paço. Historians have usually missed this crucial point, one that Gouvêa Pinto forcefully underscored a decade prior to Brazilian independence:

And, finally, it is to be noted that the spurious offspring [i.e., *quaesito*] can be legitimized *por Provisão Régia*, in order to succeed *ab intestato*, and as such become equipped in order to be able to succeed like a natural [offspring], in the absence of descendants, expressly as [stated] in the *Ordenações*, Book 4, Title 36, Section 4.[43]

Candido Mendes seconded Gouvêa Pinto when he retrospectively surveyed colonial and early imperial legal practice in the 1860s. The Tribunal of the Mesa do Desembargo do Paço had played the indispensable role, he insisted, in the *quaesito*'s matrilineal inheritance, given that crown legitimization conferred concurrent *ab intestato* succession rights.[44]

In practice, unmarried mothers who lacked legitimate children, like the priests in Mariana studied by Lewcowicz, wrote wills recognizing their offspring of unknown fathers for the purpose of making them their heirs in succession. Strictly speaking, as with the case of Mariana's clerical testators, the wills they executed could not confer any legal rights in *ab intestato* succession, except where the Tribunal of the Desembargo do Paço concurred. The explanation for why technically null dispositions were written into wills is traceable to the trust those maternal testators placed in their own relatives to concur. The mother was confident that her parents or close collateral kin would not challenge the maternal succession rights she conferred on the *quaesito*. Alternatively, a small proportion of mothers may have intended succession rights to follow from the *quaesito*'s legitimization by the crown at a future date. Basically, until 1831, the vast majority of such wills executed a de facto right to bestow matrilineal succession. Only when historians read them in conjunction with the legal rules of heirship—and consult the related inventories and *partilhas*—will we better understand how an extra-legal strategy of matrilineal heirship operated with respect to *quaesitos* in late colonial and early imperial Brazil.

What of the patrimonial fate of other spurious offspring when their fathers did not legitimize them? Was the exclusion of those who were incestuous, adulterine, or *sacrilegious* from inheritance as dire as Candido Mendes pronounced in his famous commentary on the Philippine Code? No, far from it. Gouvêa Pinto emphasized that the two commonly cited *ordenações* pertaining to succession rights, those of Titles 92 and 93, of Book 4, stipulated on what "only was relevant to legitimate succession." Rights for spurious offspring excluded from the latter might still follow, he explained, "even though we possess no specific law that declares it." He pointed to testamentary succession as an attractive alternative for spurious offspring: "We have subsidiary laws and their interpretations that do declare it, and we have the *Ordenações*, Book 4, Titles 92 e 93."[45]

Wherever necessary heirs did not exist, spurious offspring could be instituted as testamentary successors by the parent, provided the Tribunal of the Mesa do Desembargo do Paço concurred, meaning almost always that crown legitimization was accompanied by concurrent rights in testamentary succession. By "subsidiary laws," Gouvêa Pinto had in mind not only statutory law but also administrative regulations and procedures, including the rulings known as *assentos*, issued by the Tribunal of the Mesa do Desembargo do Paço. They guided that high court of privilege in conferring legitimization certificates.[46] Crown legitimization thus permitted the parent to use a will to institute the spurious child as a testamentary successor to his or her *legítima*. In this situation, the high crown tribunal would be petitioned for the right to nominate a variant of a universal heir. Gouvêa Pinto, citing Lobão, warned readers that judicial consultation with the necessary and collateral heirs was still mandatory prior to awarding rights in succession.

By the eve of Brazilian independence, consequently, Luso-Brazilian law offered ample means for reversing the bastardy of spurious offspring and equipping them with succession rights. The *quaesito* clearly enjoyed a superior status for not being identified in terms of a discrete sub-category of paternal spuriousness. Thanks to matrilineal rights in *ab intestato* succession, his *qualidade* as a bastard in the paternal line was considerably mitigated. On the other hand, crown legitimization presented an alternative few could afford. Beyond the reach of a royal bureaucracy increasingly dedicated to policing crown legitimization, unmarried mothers, like Mariana's clerics, wrote wills instituting their paternally spurious children in contravention of law. Customarily, they instituted their maternally natural offspring de facto as *ab intestato* successors without seeking approval from the Tribunal of the Desembargo do Paço, except when patrimony was very substantial or their identity prominent. Of course, they had to rely on the complicity of parents and other *ab intestato* heirs not to challenge their wills—as well as on judicial and administrative inefficiency or neglect.

If wills tailored ad hoc strategies of heirship to fit the domestic arrangements of matrifocal households, priests, or even a husband's adulterine brood, rather than observing the precise strictures of inheritance law, then those documents deserve greater attention from social historians as further demonstration of the creative ways through which Brazilian family organization increasingly sustained growing numbers of non-legitimate members.

This discussion has focused on how damnable birth and gender determined patrimonial rights, including where rules of heirship could be suspended by the intervention of the monarch who conceded solemn legitimization. Before drawing conclusions about the nature of change in late colonial Brazil, both damnable and illicit birth must be assessed vis-à-vis estate. Whether a parent was a noble or a commoner acquired greater relevance for patrimonial rights as Brazil moved toward independence. Therefore, the utility of crown legitimization also gained importance. Eventually, the circumstance that more parents enjoyed a minimal nobility influenced imperial legislators to pursue reform of the patrimonial rights of individuals born outside wedlock.

CHAPTER 4

Estate in Succession Law

Birth and Nobility

———•◆•———

> I have in my possession evidence for the legitimization conceded
> by the king, D. Sebastião, to the natural children of Jeronymo de
> Albuquerque in 1561. It is in such poor condition that the names
> are not legible and very little can be discerned [from the docu-
> ment]. It is certain [nevertheless] that those who were *perfilhados*
> numbered thirteen, and that only eight of them were born to D.
> Maria do Espírito Santo Arco Verde.
>
> Borges da Fonseca, *Nobiliarquia pernambucana* (1748–1786)[1]

From 1561, when the "Brazilian Adam," Jeronymo de Albuquerque, traveled
to Lisbon to petition Queen Regent Catarina for royal legitimization of a favored thirteen of his natural children, Brazilian parents of noble rank sought
the "mercy and grace" of the monarch. Only the sovereign could suspend the
provision of the *Ordenações do Reino* that denied their natural children *ab
intestato* succession rights. In Jeronymo's case, a successful petition that
conferred *perfilhação solemne* on the eight children he had fathered with the
Indian woman, Arco Verde, proved part of his strategy for a legitimate marriage. In 1561 or 1562, he contracted a very late first marriage with a Portuguese noblewoman, Felipa de Mello. Subsequently, the will Jeronymo executed in 1584 made clear that his creation of an entail, on behalf of his eldest
legitimate son, João de Albuquerque, had deprived all of his children of patrimony, whether they were natural or legitimate. Nevertheless, crown legitimization placed his eight natural children with Arco Verde on the same social footing with the eleven legitimate children he fathered in marriage with
Felipa de Mello. In fact, it equipped his eldest and favorite natural daughter,
Catarina de Albuquerque, to marry her father's preferred candidate, the
Florentine nobleman Felipe Cavalcanti. Similarly, her two older, full brothers were equipped to marry the women of noble rank their father selected as
their wives, none other than the younger sisters of his new Portuguese wife.
Finally, Jeronymo's will made clear, however much he regretted "robbing"

his children to create an entail, that his older, natural sons received the patrimony of land in Olinda he had been given by Pernambuco's founding donatary, his brother-in-law, Duarte Coelho.[2]

That rights in inheritance depended on the criterion of a parent's legally defined estate acquired greater importance during Brazil's final half century as a colony. Whether a natural offspring's parent enjoyed commoner or noble rank continued to matter not only for succession rights but also for equipping those children with the parent's names and honors. The intersection of the variables of birth and estate, and, in some contexts, of gender, further differentiated rights in succession. The key distinction in law turned on whether a parent was simply a commoner—termed a "*peão*" in the *Ordenações Filipinas*, and a "*plebeu*" in imperial parlance—or claimed noble rank. Unlike the natural offspring of a commoner, those fathered by someone of noble rank were prohibited from succeeding paternally. Apart from the titled nobility, the *Ordenações* construed nobility variously, discriminating among *fidalgos* (*filhos d'algo*) who were of minimal gentle birth, *escudeiros* who held the slightly higher rank of squire, and *cavalleiros* who were equivalent to knights.[3] In the context of the Philippine Code, these sixteenth-century gradations of nobility spanned the lower rungs of a status ladder in the gentry that reached upward, through the "royal vassals" who defined an "upper-middle nobility," but fell short of the higher nobility of titled barons, viscounts, counts, marquises, and dukes.[4]

LEGITIMIZING THE NATURAL OFFSPRING OF A NOBLE PARENT

Where inheritance rights mattered by the end of the eighteenth century, noble fathers great and small amounted to the same legal condition. The *Ordenações Filipinas*, Book 4, Title 92, Section 1, applied to the least degree of nobility as well as to the greatest: the natural offspring of a nobleman or noblewoman could not be called to *ab intestato* succession. This rule obviously conflicted with the rule that only the children of "damnable and punishable" birth—spurious offspring—were excluded from *ab intestato* succession. All natural offspring were by definition of illicit birth, so why were the natural offspring of nobles treated identically with those of spurious birth? Jurists responded that the *Ordenações Filipinas* treated the natural children of nobles ambiguously, but because several *ordenações* failed to discriminate them carefully from the spurious offspring of a noble parent, they were obliged to conclude they should be treated as generically equivalent to bastards.[5] Natural offspring could not succeed a noble parent, due to the precept that nobility "repudiated" the quality of infamy synonymous with bastardy. Nobility therefore demanded heirs of legitimate birth, heirs who possessed honor, a quality intrinsic to any noble's *fama*, or public reputation.[6]

Simple recognition broke the bastardy of a noble parent's natural (or spurious) offspring, but it conveyed only the noble parent's names and honors to the child, or, where relevant, a coat-of-arms. A noble parent could break the legal bastardy of a natural child by means of a private or public affidavit, or posthumously by a declaration in a will, but such simple legitimization alone, even though it bestowed honorable reputation, was insufficient for succession rights to follow. Only when the act of *perfilhação* was "solemnly" confirmed by the Tribunal of the Desembargo do Paço, and it bestowed concurrent succession rights, could a noble parent's natural offspring be equipped for heirship.[7]

Book 4, Title 92, of the *Ordenações Filipinas*, which equipped the natural offspring of a commoner parent as an *ab intestato* successor, explicitly excluded the natural offspring of a noble parent from succeeding *ab intestato*. Section 3 of the same title provided that where the noble parent lacked legitimate descendants, but ascendants lived, then the parent could leave part or all of the *terça* to the natural child, if a will was used to dispose the legacy. Alternatively, if the parent's legitimate ascendants were deceased and no legitimate descendants were living, then the same section provided that the noble parent could use a will as an instrument of testamentary succession to leave the *legítima* to the natural offspring. Such an arrangement was consistent with the right of universal heirship. Consequently, as we have seen earlier, Section 3 stipulated that, in the absence of legitimate descendants and ascendants, the noble parent could "dispose of the estate in another manner, whatever is considered [appropriate]."

This option of complete testamentary freedom to dispose of the *legítima* implied the parent could nominate a spurious offspring, as well as a natural one—or any other individual as heir—to the *legítima*. Despite such a presumption of testamentary succession, the noble parent's freedom to nominate the heir was encumbered. Approval from the Tribunal of the Desembargo do Paço was required, because this *ordenação* was interpreted to mean that crown legitimization had to take place before either a noble's natural or spurious offspring could receive rights as a testamentary successor.[8] Even prior to 1750, when the procedures were overhauled, legitimization by the crown was presumed preliminary to bestowal of succession rights of either type, "according to the custom of the realm."[9]

Yet many Brazilian wills were written that presumed testamentary succession rights would follow from a father's or a mother's use of a will for estab-

lishing simple *perfilhação*. Mathias de Crasto Porto's 1742 testamentary declaration of paternity revealed how testators who were minimally noble used
wills to bestow simple legitimization on their natural offspring. As we have
seen, they left tacit the circumstance they were minimally noble, an omission
contributing to this strategy of heirship. By means of his notary's imprecise
language, Crasto Porto availed himself of the option offered by Book 4, Title
92, Section 3 of the Philippine Code to institute his natural offspring as his
testamentary successors. Moreover, in the 1740s he could be confident that
the requirement of concurrent crown legitimization would not be enforced:

I am not married, nor was I ever, and I have always lived in the bachelor state; however, I have the following children, who, now, being born natural, I make legitimate
so that, as such, they will be able to be my heirs and thus I institute them [as my suc-
cessors] . . . .[10]

Despite their exclusion from *ab intestato* succession, Title 92 of Book 4
was straightforward on the position of a noble parent's non-legitimate offspring. The procedure of testamentary succession, following from crown legitimization, could equip either the natural or spurious offspring to be instituted as an heir—as long as there was an absence of all necessary heirs.
Unfortunately, the Philippine Code did not stop here. Title 36, Section 4, of
Book 4 introduced dissonance by invoking what amounted to a contradictory precept derived from Iberian customary law. Namely, after reaffirming
that descendants took precedence over ascendants on the ladder of intestacy,
Section 4 proceeded to contradict Title 92: "Lacking legitimate descendants
at the death of [the parent], even if legitimate ascendants exist, the natural
offspring will have the right [to succeed], even if the father is a *cavalleiro*."
Thus, in the absence of legitimate descendants, Title 36, Section 4, permitted
the natural offspring to succeed to the *legítima* of either a noble father or
mother—and when ascendants were still living. Nevertheless, legitimization
before the Tribunal of the Desembargo do Paço was mandatory, perhaps
precisely because of the ambiguity the two titles introduced.

As for the noble parent's spurious offspring, Title 36, Section 4, compounded the ambiguity vis-à-vis natural offspring, when it stipulated that
"the spurious offspring shall not have this right [to *ab intestato* succession in
the absence of legitimate children, but when ascendants may be living] unless legitimized by Us, in such a way that succession will be *ab intestato*, and
in no other way." This *ordenação* therefore disregarded the option of testamentary succession for the noble parent's spurious offspring. Gouvêa Pinto
was therefore obliged to conclude that spurious offspring legitimized by the
crown could become *ab intestato* successors "equal to natural offspring" rec-

ognized by the parent, as long as no legitimate children existed.[11] The circumlocutory logic of Title 36, when contrasted with Section 3 of Title 92, or Title 93, governing spurious offspring, produced a juridical consensus that the *Ordenações* generically equated the natural offspring born of a noble parent with the latter's spurious offspring. As the Philippine Code also noted in a sixteenth-century context, legitimization certificates provided "restitution of *fama*," or public reputation, on behalf of those born of "infamy"—the lack of honorable public reputation that was the inherent fate of all bastards. Consequently, *fama* being intrinsic to the noble condition, wherever a parent was noble, both natural and spurious offspring had to be so equipped via crown legitimization in order to succeed, either *ab intestato* or by testamentary succession.[12]

What is puzzling, of course, is the reference in Title 36, Section 4, to *ab intestato* rights for spurious offspring, rather than testamentary rights: "And the spurious offspring shall not have this right [of succession], unless legitimized by Us in such a manner that he can succeed *ab intestato*, and in no other way." In fact, this *ordenação* asserted the privileging of local custom, by favoring with rights the parent's non-legitimate descendants over his or her ascendants who might still be living. Title 92, on the other hand, rigidly asserted the Roman law principle that privileged only the legitimate line, setting aside the noble parent's non-legitimate issue, whether natural or spurious. The contradictory treatment that the *ordenações* of Titles 36 and 92 respectively applied to a noble parent's natural offspring, in situations where the noble parent's ascendants still lived, helps to account for the ambiguity in legal commentaries. They proved confusing or silent on the important question of which kinds of illegitimate offspring were entitled to *ab intestato* rights when legitimized. The Philippine Code had simply reaffirmed two contradictory points of legal doctrine, leaving them intrinsically in conflict. The silence of legal commentators proved even greater when a noble parent's offspring was spurious rather than natural.[13]

Adding to the complexity, the case files of the Tribunal of the Mesa do Desembargo do Paço in Rio de Janeiro revealed examples of legitimized individuals who received concurrent rights in *ab intestato* succession even when legitimate half-siblings existed. Crown legitimization raised them to the same plane as their legitimate siblings. What circumstances explained the bestowal of *ab intestato* rights on legitimized children who already had legitimate half-siblings? And what were the motives of their parents, or the offspring themselves, in petitioning for those succession rights? The answer to these questions can shed light on the seemingly inconsistent determinations made by the Tribunal of the Desembargo do Paço. The rulings of that high crown court of final appeal did not always neatly fit the legal rules prescribed by the *Ordenações Filipinas*, the Paço's *Regimento*, or the inferences of legal commentaries. Why those rules were overridden, and the sovereign's "mercy and grace" granted, can be explained by a mixture of both legal logic and social change.

Coveted Rights: Ab Intestato Succession

Whenever they devoted attention to crown legitimization, legal commentators devoted overwhelming attention to testamentary succession, not *ab intestato* succession. They did so emphasizing that testamentary succession was a right conceded by the *Ordenações* to legitimized individuals when their parents lacked necessary heirs. Otherwise, jurists made only passing reference to *ab intestato* succession rights awarded concurrently with crown legitimization. In only two situations, however, did *ab intestato* rights occupy their exclusive attention. Each assumed an absence of legitimate offspring: the natural offspring legitimized by a noble parent and the *quaesito* whose legitimization was matrilineal, not patrilineal.

It is easy to see why law logically accommodated both situations as worthy of *ab intestato* rights, because, in each case, the candidates arguably *were* natural offspring, not spurious. In the first situation, illicit birth was ipso facto; in the second, law presumed illicit birth to be matrilineal. As we have seen, on the one hand, the *ordenação* of Book 4, Title 36, Section 4, also permitted that *ab intestato* rights could follow legitimization in yet one other situation: when a noble parent had spurious offspring, provided no legitimate children existed. Presumably, the inference to be drawn from what was prescribed for spurious offspring was that a parent's noble estate implied succession rights should be *ab intestato*, rather than testamentary, at least when no legitimate or natural offspring existed. Therefore, a natural offspring deserved the same rights as a spurious offspring. Crown legitimization best approximated the criterion of legitimate birth by equipping the noble's spurious offspring to succeed *ab intestato*, as if he or she were indeed legitimate. By the same token, in the second case, the matrilineally illicit *quaesito* was treated as if the father's condition was irrelevant, justifying the award of prized *ab intestato* succession rights. Yet the consistent thread of logic in both cases is the absence of legitimate children. Otherwise, the *Ordenações* clearly intended testamentary succession rights should follow in all other situations.

Ab intestato rights conferred greater prestige than testamentary succession rights because the latter fell short of offering the legal verisimilitude enjoyed by legitimate children. Testamentary succession rights depended entirely on the parent's volition. They offered the choice of leaving the legitimized child either a portion of the *legítima* or its entirety. Alternatively, the child might be excluded altogether from testamentary succession, in effect, disinherited. The parent was not required, as in *ab intestato* succession, to justify disinheritance. Nor could the child contest the disinheritance.[14] Consequently, the greater prestige of *ab intestato* succession inherently rested on rights in forced heirship, those identical to what legitimate children enjoyed. Of course, some parents found testamentary succession more congenial, precisely for being revocable or for allowing discretion in determining how much patrimony they would leave a legitimized child.

Whenever petitioning parents sought crown legitimization concomitantly with succession rights, and they already had legitimate children, then their situation did not fall under either Title 92 or 36 of Book 4 of the *Ordenações*. Moreover, legal commentaries declined to comment on the anomaly of their situation. The silence of that literature suggests that law was fairly clear. Nevertheless, that class of petitioners, not entirely new, began to occupy more of the Paço's attention after 1808. Parents with legitimate children sought the mercy and grace of the sovereign for a situation unforeseen by the Philippine Code. In effect, those parents appealed for Titles 92 or 36 to be suspended, because they already had legitimate children who were their *ab intestato* successors. Contrary to the *Ordenações*, they wanted their natural or spurious children legitimized, and with *ab intestato* rights, the same rights their legitimate children enjoyed. As parents of adulterine children or as noble parents of natural children, they looked directly to the regnant precept that jurists cited for redress: "to the monarch belongs the power to restrict or extend the rights of the offspring." In other words, they sought the sovereign's mercy and grace as the only loophole the Philippine Code offered for legitimizing their children with concurrent succession rights. Research conducted in the Rio de Janeiro archive of the Mesa do Desembargo do Paço supports the practice of petitioning for succession rights on behalf of non-legitimate children when the parent already had living legitimate children.

In the preceding chapter, passing reference was made to how the royal judge of the first instance known as the *ouvidor* might disregard testimony from legitimate heirs he consulted, when the latter objected to *ab intestato* rights being awarded to a legitimization candidate. One such case concerned a legitimate daughter who objected to the *ouvidor*'s recommendation that her father's five natural offspring be legitimized and equipped for *ab intestato* succession. A lieutenant-colonel in the army, the deceased father had possessed minimal nobility, explaining why his five natural children could not be his *ab intestato* successors. The situation did not fit the situation pre-

scribed in Book 4, Title 36, Section 4, of the *Ordenações Filipinas*, because he
had a legitimate daughter. Nevertheless, the crown judge overruled her objections. He justified his decision as one constituting a direct appeal to the
sovereign's prerogative to dispense the law, invoking the "royal grace" whose
function was, he explained, "to overcome such legal difficulties."[15] His recommendation to legitimize with concurrent *ab intestato* succession rights
was accepted by the high judge of the Desembargo do Paço. It ignored
Lobão's famous caveat that legitimization with concurrent succession rights
should not do harm to the pre-existing rights of forced heirs, because the
sovereign's mercy and grace overrode existing law.

The rising demands of patronage may well explain the *ouvidor*'s decision
to depart from the guidelines set by the Desembargo do Paço's *Regimento*.
However, this case probably suggests more than the absoluteness of the sovereign's prerogative. It points toward pressure to bend or ignore the ordinary
situation for crown legitimization in order to accommodate a growing
population of non-legitimate offspring. More than merely demographic
change was at work, because noble status itself was becoming more diffused
in late colonial Brazil. In other words, a growing proportion of parents,
above all, fathers, found that their natural offspring were excluded from *ab
intestato* succession simply because they enjoyed, or had acquired, minimal
nobility. Above all, expansion of the colonial militias and the presence of the
royal officer corps on Brazilian soil, thanks to the Peninsular army's 1808
exodus to Rio de Janeiro, accounts for this trend. Nizza da Silva's valuable
analysis of the 114 petitions for crown legitimization filed with the Tribunal
of the Desembargo do Paço in Rio de Janeiro, beginning in 1808, revealed
that 51 of the petitions, or 45 percent, requested legitimization for the children of officers in the army or the militia.[16] Greater demand for legitimization, for stretching rules of heirship to include such natural offspring, introduced more tension and conflict into court proceedings and strained the
procedures laid down by the *Regimento* of the Tribunal of the Desembargo
do Paço.

Nor did patrimonial motives alone explain the strong incentive that drove
noble parents to seek crown legitimization for their natural or spurious offspring, even when they had legitimate children. Parents enjoying a minimal
degree of nobility sought to place their offspring on a par with social peers
who were legitimate, even their own legitimate children. The entitlements of
ab intestato succession projected a prestige that many in a society of rank
coveted. Equipped with *ab intestato* rights, the natural child of a noble father,
for instance, was also called to succession vis-à-vis his father's agnatic kin,

and inherited the paternal grandparents' *legítimas*. Testamentary succession, on the other hand, failed to extend those rights. A legitimized natural offspring who possessed *ab intestato* rights, however, could not succeed to a father's entail, for that privilege was exclusively reserved for legitimate children, whether male or female.[17] By the same token, the noble parent's coveted privilege the noble parent's coveted privilege of being honorifically addressed as "*dom*" or "*dona*," one automatically transmitted to legitimate children, was denied the legitimized offspring. Only when the parent was a noble titleholder would the privilege of being treated as "*dom*" apply, even without crown legitimization.[18] Brazilian imperial law reaffirmed these practices.[19]

Otherwise, crown legitimization, the solemn act of *perfilhação*, replicated in positive law almost all of a longer list of privileges and entitlements bestowed by a legitimate birthright. A parent's simple legitimization in a will or affidavit minimally repaired the offspring's social position, but failed to confer the full list of legal effects following from crown legitimization.[20] In late colonial Brazil, the right to employment by the crown depended much less on legitimate birth than had been the case until the mid-eighteenth century, but it still mattered. Prior to independence, *fidalguia* continued to be a qualification for certain entry-level career positions in royal government, notwithstanding considerable progress made in removing this barrier. Legitimate birth, or the next-best *qualidade*—legitimized by the crown—still proved to be the *sine qua non* for inheriting minimal nobility. Even minimal noble status entitled the bearer to immunity from certain taxes and revenue assessments, from torture, hard labor, and the lash. Where execution mattered, a victim of noble birth was spared the "vile" public display of his head—unless his or her public degradation occurred first, stripping nobility from the victim. The privilege of "homage prison" meant immunity from being confined in a public jail with common prisoners who were "vile" and usually amounted to the right of house arrest.[21]

In some cases, such as military cadet candidacy, minimal nobility defined a prerequisite for selection, a practice that continued after Brazilian independence. Clerking for a high judge of the Mesa do Desembargo do Paço also "required some nobility." As late as 1800, the sons of councilors of state received preferential appointment as magistrates on crown tribunals and were exempted from preliminary service on lower benches.[22] Although independence brought significant change, especially the elimination of distinctions of estate pertaining to taxation, it drastically reduced, rather than thoroughly eliminated, the credential of legitimate birth—what crown legitimization repaired—for entry into the professions and high civil service careers.

Minimal Nobility: A Reconsideration

In the 1820s, liberal constitutions in both Portugal and Brazil would abolish most attributes of nobility in the name of "equality before the law," but preserve a titled nobility on the ground of "merit and virtue." Nevertheless, how certain privileges tied to distinctions of estate survived in the nineteenth century, either in legally modified form or simply embedded in the *de facto* values of a rank society, remains a subject for historians to delineate. Whether legally or by sheer force of custom, possession of *fidalguia*, as minimal nobility, continued to matter after independence, whenever young men sought crown appointments or employment, admission or scholarships to law and medical faculties, cadet officer candidacy, ordination, and especially admission to the regular orders of the clergy. Important life choices favoring ambitious career aspirations therefore prompted petitions for solemn legitimization after independence.

Minimal nobility acquired greater significance during Brazil's early imperial decades precisely because the other exclusionary criterion—Old Christian ancestry *qua* racial ancestry—had lost its legal underpinnings. As in Spanish America, the policy of "purity of the blood"—*limpeza de sangue*—weakened irrevocably from the 1770s onward; however, it did not completely disappear in the wake of Pombal's legal reforms. The rule of descent that had excluded those with Jewish and Muslim ancestry ceased to operate, thanks to express laws and official policies that set it aside as a criterion for crown employment, especially in the judiciary. Pombaline legislation also repealed a policy of legal discrimination directed against those of Native American ancestry, thanks to efforts by the so-called *jurisnaturalistas*—jurists who drew on natural law.[23] Men of Portuguese ancestry who married Brazilian Indian women no longer acquired "infamy," the legal degradation of their noble quality of birth. Formerly, loss of public reputation had annulled their noble status and privileges. Beginning in 1775, the racially mixed offspring born of such marriages became legally "equipped and qualified for any employment, honor, or dignity" without resorting to any dispensation from the crown.[24]

Possession of African ancestry in a colonial context had been similarly fused to the Iberian formula of purity of blood, which relied on exclusively Old Christian ancestry for excluding individuals of color. At the beginning of the nineteenth century, African ancestry still constituted a "defect" of birth and continued to operate as a barrier to social mobility. The 1758 Law of Military Enlistment and Militia Service had specifically declared that militia officers and sergeants enjoyed the privilege of gentlemen, implying they would be on a par with those officers who met the three-generation rule of noble descent, "even if they did not possess it."[25] In 1802, Portugal's prince regent, D. João, issued a famous *alvará* whose purpose was "to uproot the odious preoccupation that many have with differences of color as a principle producing different rights." As proof for his "black and brown vassals," the king decreed the latter were henceforth equipped for all honors and military employment.[26] Yet militia regiments remained segregated by color and the commanders of black and mulatto regiments legally still had to be white.

The observations of Henry Koster, an English merchant resident in Recife from 1811 to 1813, offer an insightful counterpoint on behavior that did not conform to the 1802 *alvará*. He mentioned that several individuals who officially passed as white had benefited from crown dispensations conceded for a defect of birth or color. In conversation with a man of color who worked for him, Koster inquired if a certain *capitão-mor* of Pernambuco's militia was not a mulatto, confident in his knowledge that mulattoes were legally excluded from that rank. The answer came back, "He was, but is not now." Confused, Koster asked for an explanation. He received only an intuitive response from his servant: "Can a *capitão-mor* be a mulatto man?"[27]

Koster had in mind the white militia regiments whose officers law similarly prescribed be white. Regarding regiments of the line, he specifically noted that their officers also had to be of noble birth and therefore legitimate, whenever promoted from cadets. Ever intrigued by how individual Brazilians manipulated the rules, he elaborated on why men who were mulattoes got to be officers of all white regiments of the line. That apparent enigma, he pointed out, found resolution in the circumstance that race might be putatively interpreted. Koster also emphasized that officers "must prove nobility of birth," and elaborated that "certain degrees of nobility have been conferred upon persons in whose families there is much mixture of blood." Thus the crown ennobled a select few individuals of color, or alternatively, legitimized and ennobled them, in order to confer the criterion that established eligibility for promotion to the commanding officer rank of *capitão-mór*, notwithstanding the candidate's mixed racial ancestry. On the other hand, he noted that promotions from the ranks were done without regard to birth—to *qualidade*. He added, however, that "a decidedly dark coloured mulatto might not be so raised," but "a European of low birth would."[28] Although skin color would not bar men from pursuing a military career, it obliged non-whites to serve under the command of whites—or at least those who were putatively white.

Racial discrimination lessened with independence, if only because it no longer rested on a secure, de jure foundation. In compensation, the criterion of minimal, or even putative, nobility continued to privilege whites over non-whites. It was in this respect that the "defect" of illegitimate birth acquired greater significance in imperial Brazil, given that minimal nobility, when it rested on descent, always presumed legitimate birth. Consequently, only crown legitimization could repair the social reputation of either a natural or a spurious offspring born of a noble parent, frequently an officer. Indirectly, therefore, illegitimate birth worked disproportionately against men of color, denying them opportunity for career advancement and education. Almost always, it followed from minimal nobility that an individual was white—or putatively white. The latter implied, in addition to legitimate birth, the *qualidade* of "legitimized by the crown." The Rio de Janeiro archives of the Tribunal of the Mesa do Desembargo do Paço have revealed how that royal high court accommodated the ambitions of petitioners whose fathers belonged to a lily-white constituency. Analysis of the petitions submitted between 1808 and 1828 exposed "the difficulty encountered by those of darker color in proving their right to inherit and the reluctance of their white fathers to give the child of color the same rights as his white [legitimate] half-siblings." During the twenty years when the Paço functioned in the Brazilian capital, only one petitioner obtained crown legitimization on behalf of an offspring of color—an army officer whose daughter had been fathered with a slave.[29]

After 1750, legal change affected the lowest rank of noble status, diffusing minimal nobility among many in the third estate. That trend and its impact has largely escaped scholarly attention, in favor of focusing on the dramatic expansion of nobility within titleholding ranks, under both D. Maria I (1777–1816) and D. João VI (1816–1826). The eighteenth-century diffusion of minimal nobility spelled important implications for Brazil's imperial society in terms of social class, lending new urgency to crown legitimization as the only means open to noble parents for conferring succession rights on natural offspring. The population of free color, virtually excluded from crown legitimization, except in a few cases where the monarch himself may have conferred legitimization, benefited only marginally from the diffusion of minimal nobility. For the most part, the social origins of the emerging middle classes of color originated in an artisanal base within Brazil's larger cities. Individual legal "condition," whenever defined by a manual occupation, therefore was taken ipso facto as the criterion for repudiating any claim to nobility by descent.[30]

DIFFUSING CIVIL NOBILITY IN LATE COLONIAL BRAZIL

Historians of Brazil have neglected to tie individual membership in the second estate, minimal nobility by descent, to rules of heirship that continued to operate after independence. For that matter, they have largely been silent on precisely how the lowest rung of noble rank, *fidalguia*, was legally defined. Nor have they taken into account how the latter figured importantly in social divisions or political status after independence. Instead, scholarly attention has been directed almost exclusively toward titleholders, who have been meticulously quantified and gradated, even though their number never exceeded one thousand between 1816 and 1889.[31] Unfortunately, it is still not possible to say how many Brazilians without titles enjoyed minimal nobility. Arguably, the stratum they defined carried political significance equal to what the much smaller echelon of titleholders wielded, because those who possessed minimal nobility largely defined the active citizenry on whom the 1824 Constitution conferred direct suffrage. Fundamentally, minimal nobility mattered even more for defining the key social divide in both the late colonial era and the Brazilian Empire, circumscribing those of gentle birth within a nexus of family and personal associations that upheld individual identities as "worthy."

How was nobility defined on the eve of Brazilian independence? And who possessed nobility that was merely minimal? Courtly speech relied on the key legal distinction between noble titleholders and all other nobles. Narrowly construed, "*nobreza*," or nobility, colloquially denoted titleholders. After independence, Brazil's monarch would ennoble individuals only in life tenure, bestowing titles enhanced by the coveted *honras de grandeza*.[32] Before independence, however, titles were heritable in the direct, legitimate line. "*Fidalguia*," on the other hand, implied a much larger population in both colony and Empire that admitted a diverse membership, but the most prestigious were those who enjoyed nobility by birth, or "by blood," that is, those said to possess nobility by descent. Although *fidalguia* was widely applied to the latter and titleholders alike in Portugal and in Spain, Brazilian usage after 1822 was less consistent than in the metropole. Normally, but not always, "*fidalguia*" pertained to the lower nobility of descent.[33] Historically, *fidalgos* in Portugal were graded according to multiple ranks that reflected a hierarchy of privilege, in addition to the way *fidalguia* had been individually acquired. Thus individuals were set apart according to either a direct grant of nobility "by special grace of the monarch," implying inscription in the registers of the royal house, or nobility was assumed to be acquired by blood (descent) and deemed merely "notable." This distinction still mattered in late colonial and early independence Brazil.[34]

"*Fidalgo*," by connoting the nobility of lower ranks in an Iberian context, amounted to what one Brazilian scholar insightfully has observed was a "generic denomination." As in France, he pointed out, "*fidalguia* encompassed a *gentilhomerie,* constituting the nucleus and foundation of a concept of social class onto which the titled nobility was superimposed."[35] This implicit connection between lower noble rank and class formation existed over the long run of the late colony and Brazilian Empire. It largely accounts for why *"fidalguia"* was preferred in colloquial speech, in direct contrast to the august *"nobreza."* The latter term, understandably, echoed more loudly in the halls of Brazil's Parliament after 1826. *"Fidalgos"* and *"fidalgas"* connoted gentlemen and gentlewomen, the lower rung of noble rank, although not all *fidalgos* were equal. Fine-tuned distinctions in the late colonial era still applied following independence, when colloquial speech began to merge *"fidalgos"* with "cavaliers." The latter term, as *"cavalheiros"* in nineteenth-century Portuguese, was used frequently in the Philippine Code to identify the *"cavalleiros"* who amounted to "gentlemen," the minimal nobles.

In the first decades after 1822, a linguistic transformation of *"fidalgos"* into the more modern-sounding *"cavalheiros"* occurred in Brazil, corresponding to the transformation of a *gentilhomerie* into an upper middle class. Earlier, wider usage of *"dom"* in the late eighteenth century had testified to a basic degradation of minimal nobility. Whether linguistic erosion reached the point in the late 1820s that Cuban novelist Cirilo Villaverde claimed for the colony of his birth—when "the king of Spain had declared the art of tailor and tobacconist to be noble," permitting *"don"* to be used even for a man of color—remains for historians of Brazil to discover.[36] Usage of *"dom"* nevertheless receded after independence, beginning in the Regency (1831–1840), and eventually was restricted as the address reserved for noble titleholders and high churchmen.

The diffusion of yet a different type of nobility—what in imperial Brazil came to be termed "civil" nobility—alternatively favored a substitution of masculine forms of address that displaced *"dom."* Establishment of law and medical faculties in the late 1820s favored the use of *"doutor"* for their graduates, as an alternative to *"dom."* Similarly, the creation of a National Guard in 1831 validated the discrete titles of military rank differentiating members of the officer corps. The latter almost always disdained to be treated as *"dom,"* although law entitled them to that form of address, because all military officers ipso facto continued to be noble until 1889. Only with the advent of a republic did reliance on *"dom"* become confined to prelates of the church. The feminine form, however, has endured to the present. *"Dona"* was initially reserved for the daughters and wives of men possessing nobility, either by descent or by a title, including members of the officer corps. During the early republic, it gradually became extended to women in the middle classes. Finally, in the second half of the twentieth century, the honorific *"dona"*

could be routinely attached to any woman's given name, irrespective of social class, unless the speaker was inclined to be hierarchical.

The fact that *fidalguia* endured as a social construct throughout the Brazilian Empire (1822–1889) has belied its survival as a legal condition. In fact,
both manifestations were directly traceable to the late colonial period. Politicians in Brazil's Parliament liked to speak of "*nobreza*," even when referring
to a minimal nobility, because their debates counterposing "commoner" to
"noble" frequently discriminated membership in the latter estate. Often, they
had in mind not only *fidalguia* of the minimal sort, nobility by descent, but
also a different type that became very important in Portugal after 1750. Then
they spoke of "civil nobility," what corresponded to nobility "by the law"
from Pombaline times onward. It defined a minimal nobility lower in status
than natural nobility. The distinction between the two types, which jurists
actually analyzed as a threefold distinction, deserves attention in consideration of who was noble for purposes of inheritance law.

Birth or descent provides a useful starting point for understanding the
elusive issue of what it meant to be minimally noble. How was one born to
fidalguia? Customarily, children inherited it from their parents, as long as the
latter were legitimately married.[37] Thus birth, *qualidade*, mediated minimal
noble rank, because law construed *fidalguia* based on heredity as "natural
nobility." At independence, a definition of *fidalguia* by descent that followed
a rule of three generations was received in Brazilian positive law from Portugal. That is, natural nobility was heritable from the original holder by his or
her children and grandchildren, with the fourth generation obliged to re-
quest its renewal.[38]

How then did individuals prove they were noble? The answer to this
question had become problematic for Portugal's judiciary by the dawn of the
nineteenth century, precisely due to the inheritance position of the natural
offspring of minimally noble parents. Writing in 1805, royal jurisconsult
Lobão commented that the definition of a noble had become a subject "of
agitation in the courts." Disputes over the meaning of minimally noble rank,
he noted, "took place daily."[39] He referred to legal conflicts over Title 92 of
Book 4 of the *Ordenações Filipinas*. They pitted individuals of illicit birth fathered by a noble against their legitimate half-siblings for the prize of the
paternal *legítima*. Natural offspring went to court to assert rights in succession, arguing speciously that their fathers were not noble, but merely "half-
noble." The assertion of a claim as an *ab intestato* successor raised the thorny
issue of how nobility was be proved in court—or discounted. Lobão's exegesis of how nobility was acquired developed therefore as a complementary argument to his insistence that "nobility in the half state" did not exist. His

authoritative examination of how three forms of minimal nobility were defined in Portugal continued to be accepted by Brazilians after independence.
Equally important, Lobão gave consideration to how someone could lose individual nobility through inappropriate behavior. Borges Carneiro, writing
his authoritative treatise on Portuguese law during the first half of the 1820s,
drew authoritatively on Lobão's 1805 commentary, published in 1818. That he
wrote as a fervent liberal—just as the era of liberalism had taken hold in
Portugal and Brazil—made his endorsement of Lobão's basic distinctions
particularly relevant.

First, Lobão explained, one acquired the status or privilege of being noble,
"the *foro de fidalgo*," from a royal grant, with or without a title, as a reward
for service to the crown. Service on the battlefield represented the classic reason for bestowing noble rank. However, nobility from a royal grant implied
nobility by descent for descendants of the original grantee. After 1750, Portugal's titled nobility grew enormously, to the point where certain titles were
granted for either one or two lifetimes.[40] Yet two other means of acquiring
nobility mattered even more. Noting that since the reign of D. José I (1750–
1777), "letters," rather than "arms," accounted for more nobles, Lobão
pointed to a second class of persons who enjoyed nobility through university
degrees—medical doctors and "*licenciados*." The latter would be better
known in imperial Brazil as "*bacharéis*," or law faculty graduates. The list of
degrees in letters and science qualifying one for noble status expanded impressively from Pombal's era onward, to include not only graduates of the
traditional faculties of canon and civil law, theology, and medicine, but also
secondary teachers of Latin, Greek, rhetoric, and even elementary letters.
Even pharmacists and surgeons, as long as they were not practicing barbers,
qualified.[41] All these individuals, Lobão observed, constituted "the rest of the
kingdom's nobility, within which can be placed . . . [all] persons nobilized by
laws."[42]

Lobão's use of "nobilized by laws" expressed the essence of what in nineteenth-century Brazil would be deemed civil nobility. It drew on the juridical
language of the *alvará* of November 29, 1775, a pivotal law for synthesizing
and confirming preceding statutes that had ennobled doctors in letters and
science. However, the 1775 law extended noble status derived from the Academy to new occupational groups: "businessmen," or large-scale merchants,
and those engaging in agriculture and industry. Nobility in occupations
"nobilized by law" was predicated on the assumption an individual did not
work in the hire of another, as an employee. Nor could he engage in manual
trades—the "mechanical occupations"—and work with his hands. An agri-
culturist therefore was to be a resident landowner, however modest a farmer,

but not a day laborer; a merchant was to be a big businessman or wholesaler, but not an ordinary retailer or clerk who sold from behind the counter of his shop; and an industrialist would own and manage his factory, but not manufacture the product with his own hands; and so forth.[43] The meritorious exercise of a suitable occupation or profession now became tantamount to ennoblement. In imperial Brazil, jurists and legislators continued to refer to this kind of nobility as either "second class" or "second order" nobility. Precisely because they construed everyone nobilized by the law as "second-class nobles," Brazilians dignified such nobility as "civil"—*nobreza civil.*

The third class of persons enjoying noble rank identified by Lobão was not readily distinguishable from those nobilized by the law. Their nobility, however, was discriminated as an older form originating in membership in legal corporations dating to the Middle Ages, but expanded after 1750, especially to include a growing list of guilds. Technically, therefore, those so ennobled also possessed nobility by means of the law. Foremost in this group could be found the members of the first and second estates, the clergy and the military. Thus law took ordinary clerics in holy orders to be *fidalgos* and equipped them as *cavalleiros*, while bishops enjoyed "distinct nobility," implying many honors and privileges associated with higher noble rank. Historically, nobility had been exclusively military, accounting for why ecclesiastics, as well as jurisconsults, actually enjoyed military nobility. Military officers originally possessed nobility above the rank of sergeant. From the sixteenth century onward, militia officers from the rank of sergeant and above similarly were considered "to possess the privilege of a *cavalleiro*, in cases where they did not."[44]

As a corollary to the above, special exceptions could be made to the three-generation rule, due to the principle that, historically, in Portugal, "nobility was completely military." This notion implied that military nobility was extended even to the wealthy (*ricos homens*), in addition to the titled or the naturally noble members of the officer corps, and to common soldiers, in the same manner that it had inscribed ecclesiastics and jurisconsults. All enjoyed military nobility. Finally, the crown *regulamentos* of 1763 and 1764 specifically stipulated that officer commissions awarded by the monarch conferred nobility, following the *Ordenações Filipinas*, meaning that, as a last resort, promotion to commissioned officer from the ranks automatically conferred minimal nobility in cases where otherwise candidates lacked nobility by birth. Similarly, where officers were promoted to very high rank in the military, but lacked nobility, then late eighteenth-century statutes equipped them with the appropriate status.[45]

Finally, the third estate contributed a list of newcomer groups recently nobilized by Pombaline or Joanine legislation, by virtue of quasi-corporate group identities. Their importance as an *arriviste* nobility testified to the impressive advance of commoners to noble rank after 1750. Thus masters in the artisanal guilds qualified as noble, by virtue of their occupational attainment; however, common artisans and journeymen who worked under them—and used their hands—did not.[46] The list was still growing in 1802, when the prince regent added ownership of a silk factory to the list of corporate affiliations conferring civil nobility.[47] High posts in crown service similarly conferred automatic civil nobility, frequently the more prestigious "distinct nobility" that also enhanced natural nobility. For instance, members of the crown judiciary, most of whom possessed the diploma of *bacharel* or *doutor* of law as a prerequisite for their candidacy, were already "second-class nobles." However, appointment as a higher judge automatically conferred prestigious distinct nobility on them. The high judges of the Tribunal of the Mesa do Desembargo do Paço, consequently, were awarded the *foro*, or privilege, of a *fidalgo* of the royal palace and given the honors of a royal councilor.[48]

The historical significance of widely diffused nobility becomes obvious once one appreciates that it was transmissible to legitimate offspring. A noble parent's offspring legitimized by the crown acquired the parent's nobility. Coveted as a means for advancing the career opportunities for sons, or as the prerequisite for arranging an advantageous marriage for daughters, civil nobility became even more widely diffused in Brazil after the Lisbon court was established in Rio de Janeiro. On the one hand, civil nobility accounted for how those in the third estate successfully penetrated the historical preserves of the first two estates. On the other hand, the socio-political process of extending nobility to many in the third estate reflected no less than the growing power of the Portuguese crown. By diffusing noble status, Pombaline policy debased the prestige of both Portugal's "old" nobility and the ecclesiastical hierarchy while raising up new elites originating in the professions, commerce, and industry.

The juridical rule presumed someone to be a commoner. Whenever nobility was not conferred as a birthright, or descent proved ambiguous, whoever claimed to be noble might have to prove himself noble in a courtroom context. By the early nineteenth century, minimal nobility had become so widely diffused that individual behavior acquired greater importance for a presumption of nobility. Lobão laid special stress on comportment, offering an inverse definition of nobility that drew on the *Ordenações Filipinas*: "The exercise of a manual occupation is opposed to nobility." Thus engaging in a manual occupation defined an individual as a legal commoner, even when, as Lobão quipped, he "kept a horse"—a style expected of a noble.[49] Social behavior played the crucial role in mediating individual nobility, something courts took into account in ruling on whether an individual was noble. Anyone claiming to be noble by birth had to behave as if he or she was noble. An individual's social relations mattered for the presumption of noble status, for one was expected to keep exclusive company with other *cavalheiros*. Thus one who is noble "must be brought up by nobles and marry noble, lest one not be taken to be noble."[50]

If genuine nobles were expected to behave as such, then what mattered even more was the behavioral presumption that one was noble—when one really was not: "By custom of the realm, those are noble who among themselves and in common opinion, are taken to be the same, and thereby so become by public reputation."[51] Hence the complaints brought in court by natural offspring seeking a noble father's *legítima* on the ground that his public reputation did not support presumptive nobility. *Who* was really noble? It could not always be easily determined, for behavior might project a nobility that was merely putative. Brazil's early lawmakers joked that it was enough to own a horse and to pass oneself off as noble in order to be taken as noble. Again, public reputation—*fama pública*—played the fundamental role. Ergo, Lobão's famous caveat: "It is advisable always to keep horses, to avoid a manual trade or employment, and, above all, never to be reputed to be a commoner." Borges Carneiro concurred: Those taken to be noble *were* noble, as long as legal challenge did not prove them otherwise.[52]

How a Pombaline diffusion of nobility—and a fundamental reliance on legitimate birth—would matter in post-independence Brazil was well exemplified by the reform of Portugal's officer corps during the 1750s. Recruitment of officer cadets illustrated not only the new importance of a minimal nobility that was "natural"—inherited through legitimate birth—but also the tension arising between those who were noble by descent and those who possessed mere civil nobility—the "nobles of the second class."[53] Within a military career nexus, quality of birth became a sore point. Cadet recruitment for the officer corps illustrated how the interdependent criteria of minimal nobility and legitimate birth would operate in post-colonial Brazil to preserve the ranks of the imperial officer corps for those of European descent. Furthermore, cadet recruitment privileged crown legitimization as an instrument for entry. Beginning in 1757, the so-called Law of the Cadets defined recruitment qualifications for cadets training as officers. They were to be drawn exclusively from the sons of army officers who enjoyed *fidalguia*, nobility by descent. Although the sons of the higher nobility were exempt from proving their nobility, other candidates had "to prove their parents and four grandparents possessed *fidalguia* that was publicly known, without reputation to the contrary."[54] The rule of three generations insured that every cadet commissioned as an officer from the military academy would be a *fidalgo*.

Once the Portuguese Court moved to Rio de Janeiro, pressure quickly grew for admission to a new military academy established at Realengo. It came from the military officers themselves, when they sought to have their sons follow them. D. João VI, by the Resolution of May 12, 1818, permitted what amounted to an addendum to the Law of the Cadets. He sanctioned the loophole of crown legitimization that affirmed the sons of noble officers legitimized before the Tribunal of the Desembargo do Paço would enjoy their parent's noble privilege, ruling it equipped them for admission to the Royal Military Academy on an equal footing with the legitimate sons of officers.[55] In 1821, the Regency Council left in place after D. João returned to Portugal again bowed to Brazilian officers who petitioned on behalf of their non-legitimate sons. It reaffirmed what soon became a post-independence policy: "All noble persons who wanted to be legitimized [by the crown] . . . . would be admitted to the military academy without regard to number."[56] Nevertheless, the solemnly legitimized sons of military officers who were eligible to become cadet candidates comprised a miniscule proportion of those seeking to enroll at the military academy. Overwhelming reliance on the criterion of nobility by descent implied legitimate birth would remain the standard criterion, insuring that a cadet officer cohort would be of European descent.

INTERPRETING BASTARDY ON THE EVE
OF INDEPENDENCE

The question, "Who was illegitimate in colonial and imperial Brazil?" should remind us that the adjective "illegitimate" derives from Roman civil law. Thanks to Roman law, the *Ordenações Filipinas* referred routinely to "illegitimate offspring"; however, where they precisely discriminated succession rights, the *Ordenações* spoke of "natural offspring" and "spurious offspring"—or "legitimized offspring." Similarly, jurists and law professors employed "illegitimate," but still preferred the finer discrimination derived from canon law for interpretive reference to offspring who were "incestuous," "adulterine," and "sacrilegious"—or a "*quaesito*." Great dissonance can be introduced into late colonial or imperial legal discourse whenever the strict dichotomy, "legitimate/illegitimate," derived from Roman law, but familiar from an Anglo-American context, is imposed. Instead, a tripartite division for heirship needs to be recognized as inherent in Luso-Brazilian legal tradition: legitimate/natural/spurious. Because the "loophole" of legitimization offered a gloss on the meaning of bastardy, yet a fourth division deserves to be added, whether it was effected by subsequent marriage, testamentary *perfilhação*, or *per Rescriptum Principis.*[57]

The kernel of meaning in Luso-Brazilian bastardy lay precisely in the legal distinction that the recognized natural offspring of a commoner parent was not "damnable and punishable" but belonged on the ladder of *ab intestato* succession. The status of being illegitimate, but not spurious, crystallized the unique position this individual enjoyed. Natural offspring who were recognized enjoyed an illegitimacy that was technical rather than real, something social practice, even more than law, validated. That legal commentators classified natural offspring as illegitimate merely stretched the binary logic of the *Ordenações'* Roman law foundation to the limit. Jurists were obliged to pronounce natural offspring illegitimate, following the logical deduction that "all who were not legitimate were illegitimate." However, that deduction amounted to mere juridical formalism. Having pronounced natural offspring illegitimate, jurists then usually avoided referring to them as illegitimate elsewhere in their commentaries. By the same token, they avoided imputations of bastardy for natural offspring, even if a strictly legal logic told them that all illegitimate individuals were bastards. Eighteenth- and early nineteenth-century jurists used ingenious textual juxtaposition to stress that natural offspring were not bastards, and they relied on diverse analytical contexts to bring out the proximity of recognized natural offspring to legitimate offspring.

Mello Freire, for instance, began discussing illegitimacy by reiterating the legal wisdom that all offspring were either legitimate or illegitimate, but conceded in passing that some of the latter were natural—born of unmarried persons. Otherwise, when forced to admit a logical equivalence between bastardy and natural birth, he used historical distance to imply such usage was archaic: "Illegitimate individuals are called bastards, a name that already in the Middle Ages designated not only natural offspring *in specie* but also those who were spurious, and generally all those who would not be born of true and legitimate marriage." He nevertheless declined to make reference to natural offspring when discussing bastards, reserving the latter term for spurious individuals.[58] The gist of Mello Freire's commentary made clear that recognized natural offspring were a distinct category apart from bastards, falling very close to legitimate offspring. This interpretation complemented his iconoclastic dismissal of the importance of sacramental marriage, except for the propertied. As the following chapter argues, it reflected the greater importance he placed on de facto marriage—what he liked to construe as marriage "according to our customs."

Mello Freire's treatment of non-legitimate birth was further distinguished by a very different argument: flat dismissal of bastardy as a significant quality of birth. He played down differences in individual *qualidade*, drawing on the late eighteenth-century legal interpretation that a spurious *qualidade* no longer accounted for why someone enjoyed "infamy." As literally the lack of "*fama*"—public reputation worthy of respect—"*infamia*" fell casualty to a juridical reliance on natural law. Mello Freire therefore opened a new direction that anticipated a liberal position, because he rejected the notion that the defect of spurious birth implied a heritable condition. He argued that only positive law, when it condemned individual personal acts—such as treason and heresy—could confer infamy on an individual. If bastards no longer enjoyed infamy as a birthright, he reasoned, then they did not possess the much remarked "*mácula*," the stain of bastard birth attributed to them in popular speech, one that positive law formerly ascribed to them. Mello Freire therefore concluded that, at least among commoners, bastards differed little from legitimate children.[59] He deserves major credit for asserting this revision, one that Borges Carneiro popularized in the liberal decade of the 1820s for a readership that inscribed Brazilian legislators.

The late colonial legal exegesis of "bastardy" consistently implied a restrictive application, including how "breaking bastardy" applied only to spurious offspring. Ambiguously, "bastardy" would continue to apply to the natural offspring of a noble parent in imperial Brazil, but simple recognition by the parent removed the "stain." Gouvêa Pinto, following Mello Freire's lead, relied on natural law for circumventing the logical correspondence of illicit birth to illegitimacy—and therefore to bastardy—in order to arrive at a similar conclusion. Starting with the observation that illegitimate offspring were "those who are merely offspring as a result of nature," in contrast to legitimate children, who were the result of legal marriage, he noted there were four kinds of illegitimate children. However, that he declined outright to include natural offspring in his list proved significant. Instead, he enumerated *espúrios*—"known colloquially as *quaesitos*"—adding as well *adulterinos*, *incestuosos*, and *sacrílegos*. Elsewhere in his treatise, he paid separate attention to natural offspring, avoiding any imputation they were illegitimate, by simply noting they were "begotten by persons without impediment to marry."[60]

Borges Carneiro followed suit, concluding that natural offspring were not bastards. Eventually, the logic of Roman law obliged him to concede they were illegitimate, but the firm line he drew between natural offspring and "bastards" stuck for the rest of the nineteenth century. Thus Borges Carneiro noted first that "offspring born outside marriage are called '*illegitimos*,' '*naturaes*,' '*bastardos*.'" Then he discreetly separated natural offspring from bastards, implying they were distinct from other forms of illegitimacy. He con-

cluded that natural offspring were "*ilegitimos simpliciter*"—merely illegitimate in the elementary sense.[61] At the end of the nineteenth century, Clovis
Bevilaqua's legal textbook still endorsed Borges Carneiro's phraseology, in
tersely defining those born of illicit unions: "Those whose procreators enjoyed a situation [potentially] to marry legally at the time of their conception
or birth . . . take the name of simply natural, or *naturais em especie*."[62]

That the *quaesito* represented a matrilineal variation on being natural deserves similar emphasis as a corollary for how bastardy was reworked by jurists in the Pombaline era. Legal commentators pointed to the ambiguous
identity of individuals of unknown father, stressing that the mother's recognition made them matrilineally natural offspring. The *quaesito* posed a
problematic issue in succession law for jurists because, although convention-
ally presumed an *espúrio*, the "punishment" attached to damnable birth in
the *quaesito*'s case derived from a bastardy that was merely putative. Paternal
recognition might yet render such bastardy *ersatz*. Just as his matrilineal persona was "*filho natural*," the *quaesito* could be called to patrilineal succession
whenever the father bestowed a patrilineal persona by recognizing him as a
natural offspring. The law did not deprive him or her of paternal succession
rights; the father did—by withholding legal recognition. This assumption,
that the father, not the law, rendered a natural offspring a *quaesito*, had
prompted Mello Freire in the early 1790s to insist that the *quaesito*, *qua
espúrio*, did not deserve to be labeled a bastard:

The name "bastard," which comes from the Greek "*bassára*," [or] *meretriz* [prosti-
tute], and additionally is used a great deal among us for indicating in general an illegitimate offspring, does not possess the characteristics of an "*espúrio*" [*quaesito*], i.e.,
the offspring who does not have a certain or a confessable father."[63]

Therefore, from the late eighteenth century onward, Portuguese jurists,
like their Spanish counterparts, were increasingly disposed to consider illegitimacy in unilineal terms, vis-à-vis one parent.[64] Again, the reason was the
propensity of fathers to conceal paternity, leading jurists to conclude that the
child's *qualidade* deserved definition through the mother—as a natural offspring. Although the father was left as the anonymous transgressor of canonical prohibition, what deserves emphasis for changing social behavior is
that a unilineal rule worked to repair the honor of both the unwed mother
and her child. Jurists began to argue the label "*quaesito*" projected "uncertainty" over the father's identity, rather than "unknowability." The new
accent, that the father was not "unknown," but "uncertain," captured the
enigma in individual identity, throwing into question whether the child
really was spurious. It raised doubt, suggesting he or she instead might be

paternally natural. The very term "*quaesito*" similarly dissipated earlier juridical certainty that a "crime" explained the individual's birth, a conclusion, on the other hand, that "*espúrio*" roundly confirmed.

Such esoteric juridical logic mattered a great deal after 1800, because it restricted bastardy's reach in social terms. Growing linguistic reliance on "*quaesito*," for instance, responded to the rise in baptisms that priests registered "of unknown father." The label "*quaesito*" logically tended to confine people who were knowably spurious, those who were canonically incestuous, sacrilegious, or adulterine, and deemed "the fruit of a crime" to a residual population that was indeed minuscule. Hence the juridical presumption of generosity for the vast number who remained paternally "uncertain"—in fact, "unconfessable." Moreover, the mothers of children who were baptized "of unknown father" invariably were considered to have borne a natural offspring. Eighty years after Mello Freire asserted that a *quaesito* deserved evaluation as a maternally natural offspring, not a bastard, Candido Mendes de Almeida quoted him to good effect. In citing verbatim the Portuguese jurist's analysis of the *quaesito*, Candido Mendes' exegesis perpetuated Mello Freire's restricted meaning of "bastard" in an 1870s context.[65]

The *quaesito*'s potential status as a natural offspring implied yet another outcome, hinting at a fundamental difference between Anglo-American and Luso-Brazilian law. His or her parents might subsequently marry, conferring belated legitimization, even years after the *quaesito*'s birth, and on behalf of entire sibling sets. In England, Clovis Bevilaqua correctly pointed out, legitimization by subsequent marriage "had failed to succeed." Indeed, Blackstone boasted of the superiority of English law over both Roman civil and canon law on precisely this point, reiterating the "indispensable condition" that in English legal tradition a legitimate child "shall be born after lawful wedlock." Granting that "our law, though not so strict as to require that the child be begotten [in lawful wedlock]," Blackstone opposed legitimization by subsequent marriage on the ground that it was "a great discouragement to the matrimonial state." English legal tradition encouraged couples to make "early reparation of the offense" of begetting a child prior to marriage, Blackstone explained, by marrying a few months after conception. He triumphantly noted, consequently, that under English law, legitimization by subsequent marriage "could only happen once." Otherwise, were it to be delayed, or applied to more than one child, it would lead to uncertainty of paternity and "opened the door to fraud."[66]

Bevilaqua pointed to the Statute of Merton as the triumphant assertion of unchanging English law on this cardinal point: Bastard birth was immutable in English law. Yet, "in spite of the adverse influence of English law," he discovered that in seven states of the United States, legitimization by subsequent marriage was legal by the 1890s. Alternatively, legislatures sometimes conferred it paternally. Moreover, where matrilineal succession mattered in North America, he noted, "the laws are very liberal regarding bastards," Bevilaqua observed. However, in Portugal and Brazil, juridical reliance on subsequent marriage for legitimization surpassed any comparison with the United States. The following and concluding chapter explores late eighteenth-century arguments crafted principally by Mello Freire that asserted even adulterine and incestuous offspring could acquire legitimization by subsequent marriage. They inspired Brazil's first generation of imperial legislators to introduce radical proposals for legal change.[67]

The fluidity inherent in Luso-Brazilian rules of heirship closely mirrored social realities embedded in Iberian life over centuries. Jurists were logically obliged to assert, given Roman law, that "all who were not legitimate were illegitimate." Yet the fact of long entrenched social practices—"our customs," diverging from the logical purity of Roman law—explained why those jurists preferred to focus on the legal chasm separating natural offspring from spurious offspring in terms of succession rights. They emphasized how law "broke" bastardy for spurious offspring as much as they underscored that natural offspring enjoyed *ab intestato* succession rights. When Trigo de Loureiro became the first Brazilian jurist to publish a legal commentary on Mello Freire, in 1851, he synthesized what was a uniquely Iberian gloss on illegitimacy. He did so emphasizing its salient characteristic: reversibility. In parsing Mello Freire, the Portuguese *émigré* who was a professor at the Olinda Law Faculty spoke directly to the social attitudes he had encountered since arriving in Brazil, around 1820:

Once recognized by their fathers, by means of a public affidavit or a will, legitimized by a [solemn] legitimization certificate, or simply declared by a judge to be the [natural] offspring of a certain father, the bastard offspring of the highest Brazilian citizens do not differ from those who are legitimate or legitimized by means of subsequent marriage in what pertains to gentle birth, to child support . . .[68]

The last three chapters have examined four special features of what was a Luso-Brazilian inheritance system. Together, they permit sophisticated interpretation of what were also important key facets of Brazilian family patterns during the early decades of independence: 1) the *ab intestato* succession rights enjoyed by recognized natural offspring; 2) the legitimization of natural offspring by virtue of their parents' subsequent marriage; 3) the special provisions, via crown legitimization, for equipping all spurious offspring and the natural offspring of a noble parent as heirs in succession; or otherwise, the advantage of simple legitimization for reversing a "defect" of birth; and 4) the conditional matrilineal succession rights enjoyed by the *quaesito*, dependent on the absence of legitimate or natural offspring. Each of these features, by virtue of the generosity of rights in heirship they implied, suggested a reason why imperial Brazil would continue to demonstrate a low rate of marriage throughout the nineteenth century. In other words, marriage would prove to be marginal in many important family arrangements because couples took into account special provisions of the inheritance system. Wide flexibility in the rules of heirship implied perhaps not a "vicious" circle, but one that was exceptionally accommodating. Even those with substantial property might find it unnecessary to marry. Indeed, in a restricted number of situations, postponing or declining marriage altogether could represent a deliberate strategy of heirship advantageous to non-legitimate children.

After independence, Brazilian legislators would take into account the flexibility that rules of heirship demonstrated in their legal tradition. They would approach them from the evolutionary context expounded by late eighteenth-century Portuguese jurists, while attempting to introduce new political values consonant with their own century. Basically, however, an eighteenth-century Luso-Brazilian legal tradition disposed imperial legislators to view bastardy as mutable. Legitimacy, on the other hand, accommodated several variants of legitimization, and mattered largely for practical arrangements pertaining to property. By the 1820s, radical legal doctrines traceable to Mello Freire abounded on the subject of illegitimate birth. Accustomed to a multiplicity of family patterns formed outside legitimate marriage, the liberal legislators who dismantled Portugal's colonial state consciously followed in the footsteps of Pombaline reformers. They looked to an eighteenth-century legal tradition that markedly diverged, on the one hand, from the *Ordenações Filipinas* and Roman law, or, on the other hand, from canon law. Instead, that tradition posited a legal nationalism accommodating the absolutist state and juridically validated the greater emphasis accorded to "our customs." The eighteenth-century jurists who reformulated the legal underpinnings of the Portuguese state paid special emphasis to refashioning private law, by revising or refining the rules of devolving devolution, including dowry and entail. Therefore, Brazilian liberals, when they proclaimed themselves reformers of inheritance law and advocated rights for non-legitimate individuals, appealed to a legal tradition that enjoyed political legitimacy long before the Lisbon court embarked for Rio de Janeiro. Above all, they evoked the iconoclastic heritage of Mello Freire dos Reys.

CHAPTER 5

The Pombaline Tradition

Legal Nationalism

————•◆•————

From the above-noted superstitious generality of the said laws called *Imperial*, it is customary to extract other rules in order to interpret my laws. . . . It is understood that these *National Laws* should be restricted when they are contrary to Roman law . . . . I order otherwise.

Henceforth the assumptions of the tribunals and ministers will not mention knowledge of sin, but of crimes . . .

The Law of Right Reason, Aug. 18, 1769[1]

Throughout the first four decades following Brazilian independence, legislators referred matter-of-factly to law in force as *"direito pátrio"*—national law. They did so not to point to laws adopted after Portuguese rule ended in 1822, but to invoke a legal tradition inherited from eighteenth-century Portugal. When, for example, they attempted to abolish entail, beginning in the late 1820s, legislators resorted to *direito pátrio* as juridical authority for arguments that were pro and con. The appeal of national law was "bipartisan," for the so-called "royalists" who opposed the liberals nonetheless endorsed legal nationalism. Parliamentary debate implied the term connoted a received legal tradition formerly synonymous with Bragança absolutism, one whose cornerstone resided in the 1769 "Law of Right Reason." By severely circumscribing both Roman and canon law as authoritative subsidiary sources for positive national law, that famous statute had proclaimed the preeminence of national law made by the Portuguese crown.

In repudiating entail, for instance, Brazil's liberal legislators drew on *direito pátrio* to assert that a Luso-Brazilian system of intestate succession imposed a "natural equality" of rights among the necessary or forced heirs, citing as their evidence the 1754 law on which their system of *ab intestato* succession had been redefined. "The law of the *morgado*," objected the marquis of Caravellas, "should be abolished for being in contradiction to the General Law." The statute he cited was the Law of August 3, 1770, whose preamble roundly condemned secular entail—the *morgado*—for being opposed to natural law—that is, what the political lexicon construed as "the General Law."[2] The conservative defenders of entail, on the other hand, similarly appealed to national law as part of a consensus they shared with their opponents. The *morgado* did not contravene precepts enshrined in *direito pátrio*, objected the viscount of Cayru, for the Law of August 3 nevertheless sanctioned the entailment of family patrimony as a privilege tied to the founder's minimally noble rank.[3] He, like his liberal opponent Caravellas, incontestably accepted as the common plane for debate a body of positive law stretching back seventy-five years, initiated in the early administration of Portugal's first minister, the count of Oeiras (Sebastião José de Carvalho e Mello), better known subsequently as the marquis of Pombal.[4] Since the 1770s, *direito pátrio* had stood for legal nationalism, due to how it was officially diffused not only in statutes by the Law of Right Reason but also as the official ethos of the crown's 1772 legal reform of Coimbra University.

Both Caravellas and Cayru were graduates of Coimbra University's faculty of civil law, as were many of their colleagues in both chambers of the legislature. Caravellas, who enrolled around 1790, a good decade after Cayru, became celebrated as an enthusiastic convert to legal nationalism. He abandoned a career in the church after taking his degree in theology at Coimbra, precisely in order to take a second degree in what one hagiographer styled "*direito civil pátrio*."[5] The polemicizing dictionarist may be excused for distorting the special value Brazilian liberals derived from invoking *direito pátrio*, exclusive from any reference to "civil" law. Coimbra law degrees continued to be awarded in either canon or civil law, but never in "national civil law." Cayru, a diehard defender of entail, was an economic liberal and popularizer of Adam Smith who greatly admired Edmund Burke, while Caravellas stood as his generation's most vocal, senior opponent of the "distinctions" inherent in a society of estates. Legislators, whether "royalist" or liberal in the 1820s, willingly associated themselves with a Pombaline agenda of reform they recognized as legal nationalism, meaning that they viewed the broad utility of Roman civil law during most of the eighteenth century as passé. They were equally adamant that canon law should occupy a much smaller space in national juridical norms. Rhetorically, in other words, their fervent endorsement of *direito pátrio* proclaimed a greatly diminished reliance on the *Corpus Juris Civilis*, not to mention the *Corpus Juris Canonici*, as subsidiary sources of law in a liberal era where "the Legislator" was now the Parliament.

DIREITO PÁTRIO: A POMBALINE
LEGAL TRADITION

After 1750, the Portuguese absolutist state relied fundamentally on national law, law made by the crown, and a reformulation of legal culture, via university reform, as the dual means for ensuring that neither Roman civil law nor canon law would be applied in royal courts, except in two situations: where already directly incorporated in statutory law in force, such as in the *Ordenações*, or when consulted as a subsidiary source in what would now be severely restricted contexts. By the early nineteenth century, Portugal's legal culture had been impressively recast and, more important, it had gained an institutional acceptance that firmly anchored it in the minds of Brazil's earliest cohort of imperial legislators. Those lawmakers usually declined to speak of "civil law," preferring instead the watchword of eighteenth-century juridical culture many had imbibed at Coimbra University: "national law"— *direito pátrio*. The accent was far from rhetorical, however. In the area of private law, which subsumed both the family and the inheritance system, juridical interpretation in the second half of the eighteenth century successfully challenged prevailing legal norms derived from the *jus commune*. Thus crown statutes or judicial-administrative rulings supplanted Roman and canon law principles and rules. Although reformulation of positive law and juridical culture enunciated in the name of national law coincided with the reign of D. José I (1750–1777), the shift toward greater reliance on national law embodied the policies of his first minister, the marquis of Pombal. It signified the preeminence of the *Ordenações Filipinas* and complementary statutory law made by the Portuguese crown, above all, consistent application of the latter in the royal law courts. "National law" thus implied that royal law, especially new legislation, would render obsolete a historical reliance on both Roman civil law and canon law where the gaps in national law needed "filling in." Therefore, legal nationalism also captured how many sections of the *Ordenações Filipinas* were modified or discarded during the era of Pombal, in favor of new statutes that drew authoritatively on sources independent of either Roman or canon law. This circumstance accounted for a good deal of the zeal with which liberal reformers in Brazil later approached the same task after 1822.

Political discourse in early imperial Brazil implicitly took into account the fact of *direito pátrio* in parliamentary debates. The new juridical emphasis aptly translated as "legal nationalism," because, earlier, it had amounted to a fundamentally political doctrine within Portugal's eighteenth-century juridical evolution. Curiously, however, political historians of imperial Brazil have not paid specific attention to the centrality of a Pombaline legal tradition, despite the loud resonance it registered in official discourse, for explicit reference was made to "*direito pátrio*" in the speeches and debates of imperial legislators. Nor have historians of Brazil connected the much remarked regalism that shaped issues of national politics from the 1820s to the 1850s to the Portuguese legal nationalism inherited as a late colonial legacy. Sometimes historians have so misunderstood the origin of *direito pátrio* that they have assumed it was a product of the independence era; they have construed the term as embodying anti-Portuguese reaction. Far from being a notion that emerged in the crucible of Brazil's independence, *direito pátrio*, like the much more recent liberal constitutionalism that accompanied the break with Portugal, emanated directly from Brazil's colonial past. Beginning in the late 1850s, however, Brazilian legal culture ceased to uphold "national law" exclusively, for a reliance on Roman law began to reemerge. In addition, positivism, as well as German legal science, severely tempered the rhetorical endorsement of "*direito pátrio*," causing the accent on "national law" to fade. With the arrival of the First Republic (1889–1930), and the renewed reliance on Roman law, eighteenth-century legal nationalism came to be regarded as a century of deviation from what otherwise had been an overarching civil law tradition.

Historiographic neglect, reinforced by the Brazilian legislature's failure to adopt a civil code throughout the Empire, has meant that the legal culture inherent in early liberalism has been ignored in the scholarly literature. Yet legal nationalism defined a fundamental feature of parliamentary discourse in the first four decades of Brazil's independence, while its other face, regalism, testified to the endurance of a Pombaline political tradition. From the beginning, the roots of *direito pátrio* had been planted in private law. As we have seen, one of the earliest applications of legal nationalism had been the adoption in 1754 of a new law of *ab intestato* succession. The transmission of property, according to arrangements of diverging devolution that depended on marriage, birth, and death, accounted for why the roots of legal nationalism ran deep. "National law" was applied to the rules of heirship in order to supplant Roman law rules, but also to promote a state policy encouraging the greater circulation of property and wealth, at the expense of the institutional church and the higher nobility. Political motives therefore explained why the Pombaline state would restrict juridical reliance on the *jus commune* and impose new statutes to supplant juridical precepts or determinations derived from Roman and canon law.

Brazilian legislators subscribed *en masse* to *direito pátrio*, thanks to the legitimacy it received from the 1769 Law of Right Reason. As the cornerstone of *direito pátrio*, the Law of Right Reason provided an overarching juridical rationale, as well as detailed rules for recasting positive law and legal culture. This law would continue to be invoked even after the movement of legal nationalism ebbed and the Brazilian Empire had been replaced by a republic at the end of the nineteenth century. Fundamentally, the Law of August 18, 1769, targeted the utility of canon law as much as Roman law, a circumstance that wedded legal nationalism to the older regalism that the Portuguese crown had cultivated for centuries. These twin corollaries of Bragança absolutism, moreover, were conducive to the reception of liberal ideology in early independence Brazil: the nationalization of law, meaning the preeminence of positive law made by the crown and applied in the royal courts, and regalism, meaning the national monarchy's prerogatives vis-à-vis the church. The latter, exalted as the *"regalias"* of the crown, pertained to prerogatives enjoyed by the monarchical state vis-à-vis the papacy. Among them, the power to nominate bishops and other prelates for papal confirmation, as well as to authorize promulgation of papal bulls and decretals, were uppermost.[6]

The nationalization of law, in tandem with regalism, offered the official ideology for absolutism in Portugal during Pombal's long ministry (1750–1777) and afterward. The preeminence of positive law, written and imposed by the monarch through intermediaries who were his ministers, jurists, and magistrates, extolled the monarch's identity as the Legislator for the nation. Brazil's early legislators, who saw themselves as heir to that tradition, saw no conflict between that absolutist legal heritage and the liberal constitutionalism they embraced. Their gaze, consequently, looked backward, beyond the post–French revolutionary context of European liberalism, to fasten on the key tenets in an Iberian absolutism that predated 1789, when the Braganças had strengthened Portugal's national monarchy at the expense of the society of estates.

Direito pátrio especially appealed to Brazil's self-styled liberal reformers during the First Empire (1822–1831) and Regency (1831–1840), because they couched their political arguments close to home, declining to make common cause with most of the ideals of either the American or French Revolution. Instead, they appealed to a narrower, Iberian politico-legal heritage. The vast majority of them were genuinely committed to some form of monarchical government and, once western Europe found itself in the full tide of reaction to French revolutionary thought, very few Brazilian liberals could be described as republicans. Besides, unlike Spanish America, Brazil had remained juridically untouched by the Napoleonic invasion. Removal of the Portuguese monarchy from Lisbon to Rio de Janeiro in 1808 meant, among other things, that the fundamental code of 1603, the *Ordenações Filipinas*, remained insulated from the revolutionary precepts imposed by the French *Code civil* that after 1807 reshaped national law both throughout western Europe and Spanish America.

In upholding *direito pátrio*, Brazil's legislators reaffirmed the key principles of a Luso-Brazilian legal culture reaching to Pombal's dramatic reform of Coimbra University's law faculties in 1772. The fact that many of them had taken their law degrees at Coimbra University, where *direito pátrio* gained full curricular integration only after 1805, accounted for much of the continuity in Luso-Brazilian legal culture after independence. Brazil's fledgling law faculties, which graduated their first classes of *bacharéis* only in 1832, continued to inculcate *direito pátrio* through the 1850s. On the other hand, many legislators who had not been privileged to take law degrees in Portugal nonetheless acquired a passionate commitment to the tenets of legal nationalism and regalism, through study in a colonial seminary. Except for the Royal Military Academy at Realengo, seminaries were the only institutions of higher learning in colonial Brazil. As centers of heterodox learning, they attracted men whose career aspirations were not necessarily focused on the cloth.

In the eclectic ambience of the seminary, where no standard curriculum prevailed, students internalized a freewheeling brand of Jansenism that was thoroughly Lusitanian, one, however, that the Roman Curia viewed as "the heresy of Febronianism." The Vatican's condemnation followed from the perpetuation, in both Portugal and Brazil, of a pedagogical reliance on the Montpellier Catechism, a text officially condemned by the Roman Catholic Church.[7] This catechism was sanctioned by both Pombaline and Joanine monarchies in what amounted to a regalist assertion of authority that also enjoyed the support of Portugal's ecclesiastical hierarchy.[8] The Brazilian seminaries touted in the early nineteenth century as "hotbeds" of French revolutionary ideas—or crucibles of "Spanish liberalism"—had previously inculcated a Pombaline politico-legal culture supportive of the *regalias* of the Bragança monarchy and "Febronian error." Their curricula explained why papal authority was widely questioned by Brazilian legislators in a number of post-independence contexts.[9] Given the heterodox learning disseminated by the seminaries implanted on Brazilian soil, *direito pátrio* seeped into student consciousness, even when its finer points lay beyond the grasp of seminarians lacking the intellectual polish of Coimbra law graduates.

In suggesting that Pombaline legal culture deserves reinsertion within the political history of Brazil's first four decades of independence, these preliminary remarks imply a final point of historiographic omission. The meaning and significance of Luso-Brazilian legal nationalism cannot be grasped without reference to the singular and largely forgotten figure of its principal architect. The name of the jurist whose writings converted legal nationalism into a politically articulated doctrine and a venerated legal textbook was universally familiar to Brazilian legislators by the independence decade: Paschoal José de Mello Freire dos Reys (1738–1798). An elusive figure, Mello Freire today is all but unknown. As a Coimbra professor of comparative and civil law, a specialist in the *Corpus Juris Civilis*, his scholarly expertise and political skills, as much as his ideological commitment to regalism, recommended him to Portugal's first minister. As one of a number of jurists Pombal recruited to his inner circle of national policy makers, Mello Freire made most of his contributions behind closed doors. Furthermore, he survived not only Pombal's political ruin but also his era, gaining greater public recognition of his services to the Bragança state during the reign of Maria I and, after 1791, her unofficial regent and Brazil's future king, D. João VI.

RIGHT REASON AND PORTUGUESE
LEGAL NATIONALISM

An Entrenched Tradition: The Revival of Roman Law

When Candido Mendes regarded the contributions of Mello Freire from the vantage point of nearly a century, he praised him both as a teacher and the intellectual architect of Portugal's legal nationalism. On the one hand, he recalled, Mello Freire had pedagogically revealed the substance of national law "through a synthetic method in the form of a compendium," referring to the adoption of his enduring Institutes of Portuguese national law as the official textbook for Coimbra University's faculty of civil law. The synthetic method that Mello Freire advocated in the 1770s for a reformed legal curriculum at Coimbra relied fundamentally on the study of Portugal's legal history for an understanding of the diversity of sources on which national law drew. On the other hand, Candido Mendes emphasized, Mello Freire had "reduced the chaos of national legislation to a regular plane and easy comprehension." It was he who reordered national positive law, by privileging the preeminence of the *Ordenações Filipinas* and statutory law, regrounding them nevertheless in Portugal's national history and local custom. Stated differently, Mello Freire applied the 1769 Law of Right Reason as the tool for reformulating national law, denying to both Roman civil law and canon law the excessive influence they enjoyed in juridical determinations rendered in the royal courts. In Candido Mendes' estimation, Mello Freire

deserved special recognition for revising the foundation of Portuguese jurisprudence, because, through careful historical research and comparative
analysis, he reformulated national law as "a complete system."[10] That is, he
made national positive law logically reflect the preeminence of the *Ordenações* and crown law at the expense of subsidiary reliance on the sources of
Roman civil law or canon law.

The interpretive task that Mello Freire confronted was far from clear-cut.
As we have seen, Roman law was embedded, in one form or another,
throughout Portugal's multiple strands of law: in Germanic law, as the so-
called "Barbarian legislation," most recognizable in the Visigothic Code; in
diverse customary principles, where rules were often Germano-Roman; in
the local *forais* derived from municipal charters; or even in certain feudal
privileges tied to the first two estates, known as the *foros*; in canon law inscribed within the *jus comune*; and, finally, in received Roman civil law that
since the fifteenth century derived from the *Ordenações do Reino*.[11] Mello
Freire's reformulation fundamentally reimposed the *Ordenações Filipinas* as
paramount, vis-à-vis Roman and canon law, privileging how the former drew
on Portuguese custom and notwithstanding that the Code of 1603 contained
a great deal of Roman and canon law. He did so in the name of precepts
sanctioned by the 1769 Law of Right Reason.

Portuguese legal nationalism crystallized in the second half of the eighteenth century, when the new law of 1769 resolved juridical controversy by
answering one question: What was to be done in rendering judicial determinations when the *Ordenações* were silent on a point of law needed to decide a
case? Before 1769, the answer had been to turn to Roman law as the prescribed subsidiary, or secondary, source for addressing lacunae in the *Ordenações*. Moreover, the lacunae were substantial, given the absence of new
codification. That is, positive law continued to depend on Roman law rules,
due to the practice of using the latter for "filling in the gaps." As we have
seen from the introductory discussion of Portugal's civil law tradition, the
Ordenações Afonsinas had originally provided that "cases not controlled by
the laws of the realm, by the rules of the court [*estilos*], or by custom would
be governed by Roman law." This prescription implied that "the courts were
to follow the glosses of Accursius" or "the opinions of Bartolus," pertaining
to the *Corpus Juris Civilis*.[12]

The *Ordenações Manuelinas* (1521), however, restricted dependence on
Roman law as a subsidiary source of Portugal's national positive law. As we
have also seen, the Manueline Code modified the solution for the problem of
"gaps" in positive law, by articulating for the first time a rule of "right reason" (*boa razão*). It was to serve as a guide for making determinations on

points of law where the *Ordenações* and other positive laws did not apply. In this respect, it is worth underscoring that the notion, or principle, of "right reason" predated Pombal's law of the same name by several centuries. Roman law rules, according to the *Ordenações Manuelinas*, were still indicated as a subsidiary source for national law, but they were to be consulted in a more restricted sense. Only when they could be found to be based on "good" or "right" reason, meaning natural reason, were they to be employed. This meant that the glosses of Accursius and the opinions of Bartolus, which had accompanied the medieval reception of Roman law in Portugal, should have become marginal and ceased to be dogmatically applied. The problem remained, however, that neither the national legal code of D. Manuel nor the one promulgated under Philip III defined "right reason." Nor did they spell out criteria for applying the latter.[13] The total absence of such criteria suggested why, during the 1760s, Pombal found it legitimate, and politically expediential, to enshrine right reason within the "showcase" Law of August 18, 1769.

The *Ordenações Filipinas* changed nothing with respect to how the preceding Manueline code had privileged "right reason." However, the position of Roman law vis-à-vis national positive law began to change in the seventeenth century. By the first half of the eighteenth century, Roman law enjoyed its greatest influence in Portugal, for being venerated as *"ratio scripta"*—written reason. Thus it acquired authority vis-à-vis many unwritten customary practices formerly taken to be valid positive law. When Lafayette Rodrigues Pereira summed up the impact Roman law exerted between 1600 and 1769, he concluded it had been "fatal" for Portugal's legal literature, making "the ruin of juridical studies nearly complete." He had in mind advances in legal theory and juridical scholarship in France and the Low Countries, spanning the late sixteenth through the eighteenth centuries, that Portuguese jurists might have utilized in their legal interpretations. Instead, the medieval Glossators enjoyed renewed authority, and humanistic legal studies were largely lost to Portugal's juridical evolution. "The study of sources [for law] was abandoned and a sterile game devoted to the subtleties of glossing replaced the philosophical and historical meaning of texts," Lafayette lamented. The "Romanists," he charged, became "preoccupied with the majesty of imperial laws"—with Justinian's legacy. Their admiration for written reason caused "local statutes to lose their special characteristics" and be taken as "simple restrictions to the Roman text." The upshot was that in national positive law "local statutes," came to occupy a secondary plane.[14]

Although Lafayette's pronouncement was tinged with polemic, in fact, Roman law began to be employed very aggressively after 1700, in contravention of the express instruction of the *Ordenações Filipinas*. A shift also took place in how right reason was applied during the reign of D. João V (1706–1750), accounting for why the text of the 1769 Law of Right Reason explicitly objected to how "*boa razão*" had been applied. Section 10 complained that where the laws of the *Ordenações Filipinas* ran contrary to Roman law, they were being strictly construed—thus restricting their application as positive national law. But where an *ordenação* conformed with Roman law, then it was likely to be broadly construed—thereby enlarging the influence of Roman law.[15]

The progressive exaggeration of Roman law's utility for national positive law therefore explained Pombal's determination to promulgate a reinterpretation of the principle of "right reason." The jurists and judges who interpreted positive law in Portugal's royal courts had been prime movers in the new reliance placed on the *Corpus Juris Civilis*, Justinian's "imperial" legacy. Their authority found indispensable reinforcement in Coimbra University's classrooms, such that by 1750 the law professoriate stood as the principal disseminators of the revived reliance on Roman civil law. The Law of Right Reason directly alluded to the role, when it noted "there having taken place in the practice of judges and lawyers great perplexity and confusion . . . ."[16] The university was not only the repository of the civil law tradition but also of the canon law tradition similarly incorporated within the *Corpus Juris*. It is in this context of an entrenched academic tradition that Pombal's 1772 university reform must be placed. The "analytic" method of teaching, mercilessly pilloried by Portuguese expatriate Luis Antonio Verney in the 1740s, determined Pombal's direct intervention in the curriculum of Coimbra's faculties of civil and canon law. Verney had derided Roman law—the *Corpus Juris Civilis*—as irrelevantly abstruse and mocked Coimbra graduates as "the men [who] leave the universities speaking much about the laws of Justinian, which apply only in the absence of municipal law, and yet know nothing of that law that is supposed to be the applicable law."[17] His pedagogical primer, *Verdadeiro Método de Estudar*, first published in 1746, exposed how Portuguese jurists had reduced the *Corpus Juris Civilis* to a dry, rote text, rather than appreciating it as the embodiment of "living law."

In addition to the new authority that Roman law enjoyed among Portugal's jurists and law professors, canon law and the ecclesiastical courts posed a formidable parallel challenge to the preeminence of national positive law in Portugal. Today, legal histories usually fail to discuss the twin targets of "right reason," ignoring canon law altogether. The historical focus of legal textbooks tends to be narrow, on the civil law roots of contemporary jurisprudence. Yet the Portuguese crown was no less zealous in stripping canon law of its former role vis-à-vis national positive law than in rendering Roman civil law marginal. By the same token, the 1769 law sought to curtail the pedagogical influence of the canonists who dominated Coimbra University, for the faculty was composed entirely of clerics. Not until the 1730s could students routinely elect to pursue a separate degree in civil law. Previously, they were obliged to take a degree in canon law in order to study civil law. By 1724, fewer than thirty degrees had been awarded in civil law, while 1200 had been granted in canon law. More to the point, until the 1770s, a degree in canon law defined the basic credential for a career in the higher civil service and judiciary.[18]

Until Pombal imposed reform of the legal Coimbra's curriculum, in 1772, canon law predominated as a field of study, notwithstanding the rising importance of Roman civil law—what legal nationalism dismissed as "imperial law"—for interpreting national positive law. The senior echelon of Brazil's first generation of national legislators benefited from curricular reform, for, between 1776 and 1785, 115 Brazilians took their diplomas in either canon or civil law, of a total of 151 Brazilian graduates. By 1805, a total of 367 Brazilians had obtained Coimbra degrees in either law, medicine, philosophy, or mathematics.[19] In the 1770s, Antônio Nunes Ribeiro Sanches (1699–1783), one of Pombal's designated reformers of Coimbra University, proposed the radical innovation of placing the directorship of the civil law faculty under a layman, given that civil law belonged to the temporal power—to the monarch.[20] Yet the faculties did not become truly distinct until Portuguese liberals imposed another university reform in the late 1830s.

By Pombal's era, especially in the area of private law, both strands of the *jus comune*—civil and canon law—converged to limit the application of national positive law in Portugal's courts. Moreover, the third strand of the *jus comune*, the law merchant, became crucial to Pombal's reorganization of the Portuguese polity, offering further reason for him to restrict the application of Roman and canon law. After 1750, the gaps in private law demanded greater "filling in," for social change and economic differentiation enhanced the complexity of how law was to be applied. It was Book 4 of the *Ordenações Filipinas*, consequently, that most often raised conflicts between the juridical goals of the Pombaline state and the application of either Roman or canon law.[21] Book 4 treated the devolution of private property, via legal arrangements defined by entail, marriage, and either *ab intestato* or testamentary succession. It therefore raised areas of private law that were central to the policies of the Portuguese crown, above all, encouragement of the circulation of wealth or real property, increasing tax revenues, and promoting investment and entrepreneurship at the expense of the legal privileges conceded to the first and second estates.[22]

The Law of Right Reason

The Law of August 18, 1769, immortalized as the Law of Right Reason, stood as the hallmark of the legal "revolution" imposed by Pombal. Yet it did not innovate as much as it reasserted the rule of reason already embedded in the *Ordenações Filipinas*. Narrowly, the Law of Right Reason could be said to have innovated, where it spelled out discrete "rules," that is, by listing the fundamental sources for national positive law and the subsidiary sources that could be used when the latter was silent. Above all, the 1769 law qualified how right reason would be applied. Although most of the fundamental sources the law endorsed were synonymous with what the *Ordenações Filipinas* prescribed, practically speaking, the Law of Right Reason signaled a return to the primary application of national positive law in the royal courts. It set aside, in other words, the abstruse formulations of judges and jurists inclined to rely excessively on the subsidiary sources of civil or canon law. It was this utilitarian accent, implying a swing of the pendulum away from the theoretical formulations that had "confounded and diluted the cardinal ideas of [Portugal's] legislative monuments [the *Ordenações*]," that captured the essence of the Law of Right Reason.[23]

The Law of Right Reason ended once and for all the independent authority of the Glossators and the Commentators who had been so influential in the early reception of Roman law in Portugal. Section 10 of the law alluded directly to an obsessive reliance on their texts, when it condemned as "superstitious" the widespread influence of "laws called *Imperial*." The preeminence of the *Ordenações Filipinas* as the font of national law was upheld by specifically forbidding the interpretive use of learned texts and authorities whenever the same precepts already existed in the Philippine Code. Thus Roman law, at least the late "imperial" law of Justinian's *Corpus Juris Civilis*, could not be used indiscriminately as a bridge for expanding further those precepts already alien to the *Ordenações Filipinas*. Equally important, the Law of Right Reason enlarged national law by restipulating that uncodified statutory laws, called the *leis extravagantes*, as well as ministerial and judicial determinations, together with Portuguese "customs," would enjoy coequal significance with the Philippine Code as national positive law. All would henceforth supersede sources and interpretations based on Roman law.

The emphasis on the primacy of existing positive law, whether already codified, simply statutory, or implicit in judicial determinations embedded in the *estilos*, together with the explicit inclusion of customary law, restricted the application of Roman civil and canon law in Portugal as never before. In the law's oft-quoted Section 12, the king's "tribunals and judges in temporal matters" would "in their jurisdiction only follow the national and subsidiary laws, praiseworthy customs and legitimately established *estilos*." The "*Estilos da Côrte*," specifically addressed in Section 14 of the law, amounted to the cumulative determinations of the Casa da Suplicação, Portugal's high crown court of appeal. The Casa also issued *assentos*, or clarifications, designed to articulate the meaning of a given law, that carried the full force of law. Moreover, they would continue to do so throughout Brazil's imperial period, along with the *assentos* of the Desembargo do Paço.[24] The Law of August 18, 1769, placed as uppermost the application of positive law in the royal courts, implying that a routine, practical application in the courtroom was to take priority over the theoretical formulations of jurists and law professors.

Finally, the "form that is understood within this law" for applying right reason took the latter to be a residual source for positive law. Right reason would still be applicable, but only when judges and jurists exhausted the sources for national law mentioned above. In such instances, Section 10 determined that the Roman law of the Philippine Code would also have to conform to right reason—to natural reason—as well as "to fit within the spirit of the dispositions" of national positive law. This qualification anticipated the large quantity of statutory legislation that would be adopted during the reign of D. José I. In other words, existing gaps in national law, it was presumed, would now be "filled in" with new, statutory laws that conformed to natural reason. Furthermore, the latter would take precedence over specific *ordenações* derived from Roman law, suggesting that, at least on a piecemeal basis, the code of 1603 would be updated. By the same token, the *estilos* and Portuguese customary law would override former Roman law, where the latter was judged to be contrary to natural reason. In fact, Pombal's jurists anticipated a modern civil code would be adopted before the close of the eighteenth century. Although right reason meant natural reason, and therefore was a concept derived from Roman law, judges and jurists were encouraged to render their determinations based on it by first scrutinizing the multiple sources for national law enumerated in the famous law.

Therefore, despite unprecedented restriction, Roman law was far from dismissed in 1769. It was to be subjected to the litmus test of natural reason—the *recta ratio* of natural law doctrine—and only then to be authoritatively applied as a subsidiary source. Roman law also remained relevant where found in embedded in the texts of extant laws, although, as we shall see, legal nationalism meant that jurists could now downplay those texts by asserting that either customary law, or a quasi-fictive "classical" Roman law supposedly contradicted the late Roman law deemed "imperial." Otherwise, Roman law was to be used as *recta ratio* whenever it was unanimously followed by civilized peoples and nations, as, for instance, when it belonged to the *jus gentium*, the rapidly evolving law of European nations.[25] In fact, reliance on the *jus gentium* explained a great deal of the attention that subsequently Pombaline jurists would pay to European comparative law.

Less remarked today, but no less important for either Pombal's radical jurists or their Brazilian liberal heirs, was the progressive secularization of Portugal's positive law mandated by *boa razão* in 1769. The Law of Right Reason stripped canon law of its force in judicial and ministerial decisions, where, routinely, it had formerly been consulted as a subsidiary source for national law. This interpretive emphasis followed from the Jansenist thread in Portuguese regalism. Jansenism in 1760s Portugal implied no theological tenets on personal salvation, but a political position opposed to the emergence of what was regarded as a papal "monarchy." It also projected antipathy toward the Tridentine canons, because they had been used to buttress papal authority. The Jansenist current in Portuguese political thought extolled church councils as the true repositories of ecclesiastical authority and dogma, declining to accept the pope alone as superior authority. Jansenism looked to conciliar law broadly, a circumstance that explained the support or toleration it received from Portugal's ecclesiastical hierarchy. The determinations of the general councils of the church, as well as those adopted by archdiocesan conclaves in Portugal, were endorsed as supreme ecclesiastical authority—and the means for resisting the political advance of pope and Curia.

The key section of the Law of Right Reason drew justification from the "genuine confusion" reigning over how the principle of "right reason" should be applied to canon law. Consequently, the language of Section 12 drew a clear line between "sin" and "crime," emphatically proclaiming that ecclesiastical tribunals and councils were the appropriate venues for judging sinful behavior. As with Roman law, canon law stood as a glaring omission from Section 12's precisely enumerated list of fundamental sources for positive national law. The implication was that the crown justice would not be concerned with matters of sin, leaving responsibility to ecclesiastical tribunals. Hence, "when it is a case of treating what neither the law nor the *estilo* nor the custom of this kingdom prescribes, and it involves a matter of sin, we order that it be judged according to the Sacred Canons." Otherwise, crown courts exercised jurisdiction in criminal matters and might invoke *boa razão*: "When it does not involve sin," judicial determinations pertaining to crime, but lacking appropriate positive law, "should be judged according to Imperial [Roman] Laws" as the appropriate subsidiary source of law.[26]

Section 12 did not stop at addressing canon law as inappropriate for judging crime. It explicitly forbad all crown officials, especially magistrates, from consulting it to render rulings:

I order that henceforth the assumptions of the tribunals and ministers will not mention knowledge of sin, but of crimes . . . that texts in canon law be left aside by ministers, to be observed by the ecclesiastical consistories (according to their rightful and appropriate terms) . . . that my tribunals and secular judges in temporal matters will follow *only national and subsidiary laws, praiseworthy customs, and the legitimately established estilos*, in the form by which I have determined in this law.[27]

The new limitations placed on canon law as a source for positive law, it is important to remember, did not pertain to the Tridentine canons on the sacrament of matrimony. Received as law in Portugal during the 1560s, they did not come under the proscription for "sin" noted above. Instead, marriage constituted a civil contract, one that both church and crown simultaneously concurred originated in natural and divine law. However, the Law of Right Reason did open the possibility that canon law received as positive law might subsequently be modified or abrogated by the sovereign. After all, in a polity where absolutism dictated that the monarch was "the Legislator," the prerogative of changing the law belonged to him or her alone.

Legal Nationalism Enters the Academy

Under Coimbra's New Statutes of August 28, 1772, the principles of the Law of Right Reason were reiterated as integral to a university reform that was preeminently royal. The New Statutes therefore must be interpreted as proceeding directly from the 1769 law. Indeed, they emphatically reiterated the tenets of the Law of Right Reason. Where the latter applied to canon law, the New Statutes declared "the rules and precepts of Natural Reason, deriving from positive law would take precedence over canon and ecclesiastical law, leaving only one law above positive law—divine law." This conclusion was predicated on the fact that Coimbra was a royal university, founded by the monarch and subject to his direction. Coimbra professors were to make their students "see the powerful and undeniable penetration that the rules and precepts of Natural Reason have within the Public Canons of the Church, preceding all Positive Law, without excepting Divine law."[28] This goal, the undermining of canon law's juridical authority, carried important weight in early imperial Brazil, where liberals assumed that "right reason" still demanded fulfillment by further restricting the jurisdiction of ecclesiastical tribunals. Equally important, the Law of Right Reason postulated that natural law would take precedence over positive law. However, it also implied that, where appropriate, positive law would be understood as consistent with natural law.

Coimbra's 1772 New Statutes further applied the Law of Right Reason to legal studies, expanding their scope to embrace law outside Portugal. This novel accent followed from another curricular provision of the New Statutes that distinguished between those "Roman laws accepted in modern usage"— those conforming to right reason—and those that did not. Consequently, Coimbra's law students were encouraged to go abroad for the purpose of studying comparative law that conformed to "modern usage." Clovis Bevilaqua applauded the results a century later, noting that "opening the door to [other] juridical currents" had imparted "an elasticity to national legal institutions" and reinforced procedural innovation in Portugal.[29] Much as Portugal's scholars had journeyed to Paris in the fourteenth century, in order to import Roman law as a counterweight to ecclesiastical law, now the crown encouraged them to go abroad with an eye to the "elasticity" that European local law offered. Comparative legal studies offered an approved means for Portugal's jurists to draw on European juridical sources tailored to legal nationalism. In customary law they would identify the presence of an underlying natural law that nourished a complementary legal innovation. As we have seen in the Introduction, as early as 1754, a new innovative emphasis on comparative law led Portugal to redefine intestate succession and lessen prior dependence on Roman civil law in inheritance law procedures. Such a recasting of juridical precepts borrowed directly from comparative law, to wit, from French jurists who had adopted the medieval notion of *seisen*.

MELLO FREIRE'S LEGAL NATIONALISM

Texts for a New Legal Canon

As a man of the cloth, Mello Freire exemplified the priest who resisted ultramontanism and incipient claims of papal infallibility during Portugal's age of absolutism. His views, however, did not make him unique among the clerics who were counted in Pombal's coterie. Rather, uniqueness followed from his truly formidable juridical erudition. The professorial career he pursued in Coimbra University's Faculty of Civil Law, starting in 1757 at age nineteen, honed his expertise in the *jus commune* and prepared him as a synthesizer who could borrow from legal developments elsewhere in Europe. Prior to appointment as Pombal's choice for the chair of *direito pátrio* established in the civil law faculty by the New Statutes, Mello Freire held teaching chairs in Justinian's Code and Institutes, as well as in logic. Late publication, just as he reached fifty, made manifest his juridically architectonic role on behalf of Portugal's national monarchy. His reputation among future jurists, Brazilians as well as Portuguese, was sealed in the early reign of Maria I (1777–1816). Mello Freire would therefore be appreciated as Portugal's consummate "*estrangeirado*" jurist—one whose "foreignized" learning incorporated intellectual trends in comparative law and history from beyond the Pyrenees.[30]

When Pombal closed Coimbra University for thirty-two days in 1772, in order to implement the New Statutes, Mello Freire already belonged to an inner circle of collaborators charged with effecting university reform.[31] His appointment as deputy extraordinary to the Inquisition in both Coimbra and Lisbon, a year later, sealed Pombal's confidence in him as a firm regalist, for Mello Freire was entrusted with the task of restricting the jurisdiction of the Holy Office in secular matters.[32] Appointed to Coimbra's chair of *direito pátrio* by the same *alvará* that established the New Statutes in 1772, he continued to teach full time until 1783.[33] Judging from posthumously published dissertations that drew on his university lectures, research may yet establish that Mello Freire authored many of the most important laws promulgated under Pombal's signature.

During the final fifteen years of his life, Mello Freire gave lasting political and academic effect to the recasting of Portugal's legal constitution. Between 1787 and 1789, he produced draft texts of both a public and a criminal code, in fulfillment of crown projects to replace the *Ordenações Filipinas*. Unfortunately, the government did not permit either draft code to be submitted for approval. It dissolved the committee and shelved the code projects as revolution broke out in Paris.[34] Had the crown adopted Mello Freire's civil code project, then Portugal would have preceded both Austria and France as the first European nation to promulgate a modern civil code. The political timidity of the government later led Candido Mendes to lament that a rare opportunity had been lost for systematically revising the outdated code of 1603: "Little or nothing was done between 1772 and 1808. . . After all the fuss everything was pure loss . . . What abounded was . . . a distaste for serious works of legislation, despite the presence of worthy jurisconsults."[35]

Nevertheless, publication of Mello Freire's two major works, in press at the time he produced the code projects, insured that legal nationalism would be systematically and ideologically diffused throughout the overlapping reigns of Maria I (1777–1816) and her son and regent, D. João VI (1792–1826). In 1788, Mello Freire published the *Historiae juris civilis lusitani (liber singularis)*, the first legal history of Portugal to draw on a panoply of primary sources for that nation's juridical formation.[36] The *Historiae* offered the full canvas of more than a millennium of national legal evolution, beginning with Roman law before Justinian. It comprehensively moved to the "barbarian" law of the Visigoths, as well as traced the medieval foundations of canon and conciliar law. The late reception of Roman law that culminated in the *Ordenações Afonsinas* provided Mello Freire with the backdrop to a penetrating examination of how, in other European contexts, the reworking of national law had gradually evolved into legal nationalism.

The *Historiae* argued persuasively that national law was the product of an evolutionary development, absolutely mutable, and not divinely preordained. The New Statutes of 1772 had, for the first time, established a chair in national history at Coimbra's faculty of civil law. Analogous to the chair in national law, it testified to the new utility of historical study for teaching *direito pátrio*. Much as Verney had suggested in the 1740s, history supplied the methodology for subjecting the authority of both civil and canon law to critical scrutiny and reevaluation. The *Historiae* acquired central importance because it demonstrated that the study of history could undermine the canonists' domination of Coimbra's legal curriculum. It challenged the authority of canon law by demonstrating that, historically, dogma had been a product of conciliar determinations. Equally important, the *Historiae* upheld the *regalias* of Portugal's national monarchy and whittled away the ground on which eighteenth-century pontiffs had erected a "monarchical" argument to challenge the authority of general church councils. Using historical research, Mello Freire argued that Portugal's kings and bishops enjoyed their prerogatives by virtue of powers they had never ceded to Rome. Or, alternatively, he resorted to concordats and treaties for establishing that those prerogatives had been papally delegated to the monarchy. By the same token, the *Historiae* challenged the role of Roman law by propagandizing persuasively in favor of the preeminence of national positive law.

The *Historiae juris civilis lusitani* served as the fitting prologue for Mello Freire's *magnum opus*, the *Institutionum civilis juris lusitani*, what Portuguese and Brazilian jurists consistently referred to in the plural, as his *Institutiones*, or "Institutes." Submitted to the royal censors in 1788, a year after the *Historiae*, the *Institutiones* presented a reformulation of national positive law that followed a European trend modeled on Justinian's Institutes. A monumental work, the *Institutiones* appeared between 1789 and 1793 and were divided into four books, each with diverse tomes. Meanwhile, the *Historiae juris civilis lusitani*, delayed by the royal censors, was cleared and published in 1788—but only after Mello Freire was obliged to make a formal defense of the work.[37]

The European Context of Legal Nationalism

Mello Freire's lasting contributions to Pombaline and post-Pombaline reform of Luso-Brazilian legal tradition derived from his mastery and practical application of developments in legal science outside Portugal. Although he possessed a comprehensive grasp of a vast juridical literature, there is no evidence to suggest that he ever left his native country. His dazzling command of the legal literature published throughout western Europe, particularly of works produced in Northern Europe by German-speaking, Protestant authors, is greatly in evidence in the *Institutiones juris civilis lusitani*. Book 2, *De jure personarum* (1791), treating private law, became the most widely consulted volume due to the fact that Mello Freire addressed the ambiguity and hiati in that area of law. Book 2 also demonstrated Mello Freire's special interest in institutes of local law, meaning law pertaining to either an ethnic group, such as the Visigoths, or a political unit, one ranging from a free city to a principality to even a national monarchy. Institutes were an eighteenth-century innovation that drew on a rich literature in humanistic studies reaching to the sixteenth century. They paid special attention to the living law and critically appraised the evolution of the *Corpus Juris Civilis* in early modern Europe in order to justify its replacement by sources deemed "national."

Mello Freire also immersed himself in complementary studies of feudal law, again written mostly by German-speaking authors or their French Huguenot counterparts who, as political refugees, resided in either the Low Countries or the German Protestant principalities. For example, Dionysius Gothofredus (1549–1622), whose work was an early forerunner of the scholarly attention paid to Justinian's Institutes, was a jurist regularly cited by Mello Freire. A Dutch professor of law who taught at the University of Heidelberg after 1610, Gothofredus was "the most celebrated editor" of the *Corpus Juris Civilis*. He had worked out a tabulation of Justinian's Institutes that influenced and guided European scholars until the era of Theodor Mommsen.[38]

Mello Freire's bibliographic citations, however, fell most heavily in the first half of the eighteenth century, on authors like Georg Beyer (1665–1714), whose *Delineatio juris Germanici* (1718) amounted to the earliest Institutes of German private law. He had been a pupil of Christianus Thomasius, who gave the first lectures on German private law in Halle, between 1699 and 1701.[39] Beyer's influence can be seen on Mello Freire's broad approach, especially in his use of customary and national positive law, rather than in specific citations. Beyer tried to "set out a systematic account of German private law" wherein the rules of "Roman law received in Germany are generally omitted." His technique can be found replicated in Mello Freire's *De jure personarum*, including Beyer's precedent-setting conclusion that the *Corpus Juris* was "wrongly adduced as a source of rule [law]."[40] In arguing that accepted law differed from that of the *Corpus Juris*, Beyer provided early inspiration for the movement of legal nationalism that emerged after his death. If he provided Mello Freire with general incentive for questioning the given tradition of Justinian, then the influence of Samuel Stryk (1640–1710) on German feudal law was more narrowly discernible in an impressive number of Mello Freire's bibliographic citations.[41]

Partiality toward the local institutes of law that led Mello Freire to fasten on the Visigothic Code eventually carried him into the special turf of Germanic customary law. Especially the writings of Johann G. Heineccius accounted for how he would use customary law in *De jure personarum*. Heineccius, who offered an explicitly historical perspective on "German law, old and contemporary," had turned to Tacitus' writings on the Germans as well as to Visigothic laws.[42] He attracted Mello Freire's historical eye, because Heineccius offered a quasi-constitutional model for the Portuguese as a nation, one that predated the fifteenth-century reception of Roman law in Portugal. Furthermore, Visigothic law enshrined the calling of assemblies that eventually metamorphosized into Portugal's medieval Cortes, or Estates General. Finally, Visigothic law analogously privileged the decisions of church councils, particularly during eras when the pope's power was weak. In short, the Visigothic Code provided the means for disregarding the debt owed by Portuguese legal tradition to Roman civil law. Determined to idealize the legal legacy of a Germanic past, because it enshrined pristine custom that he construed as uniquely "Portuguese," Mello Freire and other jurists closely associated with the Bragança state promoted legal nationalism in consonance with a broader movement in western Europe. As a consequence, the triumph of the national monarchies throughout western Europe spelled the end of the *jus commune*.

The comparative legal literature led Mello Freire to a reformulation of Portuguese national law that typically displaced the *jus commune* in favor of national sources of law. Frequently in tandem with Samuel Stryk's work, he relied fundamentally on Georg Adam Struve's *Jurisprudentia Romano-Germanica forensis* (1670), because it did not restrict scrutiny to one or a few German states. In addition to modern rules of private law that were Germanic, Struve addressed those that were Roman, notwithstanding that he argued much of the law traceable to Justinian's Institutes no longer was being applied. For these reasons, as well as for the attention it paid to legal procedure, Struve's *Jurisprudentia* was still the most important Institutes of private law in late eighteenth-century Europe.[43] The same comprehensiveness attracted Mello Freire to the work of Hugo Grotius. Grotius' early seventeenth-century study of the law of Holland, a country heavily influenced by Roman law, essentially relegated the *Corpus Juris Civilis* to the background. Beyond treating Dutch law as a national system on its own, however, Grotius placed fundamental stress on natural law. Both emphases can be found in Mello Freire's writings. Frequently, he identified natural law as residing in custom, allowing him to justify the latter as a revitalized source for positive law in Portugal. Mello Freire's grasp of comparative legal history also led him to use Grotius' development of a *jus gentium*, or law of nations, as a concept that sanctioned his innovative approaches whenever they drew on legal practices common throughout western Europe.

Finally, mention must also be made of the juridical influence of Georg Ludwig Boehmer (1715–1797), Mello Freire's senior contemporary who died a year before him. Above all, Boehmer proved to be of central importance for Mello Freire because of how he challenged the sacred canons on matrimony. To wit, he enunciated a new application of legitimization by subsequent marriage. More broadly, however, he reinforced Mello Freire's juridical reliance on the laws of feudal custom. A Prussian and a Protestant, Boehmer was a subject of both the king of England and the Elector of Saxony, although he held a professorship in law at the University of Gottingen. His *Principia Iuris Feudalis* (1765), or Principles of Feudal Law, ran to eight editions, the last of which appeared in 1819. The *Principia* addressed feudal law common to all of German-speaking Europe, and thus provided an alternative source to the *jus commune* that was fundamentally European, but nationally discrete.[44] For Boehmer, the *jus commune* had to be acknowledged, although he ranked it last among the strands that defined the legal basis of modern states: "The sources of common German feudal law are the feudal law of the Lombards received throughout Germany; universal German feudal customs; [and] the common law of the empire contained in imperial sanctions, in Roman and canon law."[45] Confirmation that Boehmer inspired Mello Freire to rely on "the customs of this kingdom" and the Visigothic Code as pivotal sources of law in *De jure Personarum* can be found in the multiplicity of footnotes the Coimbra professor employed to cite Boehmer's works.

MELLO FREIRE AND THE CANONS ON MARRIAGE

Applying Legal Nationalism to Private Law

Mello Freire applied *direito pátrio* to private law with gusto. The introductory chapters of this book have referred to his reinterpretations of the legal position of natural and spurious offspring, particularly the *quaesito*. As we have also seen, Mello Freire's successors, Lobão and Borges Carneiro, whose legal commentaries appeared between 1818 and 1828, reiterated and reinforced his reinterpretations on natural offspring. His willingness to mitigate legal distinctions ascribed to the fact or absence of legitimate marriage derived from his radical stance on the sacrament of matrimony and his related reinterpretation of legitimization by subsequent marriage. Mello Freire's method of argumentation with respect to family law, dissected in *De jure personarum*, Book 2 of the *Institutiones*, often opened with "according to Roman law . . . ." He then proceeded to argue that Roman law either did not apply or did not matter in a Portuguese national context. His frequent use of the first person plural reinforced the dichotomy he constantly established between national law—"our law"—and alien "imperial law," meaning Justinian's late Roman civil law. For instance: "We can say the same of marital dower, which, understood according to the meaning of Roman law, is unknown by our laws and customs."[46]

In expounding on dowry, Mello Freire simply cast aside Roman law, privileging Germanic law's marital property regime and, implicitly, Portuguese custom: "Under Roman law a mother was not obligated to give her daughter a dowry, except in special situations. Among us, however, the *Ordenações* (Book 4, Title 46) obligates her fundamentally and equally with the father, given community property."[47] Elsewhere, Roman law might be discredited for being "uncivilized," as when he explained that children were only subject to the rule [*imperio*] and power [*poder*] of the father." Roman law's grant of dominion (*domino*) to the father, he maintained, "was never received among the Portuguese," explaining why, under Visigothic law, fathers were permitted only moderate punishment of their children. Consequently, the Portuguese were spared an unsavory feature of Roman *imperio*: "The right to sell one's children was not received law [in Portugal], even if necessity demanded it—and, earlier, the same Visigothic laws expressly prohibited it."[48]

Mello Freire's interpretations of family law proved most controversial on the subject of spurious birth, a point that later enhanced his appeal for many Brazilian liberal legislators. For instance, he reasserted the right of spurious children to paternal child support. On the other hand, he liked to flavor his juridical arguments with a touch of scandal. The sexual behavior of some of Portugal's most famous prelates became the centerpiece of his discussion, for he reeled off an impressive list of names, including those of archbishops, bishops, priors, or cathedral canons whose children had been legitimized by the crown. As if to say priests were no different from other mortals, he cited popes and diocesan councils that had issued rulings making priests legally obligated to contribute to the support of their sacrilegious children.[49]

Finally, Mello Freire called on natural law as the basis for reformulating positive family law, where formerly reliance would have been placed on Roman civil law. For example, in discussing maternal attributes of power, which, unlike the paternal attribute of power (*pátrio poder*), did not derive from Roman civil law, he addressed an important lacuna in the *Ordenações Filipinas*. Natural law, consequently, could supply the source for new national law: "The power of a mother over her children does not lie in the civil law, but in natural law; and thus only to the latter should those rights be attributed which derive from the nature of this power. For this reason she cannot ...."[50]

Legal Nationalism and Customary Marriage

Matrimony afforded Mello Freire opportunity to apply national law in a direct challenge to canon law. By dismissing Tridentine rules as indispensable for constituting legal marriage, he disclosed the central importance he placed on custom as a source for national law. Although he upheld some of the canons on marriage adopted at Trent, Mello Freire studiously avoided any citation of the Articles of Trent as an authoritative source for national law. Instead, he privileged the *Ordenações Filipinas* or the preceding Manueline Code. Well aware that the crown's promulgation of the canons adopted at Trent, in the 1560s, had preceded the national codification of 1603, he nonetheless treated marriage as a feature of national law that derived either from crown legislation or Portuguese custom. When, for instance, Mello Freire condemned clandestine marriage, he pointed to its prohibition originally incorporated in the *Ordenações Manuelinas* (1521), that is, predating Trent. Then he cited the *alvará* of November 13, 1651, reiterating the prohibition.[51] He did not, however, invoke the Articles of the Council of Trent that similarly condemned clandestine marriage.

Mello Freire argued that marriage derived from the *Ordenações Filipinas* for yet another reason: Books 4 and 5 recognized both customary and de facto unions as tantamount to legitimate marriage. Consequently, he was the last great jurist to defend the legal validity of the multiple arrangements known popularly as "marriage according to the *Ordenações*" or, alternatively, as "marriage according to the custom of this realm." By sanctioning a diversity of customary arrangements historically accepted in Portugal as valid marriage, he lent considerable juridical authority to deeply rooted notions of marriage that predated the Council of Trent by centuries. Although the *Ordenações Filipinas* gave them full legal effect, late eighteenth-century jurists increasingly regarded them as obsolete, due to the reception in national law of the rules of Tridentine marriage during the 1560s. Mello Freire chose to defend forms of marriage that were non-sacramental out of a political conviction that marriage was as much a civil act as a sacrament: "In almost every nation, it has been observed in the celebration of certain rites and solemnities for matrimony, that [they] are as much civil as ecclesiastical, that they are either essential to marriage, may take place, or may be left aside, but always [are] its essence."[52] By construing as "solemnities" the celebration of marriage according to either regional festivities or local Portuguese customs, he asserted that they carried the force of law. Following a tenet of legal nationalism, Mello Freire also argued on behalf of a "living law," one found embodied in local historical practices rather than the *ratio scripta* of written abstractions.

Appropriating the "thick description" of ethnographic detail, Mello Freire waxed subversive, given that the church rejected all forms of de facto marriage as invalid:

Among the Portuguese, just as among other peoples, the solemnities would consist principally in offering banquets, glasses of water, musical concerts, formal balls, and dances; and those who would attend these events would follow after the bridegroom and the bride [uttering] pious invocations and would make them offerings, toasting them with "to each, according to his physical strength and faculties . . . ." In Minho and Beira, the bride was taken from her father's home almost by force . . . . The nobles . . . celebrated their weddings with much greater to-do, and, for this reason, they were liable to incur larger expenses . . . .[53]

By assigning the church either a marginal role or no role at all, and concluding that the priest was dispensable, Mello Freire openly defied the official dogma of the Counter Reformation Church respecting the sacrament of marriage. The presence of a priest for administering the sacrament of matrimony had been made obligatory at Trent. The Coimbra jurist's irreverent stance, indeed his unorthodoxy, became transparent when he punned the common people's "dispensing" of the matrimonial banns, for he equated the authority of the laity with that of the priesthood. Not only was the sacrament of matrimony optional in Mello Freire's view, but it served only one group, the nobility:

The religious rites consist principally of the priestly blessing, the bans or public proclamations, which for me are not necessary to examine. The *Ordenações*, Book 4, Title 19, §2 (and the same in the *Ordenações Manuelinas*) talk about these proclamations. However, in our times, the common people are accustomed often to dispense with them and to regard them as favoring the nobility. They do not want their marriages proclaimed from the place of the high altar of the church, nor do they either, in the present time, want to celebrate [marriage] with solemnity, "before the altar" of the Lord [*a face dos templos*], but they want it to be done within their own houses.[54]

To conclude, Mello Freire left standing a historical definition of marriage in Portugal that was deeply rooted in customary behavior. In every case, it rested on the evidence of a cohabiting couple's *fama pública*—their public reputation of living together as man and wife. The juridical tide nevertheless was turning in the late 1780s. Contemporary jurists, starting with Joaquim José Caetano Pereira e Souza (d. 1818), did not always agree with Mello Freire that "marriage according to the *Ordenações*" deserved legal validity. In 1836, the Roman Curia would condemn the *Institutiones juris civilis lusitani*, partly on the basis of Mello Freire's defense of de facto marriage.[55] On the other hand, for a radical minority of Brazil's liberal legislators during the same decade, his interpretation would continue to exercise appeal.

Legitimizing Spurious Offspring by Subsequent Marriage

How Mello Freire interpreted canon law on legitimization by subsequent marriage would prove even more critical for why the *Institutiones* was eventually placed on the Index of Forbidden Books. In interpreting how national law treated legitimization by subsequent marriage, he built an argument that deliberately misconstrued canon law. He began with the general understanding: "It is common opinion that only natural offspring may be legitimized by subsequent marriage under canon law." Then he noted, again correctly, that it was common opinion that offspring who were spurious could not be legitimized by subsequent marriage. Finally, he took back the latter observation and knowingly controverted canon law: "It seems that canon law concedes that offspring born of damnable unions can be legitimized by the subsequent marriage of their parents."[56] Of course, the church did not accept this position.

What was Mello Freire trying to do? In all likelihood, by deliberately confusing logic, he sought to protect himself from ecclesiastical censure, given that his argument relied on none other than G. L. Boehmer as chief authority. Although, as we have seen, Boehmer's *Principia Iuris Feudalis* greatly influenced Mello Freire's interpretation of custom as inherently received law, his utility on the fine points of legitimization by subsequent marriage derived from a specific treatise he authored on legitimization, entitled *Qui filli sint legitimi*. Boehmer's appeal to Mello Freire lay in his flat refutation of the canonical position that subsequent marriage could not legitimize children born of "damnable and punishable" birth—those whose parents' dire impediment made them spurious offspring. Boehmer, however, was a

Protestant, meaning that for him to argue that spurious offspring could be legitimized by subsequent marriage was an easier political task than for a Catholic jurist like Mello Freire to do so.

Although usually he declined to speak of canon law, Mello Freire was obliged to engage it on this point. It was common knowledge that canon law permitted legitimization by subsequent marriage only for natural offspring. Resorting to Boehmer, Mello Freire simply argued that the legitimization of spurious offspring by subsequent marriage was currently "accepted in the courts, with approval, as axioms of canon law." In other words, he posited that the courts validated what basically represented an incorrect reading of canon law, although he also acknowledged that Boehmer "distanced himself from the axioms of canon law." Yet when Mello Freire cryptically insisted, "But we also *use* this law in our courts," he implied canon law. What did he mean?[57]

Although Mello Freire might have been implying that the courts accepted social practice—custom as a source of law—he gave no indication he meant the latter. Rather, his allusion is better read with an eye to the Tribunal of the Mesa do Desembargo do Paço, for that was the only court where couples who married after establishing a family could petition for the legitimization of their spurious children. In this context, Spanish practice is instructive. Royal bureaucrats in Bourbon Spain who struggled with the same issue of legitimization by subsequent marriage, during the 1780s and 1790s, occasionally bestowed crown legitimization on canonically incestuous children whose parents married after their birth. The instances were rare, and the few exceptions granted by the Camara de Gracias y Justicia, as Twinam recently has revealed, spun exceedingly fine arguments.

What was significant about a Spanish context for Portuguese juridical determinations was that the exceptions granted by the Bourbon crown jurists did not contravene canon law. In more conservative Spain, the crown Camara charged with recommending such action did so only in extremely compelling situations, and where legitimization would enjoy strong support in public opinion. Again, public reputation, the *fama pública* of both parents and children, proved pivotal for granting exceptions to canon law. The jurists in the Spanish Camara, however, avoided any outright contradiction of canonical rules, in favor of "stretching" individual circumstances in the facts of each case. Usually, they found a "loophole" that rested on a prior episcopal dispensation to marry—and the fact that the parents had already acted on the latter. Sometimes, in such cases, the parents had older children who were spurious and young ones who were legitimate, a circumstance that divided siblings in reputation and inheritance rights. That royal bureaucrats in Spain preferred to build on a dispensation already granted to the parents by the church was notable, because they granted legitimization only on behalf of children who were canonically incestuous—never for those who were adulterine.[58] Mello Freire, however, did not restrict himself to that narrow limitation.

What of the analogous petitions in Portugal, asking for legitimization of spurious offspring whose parents had married after their birth, thanks to a dispensation? How did the Desembargo do Paço rule? Was Mello Freire's argument derived from Boehmer applied by Portugal's high crown judges? Unfortunately, no answer can be offered, for the direct evidence awaits discovery. The whereabouts of the Lisbon archive containing the decisions of that high crown tribunal has not been determined.[59] Alternatively, however, the archive for the Tribunal of the Desembargo do Paço established in Rio de Janeiro between 1808 and 1828 offers several tantalizing clues that favor Mello Freire's radical interpretation of legitimization by subsequent marriage.

In a case brought before the Desembargo do Paço in 1815, an adulterine son was legitimized whose mother was a widow when he was born, although his father was married to a different woman at his birth. After the father's wife died, the adulterine son's parents married, thanks to an ecclesiastical dispensation. Typically, the ceremony was performed at night, because the dire impediment of marrying the person with whom adultery was committed had been dispensed. Yet what prompted the widowed mother's petition— and her expectation of legitimization—was precisely the death of her second husband, the father of her adulterine son, only four years after her second marriage. Furthermore, there were two unusual twists in the mother's petition. First, it produced a notarized affidavit made by the half-sister of her adulterine son, consenting to the legitimization of her adulterine half-brother. Second, the mother offered a notarized declaration of paternal *perfilhação* on behalf of her adulterine son. It was a bizarre affidavit, because the father had not executed it; the mother herself did so. The adulterine son's half-sister testified as a witness to her mother's declaration of her deceased husband's paternity. Of course, law denied an adulterine son judicial recourse for establishing his filiation to his father. In this case, his widowed mother attempted, and succeeded, in having the Paço establish it on her behalf. The affidavit ascribing paternity represented a step vital for crown legitimization, because it stated that the father's wish had been to have his son enjoy his honors as a military officer, his family name, and, not surprisingly, his right to inherit paternally. Hence, the affidavit of *perfilhação* served a second purpose. It converted hearsay evidence into the father's notarized intent to legitimize his child and make him his heir, and despite the fact that the mother declared *perfilhação*. The Desembargo do Paço granted the legitimization, even for an adulterine son, although the individual case spoke to highly unusual circumstances.[60]

In another case, crown legitimization was bestowed on a canonically incestuous child, but the incest involved the child's father's prior sexual relations with a cousin of the mother, before marrying the latter. Nizza da Silva concluded that the legitimization was due to an episcopal dispensation, "which, having removed [the stain of] incest, permitted the Paço to grant the petition."[61] Such action on the part of the Tribunal of the Desembargo do Paço more closely approximated the norm in Spanish cases, where a dispensation to marry was hardly sufficient, in the eyes of the church, to justify legitimization. In other words, the royal court conferred what canon law withheld from the couple's children. In the absence of a form of marriage that was exclusively civil, the Desembargo do Paço resorted to a definition of marriage that more closely approximated the latter than a canonical definition.

Although Boehmer successfully argued the primacy of national positive law over any canonical determination, Mello Freire was obliged to fall back on a polemical, rather than a juridical, argument. In referring to the *ordenação* on legitimization by subsequent marriage (Book 2, Title 35), he initially acknowledged that "this *ordenação* may not be clear, nor remove the issue." Legitimization of spurious offspring by subsequent marriage therefore would have to be deduced apart from the *Ordenações*. As a result, he explicitly discarded the canonical notion of "simultaneity," one used to justify why individuals who were of illicit birth managed to escape the stain of spuriousness. Simultaneity rested on a legal fiction, that a marriage could be deemed retroactive to the time of, or simultaneous with, a natural offspring's birth or conception—providing, of course, no impediments to marriage existed between the parents.

In place of simultaneity, Mello Freire innovated, by arguing that the fact of marriage—both a civil act and a sacramental rite—remedied "defects" of birth. Thus he construed marriage in positive law as the means for removing the "defect" of spurious birth, what jurists until his own era pronounced as the "stain" (*macula*) of spuriousness: true bastardy. Because marriage according to Trent coincided with marriage in positive national law, he implied that it permitted jurists to interpret legitimization by subsequent marriage as applying to spurious as well as to illicit birth, thereby eradicating the stain of bastardy:

I am of the opinion that children born prior to marriage, even those who are spurious [*sacrílegos*], adulterine, or incestuous, can be legitimized by virtue of, and by the force of law, the preceding impediment being brought to a halt, and, following from true and legitimate matrimony. I judge completely inept and suggested by no rule that which is accustomed to be said commonly, with complete freedom, about the retroactivity of marriage to the time of the child's birth—concerning the fiction of simultaneity or of the marriage.[62]

With this terse and elliptical pronouncement, Mello Freire opened a debate that in Brazil would run to the twentieth century: Could the subsequent marriage of adulterine children's parents render them legitimized?[63] During the 1830s and 1840s, as we shall see in the following volume, Brazilian legislators found his argument compelling, believing Mello Freire when he said that canon law permitted such legitimization. For Mello Freire, however, what mattered was the national law imposed by the crown. This alone accounted for why he could deliberately misconstrue canon law and claim that national law extended legitimization by subsequent marriage to spurious offspring.

What mattered about Mello Freire's radical interpretation of legitimization by subsequent marriage for spurious offspring, on the part of liberal reformers in imperial Brazil who wanted to redefine procedures for paternal recognition, legitimization, and heirship, was the assumption that Mello Freire had been right. Especially when they believed—erroneously—that canon law sanctioned his position, they would seek to write it into national law in the late 1830s. As late as the 1870s, the authoritative guide written for judges and their clerks by the Portuguese jurist Carlos de Menezes, which was adapted for use in Brazil's lower courts, devoted favorable attention to the issue. As the annotator noted, the issue continued to be intensely debated, with judicial opinion divided. Menezes cited one ruling of the Relação of Rio de Janeiro, in support of a lower court's endorsement of Mello Freire's interpretation, to demonstrate the argument could be sustained.[64] Mello Freire himself, on the other hand, did not recoil from reinterpreting, or misinterpreting, canon law because his reformulations enabled the absolutist state to play a more powerful role vis-à-vis marriage and the family. Nor was he immune from acting as a polemicist on behalf of the view that a modern state should not bow to canon law in regulating the private sphere of marriage.

A NEW LEGAL CANON:
THE INSTITUTIONES JURIS CIVILIS LUSITANI

Pombal's death, in 1782, released Mello Freire from the academic venue where he had labored in relative obscurity for a quarter century. Although his move to Lisbon in 1783 signified a return to royal favor, it is likely that

Mello Freire left Coimbra because reform of the legal curriculum had been stymied by the canonists. In the aftermath of the removal Dr. Francisco Lemos, Pombal's hand-picked rector, university reform was compromised, one of the events the poet Francisco de Mello Franco had in mind when he decried the new government of D. Maria I as the "Reign of Stupidity [*o Reino da Estupidez*]."[65] A growing list of royal appointments established the crown's confidence in Mello Freire and testified to the value his juridical talent offered the monarchy: an honorary judgeship on Portugal's highest court of appeals, the Casa da Suplicação, in 1785, followed two years later by nomination as deputy to the Royal Board of Censorship (an agency created by Pombal to neutralize the secular influence of the Inquisition); then promotion to magistrate of the Casa da Suplicação and membership on the Committee for the Organization of Civil and Criminal Code Projects[66]

Permanently freed from duty in Coimbra's cloistered halls, Mello Freire embarked on publication. Within four years of arrival in Lisbon, he presented his legal history of Portugal to the board of royal censorship and then quickly followed with his Institutes of Portuguese civil law. In 1788, the board cleared the path for publication of both, the principal works that would immortalize him as a jurist: the *Historiae civilis juris lusitani* (1788) and the *Institutionum civilis juris lusitani* (1789–1793). The *Historiae*, whose conclusions anticipated and infused the reasoning of the *Institutiones*, proved more problematic for the censors than the *Institutiones*, given the stunning evidence it marshaled on behalf of a conciliar interpretation of church authority. Hence, it was deemed politically subversive in the eyes of the church. The Jansenist current in Mello Freire's interpretation, evident in both of his works, later proved congenial to the political views of many in Brazil's first generation of imperial legislators.

The *Institutiones* were intended as a student compendium—a set of textbooks—but it would take sixteen years for them to be adopted as the official curriculum in Coimbra's Faculty of Civil Law. Although Mello Freire wrote most of his dissertations in the vernacular, a standard practice by the late 1780s, publication of his two major works in Latin belied the new trend. Very probably, the choice of Latin followed from the need to obtain publication permission from the Royal Board of Censors and the author's calculation that his controversial ideas would more likely gain approval if Latin limited their circulation. Mello Freire thus was the last great royal jurisconsult to be read in what Candido Mendes pronounced a "consummately elegant" Latin.[67] The first book of the *Institutiones* appeared in 1789, followed by the second and third books in 1791; the final book was published in 1793.[68] What is sometimes referred to as a "fifth book," published in 1794, consisted of the shelved, criminal code project of 1787–1788.[69] Reprintings for each of the four books of the *Institutiones* began as soon as Book 2, the most widely read, rolled off the press. The latter, *De jure personarum*, remained in print until the second half of the nineteenth century as the most useful and controversial book, given Mello Freire's approach to the private law of the family.[70]

Mello Freire's *Historiae* and *Institutiones* saw publication during the initial unfolding of the French Revolution. The fame and intellectual prestige their author achieved underscored his utility to the throne, for his radicalism did not question either royal absolutism or divine right. Recognition, in the form of crown appointments to high judicial office, culminated in his promotion to royal jurisconsult in 1797. Once D. João began to exercise de facto sovereignty on behalf of the mentally incompetent Maria I, in 1792, Mello Freire's political position became no less than "mainstream." In the early Age of Revolutions, he remained a thoroughly committed absolutist. Like his Spanish counterpart Jovellanos, he declined to be moved by the newfangled, liberal idea of a written constitution.[71] A political conservative on the threshold of a liberal era, Mello Freire advanced his career because his radicalism was directed against either the authority of pope and Curia or ecclesiastical privilege and canon law. In the early 1800s, when the papal nuncio in Lisbon deplored that Jansenism survived in post-Pombaline Portugal, he blamed Coimbra University's reinstated rector, D. Francisco Lemos, together with Portugal's equally regalist bishops. But it was Mello Freire's juridical writings that by then were inspiring law students. According to the nuncio, the recent curricular reform, of 1805, disseminated "the Febronian and Jansenist maxims," turning the university into "a true seat of pestilence."[72]

Mello Freire's 1797 appointment as royal jurisconsult placed in his hands authority to impose legal nationalism in practical contexts. The post conferred direct responsibility for overseeing crown justice at all levels. The jurisconsult's charge was to instruct judges, prosecutors, and crown lawyers in the royal courts on the proper application of positive law. This role implied eminently practical effects, given the opportunity to impose national law in a courtroom context. He, and especially his successors, would act to insure that juridical determinations made in the royal courts reflected the primacy of national law. The office of jurisconsult also entailed the authorship of learned treatises and dissertations, for they were employed in the courts for interpreting precise matters of law. Although Mello Freire died before this task could be fulfilled, the renowned jurisconsults who followed him—Corrêa Telles, Lobão, and Borges Carneiro—would apply the *Institutiones* in practical courtroom determinations. Fittingly, Mello Freire was also the last cleric to hold the important post of royal jurisconsult in Portugal. His ideological association with the monarchies of both José I and Maria I accounted for why he acquired a final appellation immortalizing him as the counselor of kings: "Paschoal José de Mello Freire dos Reys."[73]

Mello Freire's lasting impact on Brazilian family law is still to be discerned in the footnotes of contemporary textbooks and legal commentaries, where he continues to be cited to the present day. As we have seen, his immediate legacy for liberal reformers in imperial Brazil lay in the impact of his position that neither natural offspring nor *quaesitos* were to be regarded as bastards by the law. In lending his substantial prestige to Pombal's efforts to remove discrimination in crown appointments and employment on the ground of bastard birth, he was the preeminent jurist who dismissed the medieval notion of infamy (*infame*) as inherent in spurious birth. Both positions were closely tied to his emphasis on natural law—the equality of all children in nature—and his stance on marriage as an act solemnized by national customs as much as by the canons laid down by the Council of Trent. Otherwise, it was Mello Freire's injunctions on a father's duty to support both his spurious and natural offspring that jurists quoted in the nineteenth and twentieth centuries. Despite these important contributions in the area of private law, Mello Freire must be viewed in the long run as no less than the founder of national law in Portugal, the first to recast that nation's law as a modern structure. In that respect, he stands as the major architect of Brazil's early legal culture, given that, in the hands of liberal standard-bearers, the *Institutiones juris civilis lusitani* transcended the age of absolutism and offered either the template or the intellectual approach adopted by all major legal commentaries published in Portugal, precisely the literature that Brazilians consulted through the 1850s.

Conclusion

A Pombaline Legal Tradition for a Liberal Era

———◦◦◦———

[Paschoal José de Mello Freire] reduced the chaos of National
Legislation to a regular plane and easy comprehension . . . . In
possession of the vast ideas of the marquis of Pombal, he applied
philosophy to jurisprudence . . . and interpreted the ancient laws
in the spirit of the century in which he was living and in which
they had to be executed. His writings introduced new intellectual
tastes and created a new school of National Jurisprudence.

Professor Antonio Joaquim Ribas, 1865[1]

Writing in the late 1860s, when Brazilian jurisprudence had again begun to
privilege Roman law, Candido Mendes de Almeida emphasized that Mello
Freire had been "an eminently innovative spirit." He lamented the lost opportunity for national codification in the eighteenth century and observed
that "had Mello Freire been given a free hand, then he would have made of
his epoch a *tabula rasa*" for replacing Portugal's legal constitution.[2] In Brazil,
Mello Freire's legacy endured intact until challenged in the late 1850s by the
genius of Teixeira de Freitas, the jurist who first pushed the pendulum of juridical reinterpretation in the old direction of Roman law. Mello Freire's
lasting contribution to Luso-Brazilian jurisprudence was to modernize Portugal's eclectic and conflicting corpus of laws, what in his own time had become an obstacle to modern state building.

Short of replacing the *Ordenações* with a modern civil code, the *Institutiones juris civilis lusitani* provided the next best alternative. They eliminated irrelevant sources of law and reconciled the essence of a national legal tradition, where formerly there had been a veritable jumble of sources. The codi-
fications of Portuguese law known generically as the *Ordenações do Reino* had
successively carried forward many limitations embedded in the initial *Ordenações Afonsinas*, for the latter had relied on medieval compilations of royal
law, in addition to Roman and canon law or custom. Technically an early
modern national code, the *Ordenações Filipinas* remained faithful to the late

medieval society of estates that supplied so many of its precepts and rules. Corporate privilege, embedded in its provisions, no longer represented an unqualified good by the late eighteenth century. Although the national code of 1603 had imposed important limits on the authority of seigneurial custom, and paid new attention to Portugal's agrarian economy, it did so at the expense of the commercial classes that became central to Pombal's grand design.³ Many *ordenações* also conflicted with each other, a case in point being the contradictory definitions of legal marriage mentioned in the preceding chapter. Other *ordenações* were simply out of place in a late eighteenth-century polity or inappropriately silent on points of law that mattered.

Nullification of individual *ordenações* defined the principal task for a Pombaline generation of crown jurists. In replacing the discrete provisions of the Philippine Code with new legislation, either statutes or administrative orders authored by the king's ministers, crown policy targeted the courtroom as the practical beneficiary of national law. Legal nationalism privileged the living law imposed in crown courts, a circumstance that also explained a new emphasis on legal procedures. The 1769 Law of Right Reason therefore became indispensable for overriding or replacing portions of the *Ordenações Filipinas* as a piecemeal process, by providing the necessary *raison d'être* for reformulating juridical precepts or procedures. Although Mello Freire's *Institutiones* explicated how this process worked through the 1780s, by connecting new legislation to precepts spelled out in the 1769 law, his Institutes also provided theoretical and comparative demonstration for a practical application of right reason. By supplying a myriad of illustrations, the *Institutiones* illustrated how the Law of Right Reason could be applied, especially in all areas of family and inheritance law. They also introduced a pivotal reliance on natural law for supplanting Roman or canon law, but, at the same time, they cited custom as a fundamental authority for positive national law. For a nineteenth-century audience, Mello Freire's magnum opus popularized the relevance of natural law in a Portuguese-speaking world as much as it propagandized on behalf of legal nationalism.

When the Portuguese court moved to Rio de Janeiro in 1808, Mello Freire's legal nationalism accompanied the exiles who reconstituted royal government, as an ingrained strand of their political culture. Quite literally a part of the royal library transported to Brazil by the Bragança flotilla, the *Institutiones* and *Historiae* were disseminated in Portugal's new tropical capital as the key texts of a secularizing dogma. By independence, in 1822, Mello Freire's major works were familiar reading for two senior generations of Brazilian legislators who had attended Coimbra University, even when their training in civil law had been obtained prior to 1805, when the *Institutiones* became mandatory reading. A few of them, like the viscount of Cayru, held degrees dating to the early 1780s, when Mello Freire had been a Coimbra professor in residence. In authoritatively invoking the name of "Dr. José Freire" on the floor of the national legislature, Brazilian lawmakers did so as much for political as for juridical reasons, believing that his reformulation of national law stood as the necessary complement to modern statebuilding. In this regard, they venerated Mello Freire as much for his regalism as for his insistence that canon and Roman law should remain secondary sources for national law.

Undoubtedly, those who were well trained in law appreciated that Mello Freire compared favorably to the great seventeenth-century jurisconsult who inspired him, Gabriel Pereira de Castro.[4] However, unlike the latter, whose focus was public law, Mello Freire applied regalism to both public and private law, demonstrating a comprehensiveness that far surpassed Pereira de Castro's narrow gaze. Thanks to Mello Freire, Brazilian liberals of the independence era found little need to incorporate many new ideological notions borrowed from the French Revolution. However much they responded to the appeal of "equality before the law," the ideological refrain sounded by liberalism for a post-1789 world, their attack on corporate privilege reached to the preceding era of the marquis of Pombal.[5]

When Brazilian jurists summed up Mello Freire's contributions in the 1860s, they agreed on his talent as a synthesizer and acknowledged that his juridical perspective had endured. Professor Antonio Joaquim Ribas, who pronounced Mello Freire "incontestably, the great jurisprudential scholar of the eighteenth century," praised his "profound and synthetic intelligence" which placed him "in the forefront of national jurisconsults." Writing when Roman law had started to reclaim important attention in imperial legal culture, Ribas could still pay homage to Mello Freire's genius in the 1860s. He wanted his students to appreciate that, although Mello Freire systematically subordinated Roman civil law to national positive law, he nevertheless wedded it to the latter. In his 1865 textbook, whose title verified the new importance accorded *civil* law in Brazil, Ribas praised Mello Freire as the jurist whose talent Portugal's eighteenth-century sovereigns had known how to use to political advantage.[6] On the other hand, his more influential colleague, Lafayette Rodrigues Pereira, offered blunter confirmation of how difficult it was going to be for law professors to dismiss or replace Mello Freire's legacy by restoring the authority of Roman law. Lafayette's terse comment confirmed that more than a century of legal nationalism would be difficult to undo: "Among us Brazilians, there is not much taste for the study of civil law."[7]

Mello Freire's death, in 1798, meant that the task of transmitting the legal precepts embedded in the *Institutiones* to a younger generation of jurists and law students fell to his erstwhile student, Manoel de Almeida e Souza de Lobão (1745–1817). Known simply as "Lobão," after the small town near Viseu where he lived and practiced law, Almeida e Souza was a near contemporary of Mello Freire, having graduated from Coimbra University a decade after him, in 1766. Unlike the professor, he did not take holy orders, notwithstanding his doctoral degree in canon law. Possessing a lifelong distaste for Coimbra professors, Lobão pursued a career as a lawyer in the royal courts. His practical bent led him to render Mello Freire's abstracted commentary with valuable insights for the courtroom. What became known among jurists as the *Notas à Mello* amounted to Lobão's juridical formulations and highly personalized interpretation of Mello Freire's *Institutiones*. His *Notas à Mello* converged fortuitously with the diffusion of liberal notions that was set in motion by the Spanish Liberal Revolts of 1812 and 1820. Dramatized for a Luso-Brazilian world on the national stage of the Lisbon Cortes, from 1820 to 1822, the liberal challenge to absolutism in Portugal emphatically repudiated the ancien régime. Legal nationalism, however, offered an ideological matrix that facilitated rapid accommodation of a liberal agenda. Given that Lobão's three volumes of "practical and critical notes" on Mello Freire's *Intitutiones* saw publication between 1818 and 1824, his *Notas à Mello* proved critical for a political generation seeking to adapt legal nationalism to the tenets of Portugal's early Liberal Revolution.[8]

Intended for the apprentice lawyers and judges who were Lobão's charges as a royal jurisconsult, the *Notas à Mello* made Mello Freire's legal interpretations widely accessible in the vernacular for the first time. Equally important, Lobão's commentary both reinforced and rejected his predecessor's views. His pungent comments obliged readers to descend the ivory tower that had been Mello Freire's platform and invited them to enter the practical world of courtroom procedures and legal maneuvers. Another university reform, enacted by the *alvará* of May 10, 1805, finally sealed the inculcation of Mello Freire's juridical thought in Coimbra University's legal curriculum. The four volumes of the *Institutiones*, together with a fifth volume containing the *Historiae*, were officially adopted as a student compendium.[9] Mello Freire's draft of a criminal code project, similarly confined to Latin, also became required reading for civil law students in 1805.

Mandatory for third- and fourth-year law students, as its flyleaf proclaimed, the student compendium offered Mello Freire's *oeuvre* as "synthetic" lessons that effectively replaced the formerly entrenched "analytic," or Thomistic, method used by the Jesuits and their post-1759 successors.[10] The latter method, deemed Aristotelian, focused rote attention on discrete *orde-nações*, Roman law, and the Glossators, ignoring the practical application of national law in the courts. It disdained a historical perspective on Portugal's legal evolution. In contrast, Mello Freire's synthetic method looked at law as a system and assumed that history was the key for understanding how its parts fit together. Brazil's first generation of imperial legislators partook of these developments in legal and political culture directly, because, until the early 1830s, they continued to be educated at Coimbra University, primarily in civil law.

Consequently, Lobão gave the Portuguese-speaking world a lasting vernacular distillation of Mello Freire's *Institutiones* that covered both public and private law.[11] He took as his task a set of vernacular notes annotating key passages of each book of the *Institutiones*, which were left excerpted verbatim in Latin. He restated Mello Freire's most important ideas in Portuguese or, alternatively, identified and discarded those rendered politically obsolete by the impact of the French Revolution. As the full title of the *Notas à Mello* confirmed, Lobão took as his model Philipp Friedrich Müller's juridical commentary on George Adam Struve. Known as the "little Struve," Müller's popular eighteenth-century reference text was consulted by lawyers and judges in the German-speaking lands, having been extrapolated from Struve's *Jurisprudentia Romano-Germanica Forensis* (1670). The latter had remained in print until 1771. Although its "enormous popularity" lay in how it excluded, "as far as possible . . . treatment of rules deriving from Roman law," Struve's *Jurisprudencia* nonetheless exerted appeal due to how it paid attention to Roman law. Doubtlessly, Lobão valued Müller's focus on both "living law" and legal procedures in the courts. The "little Struve" was said to be all that "many a lawyer needed for his practice."[12] In emulating the latter, the *Notas à Mello* offered a lawyer's guidance for consulting Mello Freire, but Lobão also furthered his own goal as a royal jurisconsult—to impose legal nationalism in the royal courts. The impassioned lawyer from Viseu, whom Coelho da Rocha subsequently described as Mello Freire's "emulation and censor," offered what amounted to an insider's manual for anyone practicing or consulting law.[13]

Brazil's first cohort of national legislators, consequently, found in Lobão an irreverent critic of Mello Freire who sought to correct the master from the vantage point of the courtroom. His sharp commentary, punctuated with authoritative Latin excerpts from the *Institutiones*, counseled readers that, in some cases, they would be better off "leaving aside these very old notions [*antiguidades*]," usually when Mello Freire's assertions upheld the society of estates. Instead, he advised, they would find advantage in "turning to practical and modern usage (which is all that concerns me for comment)."[14] Yet Lobão's "critical notes of practical usage" more frequently converged with Mello Freire than they diverged from his interpretations. He shared the Coimbra professor's commitment to modernizing Portugal's juridical foundation through an exaltation of positive national law—at the expense of both Roman and canon law. Like Mello Freire, he was a fervent regalist. Furthermore, Lobão peppered his glosses on Mello Freire with precise citations of Pombaline legislation and administrative rulings adopted during the long reign of D. Maria I, a feature especially recommending him to Brazilian legislators who consulted him as a handy reference tool.

The *Notas à Mello* guaranteed that legal nationalism would transcend the confines of an eighteenth-century political world. Unlike Mello Freire, whom he outlived by twenty years, Lobão lived through the French occupation of Portugal, a circumstance that shaped his political perspective in the *Notas à Mello*. The antagonism that he reserved for the nobility's legal privileges distinguished his views from those of Mello Freire, although his views were acquired before the French occupation of Portugal. However, Lobão did witness firsthand the French imposition of revolutionary goals in Portugal that abolished guilds, the inquisition, and many noble privileges. Therefore, his commentary took a different starting point than Mello Freire's *Institutiones*, that of a world changed by European revolution and, much closer to home, by the Spanish Liberal Cortés and Constitution of 1812.

Publication of the *Notas à Mello* was perfectly timed for Brazilian independence. Although Lobão died in 1817, the first of the three books comprising the *Notas à Mello* saw publication the following year. The pivotal Book 2, following Book 2 of the *Institutiones*, treating private law, proved the most avidly read. Finished in 1805, the manuscript went astray in the confusion of the French occupation of Portugal, to be returned to Lobão only in 1817. Book 2, together with Book 3 that extended the private law focus to the inheritance system, was published by 1824. As early as 1821, readers of the *Gazeta do Rio de Janeiro* found that Book 1 of the *Notas à Mello*, together with six of Lobão's important dissertations on private law—including one treating illegitimate offspring—could be purchased in bookstores in the Brazilian capital.[15] Certainly, some of the Brazilian delegates to the Lisbon Cortes of 1821–1822 carried Book 1 of the *Notas à Mello* on their homeward voyage. Otherwise, its availability in bookstores in Rio de Janeiro galvanized his popularity among a much wider readership no longer confined to Coimbra civil law doctors.

A prolific writer, Lobão died before he could publish either the *Notas à Mello* or perhaps half of his treatises and dissertations. Hence, the impact of his juridical commentary in both Portugal and Brazil did not really begin to be felt until the 1820s, when the corpus of his juridical work received systematic publication. Lobão's influence continued to be pivotal for three decades following independence, given the orthodoxy of legal nationalism in post-independence Brazil. His dissertations and treatises touched directly on topics politically relevant for Brazilian legislators, such as entail, the succession rights of illegitimate individuals, the procedures for conferring paternal recognition, and legal marriage, accounting for why he remained authoritative among jurists in imperial Brazil. The *Notas à Mello* continued to be published throughout the nineteenth century, with a fourth and final edition appearing as late as 1918.[16]

As the principal diffuser of a Luso-Brazilian legal tradition, Lobão's *Notas à Mello* bridged the gap between an eighteenth-century legal nationalism grounded in absolutism and the liberal constitutionalism that, in an Iberian context, supplanted the former between 1812 and 1822. Although Lobão pointed in the direction of liberalism, it would take a different Portuguese jurisconsult to anchor Mello Freire's legacy firmly on a foundation of liberal constitutionalism. Thanks to Manoel Borges Carneiro, and, secondarily, his contemporary, João Homem Corrêa Telles, legal nationalism in Portugal was stamped as a thoroughly modern tradition for a nineteenth-century context. Borges Carneiro proved to be the jurist who, above all others, accommodated Pombaline legal culture to the Pyrrhic triumph of Portuguese liberalism in the first half of the 1820s. Already a royal jurisconsult when his political oratory dazzled fellow delegates to the Lisbon Cortes, he produced a refined synthesis of the basic tenets of legal nationalism that could be read against Portugal's adoption of the short-lived liberal Constitution of 1822.

The first book of Borges Carneiro's *Direito civil de Portugal* was published in two parts, between 1826 and 1828, in the aftermath of the death of D. João VI. That occasion presented the opportunity for Brazil's emperor, D. Pedro I, to present Portugal with a new, liberal constitution. The two years that witnessed publication of Borges Carneiro's version of what amounted to a set of Institutes were the years when Brazil's Parliament reopened and the Chamber of Deputies evolved into a liberal-dominated body. Borges Carneiro's juridical masterpiece was never completed, due to his political martyrdom under the anti-liberal regime of D. Miguel, the brother of Brazil's first emperor. He was arrested and imprisoned in 1828, soon after publication of the first two volumes of his famous legal commentary. He had dedicated them in true liberal style to "D. Pedro IV," that is, to D. Pedro I of Brazil, whom the flyleaf flattered as "father of the *patria*" and identified as "emperor and king" of Portugal—although officially Pedro assumed the throne only for five days.

Borges Carneiro died in prison, of cholera, in 1833, a mere twenty days before he would have been liberated by Pedro's peninsular revolution. However, all 3 tomes of Book 1 of *Direito civil*, written in two parts, or volumes, and covering the private law of persons, became available by 1828. Until 1835, the *Direito civil do Portugal* was accepted in both Brazil and Portugal as the most authoritative juridical reference work to provide a constitutional perspective on Mello Freire's legal nationalism.[17]

Borges Carneiro's style was thoroughly modern, displaying an impressive erudition that took into account the post-1822 modification of Portugal's absolutist polity. He relied fundamentally on Lobão's *Notas à Mello* for interpreting Mello Freire's thought, with the result that his work offered a "continuous" reading of Mello Freire from the 1780s through the 1820s. He tersely explained legal changes against the backdrop of Portugal's short-lived, 1822 Constitution, interpretively noting the abolition of the machinery of absolutism. Above all, he reiterated that the sovereign's role as "the Legislator" was an attribute that Portugal's first Constitution had transferred to a newly constituted Cortes, one no longer reflecting separate estates. Borges Carneiro explicitly acknowledged his enormous debt to Mello Freire and Lobão, by asserting the enduring relevance of legal nationalism at the outset of Book 1, where he explained that one of its purposes was "to show the difference between *direito pátrio* and Roman law."[18] He also reminded readers that the 1769 Law of Right Reason remained the cornerstone of a national legal tradition that had recently acquired the new foundation of liberal constitutionalism.

José Homem Corrêa Telles was the other influential Portuguese jurist whose legal commentary guided Brazilians in the absence of any that addressed their own law. Like Borges Carneiro, who was slightly his junior, he had been a representative to the Lisbon Cortes and an enthusiastic proponent of legal nationalism. Corrêa Telles became Portugal's senior jurisconsult and published many treatises over a span of nearly forty years. One of the earliest was his definitive exegesis of the 1769 Law of Right Reason. His *Critical Commentary on the Law of Right Reason* appeared in 1824, the same year that Brazil adopted a Constitution, and more than half a century after Pombal promulgated the famous law. Fortuitously, Corrêa Telles called attention to the relevance of legal nationalism for the new era of liberalism. However, he also deplored Portugal's lack of a civil code, giving him reason to recommend limited reliance on Roman law. Observing that he "was somewhat more emphatic on Roman law's [utility] than the Law Doctors" of the eighteenth-century, he broke rank with them by asserting, "We cannot deny a degree of extrinsic authority to it."[19]

Noting that Coimbra University's New Statutes prescribed Roman law as a subsidiary source, when "the laws of the realm are absent and when it cannot be shown that Roman laws are opposed to the latter, or to the law of civilized nations that is natural, political, economic, mercantile, or maritime," Corrêa Telles made a more compelling case for the value of Roman law than his iconoclastic predecessors:

Thus, as long as we will not have codes that are less imperfect than the *Ordenações*, which in innumerable places fail to determine what is necessary, ordering that Common Law be observed, we cannot, as do the French, deprive Roman law of everything, placing ourselves under penalty of being without any law in many areas and leaving us to combat arbitrariness. Today, even in France, it is licit to invoke Roman law, not as law, but as [the subsidiary source of] written reason—or, as some say, *non ratione imperii se rationis imperio*.[20]

He thus isolated the irony in legal nationalism, one that in Brazil would become so much more glaring as the nineteenth century progressed: Postponement of a civil code merely renewed the utility of Roman law.

Corrêa Telles' *Commentario critico* on the Law of Right Reason confirmed that the pivotal concepts associated with legal nationalism would continue to remain relevant for Brazil's first cohort of national legislators. Yet he became better and enduringly known to Brazilians for his notarial manual, which first saw publication in 1819. Together with Gouvêa Pinto's 1813 classic treatise on wills, the *Manual do tabellião* was for sale in Rio de Janeiro's bookshops by 1821. It went through four editions in Portugal by 1870. Although it became the standard reference volume employed by Brazil's notaries for the remainder of the century, not until the 1860s was an edition of Corrêa Telles' *Manual do tabellião* produced that adapted it to Brazilian law and legal practice.[21]

The *Digesto portuguêz*, which Corrêa Telles published in 1835, months before the definitive collapse of the anti-liberal forces in Portugal, soon supplanted Lobão and Borges Carneiro as the standard juridical authority in both Portugal and Brazil. The author of the *Digesto* modestly disavowed any juridical innovation, assuring his readers that he had been guided either by "the laws and the customs of the Nation," the very sources to which the Lisbon "Cortes had concurred that new law codes should conform," or by "the old Law Doctors who upheld them." Confessing that he did "not want to appear less versed in jurisprudence," he told his readers that he "had invoked the help of the old Law Doctors, who now have passed away, on behalf of my opinions." The book's subtitle paid homage to Mello Freire and Lobão by emphasizing precisely the sources privileged by those "old doctors": "A Treatise of Civil Obligations Accommodated to the Laws and the Customs of the Portuguese Nation."[22]

Mediated by Lobão's *Notas à Mello* and adapted to an era of liberalism by Borges Carneiro and Corrêa Telles, Mello Freire's systematic reworking of Portuguese law defined the foundation for legal study in Brazil's new faculties of law, from the late 1820s through the 1850s. Following the Law of August 11, 1827, establishing law faculties in Olinda and São Paulo, a curriculum for a five-year program of study leading to the degrees of bachelor and doctor of law was left to the determination of the respective law professoriates. The same law prescribed an interim reliance on statutes for those law faculties, drafted in 1826 by Sen. Luis José de Carvalho Mello, viscount of Cachoeira. A Coimbra law graduate, Cachoeira included in his provisional statutes a curriculum that remained formative for three decades. It demonstrated Mello Freire's overriding pedagogical influence.

The first two years of study were dedicated to acquiring a theoretical foundation, especially in natural law and the law of nations, complemented by the study of Roman law. Roman law continued to be accepted for study as the basis of not only the *Ordenações* but also western Europe's civil codes. However, the curriculum subjected it to vigorous historical periodization, à la Mello Freire, precisely in order to isolate "late imperial law," the source of so many "superstitious" notions. Also following Mello Freire's emphasis, Roman law was to be taken as "always subsidiary and doctrinal, never possessing extrinsic authority, as the authors of the Statutes of Coimbra University and the Law of August 18, 1769, observe." Professors were "to accentuate what in Roman law were the customs of a people, founded on right reason." Initially, the curriculum indicated Heineccius' student compendium, that "pointed out in relevant places what was German law," but what also mattered was "the application of Roman law to that practiced in the courts," implying procedural consequences. In the third year of study, the practical received emphasis, Mello Freire being prescribed as "the principal guide for studying public, private, and criminal law." Where ecclesiastical law mattered, he would be "helped by Gameiro, Fleury, and Boehmer." In the fourth year, when attention again turned to criminal law, together with the law of obligations and actions, explication of *direito pátrio* would be uppermost. Mello Freire, Stryk, Caminha, and Bentham, among others, were required reading. Political economy also figured as a fourth-year subject, when the works of J. B. Say, Godwin, Ricard, Malthus, and Smith were required reading.[23]

The fifth and final year offered a practicum, with students drawing up indictments and functioning as lawyers, judges, and clerks, in order to acquire firsthand experience in the courts. Clovis Bevilaqua acknowledged that, although the pairing of formal study and practical experience made "an excellent impression," there were "defects" in their proportionate emphases, not to mention "confusion" produced by the "state of legal science itself." By the latter, he implied no less than what in retrospect was acknowledged as the great shortcoming of the school of *direito pátrio*, the excessive emphasis on the practical context of the courtroom, to the neglect of a rigorous theoretical foundation in Roman law. For that matter, curriculum in the 1830s evinced a marginal role for the French Civil Code that had been transforming European civil law since 1807. Analysis of Roman law also stressed the latter's subordinate application in the courtroom where national positive law remained preeminent. Legal determination was to rest on law derived from either the *Ordenações Filipinas* or statutes.[24] Although Brazil adopted criminal and criminal procedural codes in 1830 and 1831, the country remained bereft of analogous codes for civil law until the twentieth century. The legal curriculum, by carefully restricting the influence of Roman law, and precisely at the moment of Brazil's national formation, significantly dismissed the national project of elaborating private law. Given that a civil code would fail to materialize, the private law of both the family and the inheritance system would have to be made piecemeal. The legal training of law students, furthermore, ill equipped them to innovate where private law was silent, thanks to the restrictions placed on the role of Roman law by the celebrated Law of August 18, 1769.

A dearth of textbooks addressing Brazilian law inspired Professor Francisco Pereira Freire to translate Mello Freire's *De jure personarum*, Book 2 of the *Institutiones*, into Portuguese. Published in 1834, his translation followed the format of Lobão's *Notas à Mello*, reproducing key portions of Mello Freire's Latin text, but offering a vernacular juridical commentary adapted to the post-1831 context of Brazil's Regency era. This meant that Pereira Freire had to distill sections of Mello Freire and Lobão relevant to Brazilian law in force and to discard what no longer applied. The author, a Portuguese expatriate who taught at the Olinda Law Faculty and held an imperial judgeship, explained to readers that he had available only two up-to-date legal commentaries for reference, those authored by Lobão and Borges Carneiro. In noting that each "lacked sufficient illustrations or precision for pedagogical purposes," Pereira Freire alluded to his motive for undertaking the translation—to provide his students with a treatise exclusively devoted to private law.[25] Yet, just as significantly, he implied the waning popularity of Latin as a language for study, notwithstanding the Olinda Law Faculty Library's acquisition of two copies of a second edition of Mello Freire's *Institutiones*, published in 1815 and 1827–1829. As a result of Pereira Freire's translation, Mello Freire's pivotal Book 2 of the *Institutiones* became available to

Brazilian students and jurists in a vernacular edition. Its value increased once the adoption of a civil code looked remote. The other three books remained confined to Latin and less influential, for public law in Brazil now proceeded from a new source: the 1824 Constitution. Alternatively, students could read Lobão's *Notas à Mello* to acquire familiarity in the vernacular with Books 1, 3, and 4 of the *Institutiones*.

Only after 1850 would the template of Mello Freire's *Institutiones juris civilis lusitani* metamorphosize into a commentary authored by a Brazilian jurist. Meanwhile, Brazilians had to make do with those written by Portuguese jurists who were faithful to Mello Freire's legacy, including the format of his Institutes. One of the Portuguese commentaries that Brazilians most frequently consulted was Antonio Ribeiro Liz Teixeira's *Curso de direito civil portuguêz*, published in Coimbra in 1845. Its title page proclaimed, furthermore, that the book faithfully parsed "the Institutes of Sr. Paschoal José de Mello Freire."[26] For the first twenty-five years after independence, Brazilian jurists, legislators, judges, notaries, and law students were bereft of any authoritative legal commentary addressing their nation's juridical identity or legal evolution. Until 1851, they relied solely on juridical authorities who were Portuguese: "We were . . . a Peninsular extension in the land of the New World. We still did not possess a real juridical culture."[27]

The absence of a civil code, as well as legal commentaries addressing Brazilian law, drove Minister of Justice Eusebio de Queiroz to give consideration to a desperate measure in 1851. He proposed that the government adopt as a national juridical standard—a substitute for a civil code—Corrêa Telles' *Digesto portuguêz*. Adapted to Brazilian legal practice, he argued, the *Digesto* would possess the advantage of offering the most comprehensive and authoritative synthesis of Portuguese national law available. Since publication in 1835, the *Digesto* had been updated and revised by the author for two succeeding editions.[28]

Although Corrêa Telles' *Digesto* possessed the attraction of having been published just as liberalism was about to triumph in Portugal, Brazilian legislators did not adopt it as a substitute for a civil code. The recently established Brazilian Institute of Lawyers, whose founder and president was the eminent Bahian jurist Augusto Teixeira de Freitas, opposed the idea, pronouncing the *Digesto* incapable of adaptation to Brazil's "social and economic conditions and peculiarities."[29] Instead, Teixeira de Freitas' *Consolidação das leis civis* (1857), especially when revised, served the same purpose for Brazilian jurists and judges as the *Digesto* analogously served for the Portuguese, who lacked a civil code until 1867. In spite of Parliament's refusal to accept Teixeira de Freitas' pending design of what incorporated both a civil and a commercial code project for Brazil—his *Codigo civil: Esboço* (1860–1865)—the latter became accepted as the companion reference to the *Consolidação das leis civis*. Until 1916, the *Esboço* was consulted along the same lines as a civil code.

Meanwhile, Brazilian jurists began emulating the Portuguese commentators to Mello Freire's *Institutiones*. The first to adopt the model, in 1851, was Lourenço Trigo de Loureiro, a professor at the Olinda Law Faculty since 1833. His title, inspired by Lobão's template, was the first to proclaim "*Instituições do direito civil brasileiro*." The title page confirmed the source of these first *Brazilian* institutes. They were "Extracted from the *Instituições de direito civil lusitano* of Paschoal José de Mello Freire." What made Trigo de Loureiro's Institutes special was that they paid attention to only "the parts [of Mello Freire] compatible with the institutes of our city [Recife] and the substance of Brazilian law."[30]

What mattered ideologically in the process of Brazil's early national formation, one crystallized in the 1850s, was legislators' consistent reliance on a juridical culture whose roots lay in Portugal and reached to Pombal's promotion of legal nationalism. For the first decades after independence, legal nationalism tied several post-1805 generations of law school graduates to a senior generation of Brazilian legislators educated at Coimbra before 1805. Thanks to the foundation of law faculties in Brazil, post-independence generations of legislators continued to be inculcated with legal nationalism. The regalism of Brazil's first emperor, as well as the liberal legislators who predominated in the Regency that governed Brazil between 1831 and 1840, sustained that cultural legacy and conveyed it to the politicians who would become prominent during the Second Empire (1850–1889). Brazilianized legal commentaries eventually perpetuated Mello Freire's legacy, authoritatively drawing on Lobão, Borges Carneiro, Corrêa Telles, Liz Teixeira, and yet another Portuguese jurist, Coelho da Rocha. They "filled the gap" in the absence of a civil code, mediating between Portugal's colonial legal tradition and Brazilian statutory law that immediately modified the *Ordenações Filipinas*. Eventually, by the 1860s, the swing of the pendulum in the direction of Roman law, not to mention the impact of a new ideology—positivism—introduced a countermovement to legal nationalism that would gradually diminish its influence during the Mature Empire (1870–1889).

For our purposes, the continuity of a Pombaline legal tradition in post-independence Brazil nourished the arrival of historical liberalism in the new nation. The efforts of Brazil's first generation of liberals to reform family and inheritance law, consequently, deserve to be appreciated within a fundamentally Pombaline context. Whether attempting to mitigate the stain of bastardy, to extend rights in succession to spurious offspring, or to promote civil marriage, Brazil's liberal legislators drew on legal nationalism as well as the unorthodox canonical interpretations of Paschoal José de Mello Freire as they became available in the vernacular during the 1820s and 1830s. When they did not do so directly, in terms of several translations of Book 2 of the *Institutiones*, then they frequently invoked those who were his standard bearers—Lobão, Manoel Borges Carneiro, and José Homem Corrêa Telles. The impressive endurance of *direito pátrio* as a Luso-Brazilian legal tradition also explained the initial disinclination of Brazil's early legislators to borrow, in the manner of their Spanish American neighbors, from the innovative French Civil Code, just as it determined their reluctance to acknowledge the jurisprudential utility of Roman civil law. This is to say that Napoleon's invasion of Portugal in 1807 proved as pivotal for Brazil's legal evolution as it did for the colony's future political identity. The consequent flight of the Portuguese court from Lisbon to Rio de Janeiro perpetuated the institution of monarchy for the newly independent colony of Brazil in 1822, but it just as effectively stamped the new nation with an eighteenth-century legal tradition that proved remarkably receptive to challenging legal distinctions based on individual quality of birth or membership in the society of estates.

Reference Matter

Abbreviations

COLLECTIONS OF LAWS AND PARLIAMENTARY DEBATES

AS *Anais do Senado do Imperio Brasileiro, 1826–1847*
CLIB *Collecção das leis do Imperio do Brasil 1808–1889*
CLP *Collecção da legislaçao portuguesa 1750–1820*, Antonio Delgado da Silva, Compiler

STANDARD DESIGNATIONS FOR LAWS, EXECUTIVE ORDERS, JUDICIAL
CLARIFICATIONS OR RULINGS CARRYING THE FORCE OF LAW

Al. *Alvará* (plural: *Als.*)*
Ass. *Assento*
Av. *Aviso*
Dec. *Decreto*
Prov. *Provisão*
Reg. *Regimento*
Regul. *Regulamento*
Res. *Resolução*

COMPONENT PARTS OF LEGAL COMMENTARIES OR THE ORDENAÇÕES
DO REINO (i.e., the *Ord. Filipinas*, *Ord. Manuelinas*, and *Ord. Afonsinas*)

L. *Livro* (Book)
Pte. *Parte* (Part, synonymous with "*Livro*")
v. *Volume* or *Tomo* (Volume or Tome)
Cap. *Capítulo* (Chapter)
T. *Título* (Title)
§ *Seção* (Section)
§§ *Seções* (Sections)
Art. *Artigo* (Article)
Par. *Parágrafo* (Paragraph)
N. *Número* or *Item* (Number or Item)
n Nota (Note)

*"Alvará" was used interchangeably with "law" (*lei*) until independence (1822). After independence, certain legal commentators retroactively converted "*alvará*" to "decree" (*dec.*), meaning "law."

ARCHIVAL DESIGNATIONS

AN   Arquivo Nacional (Rio de Janeiro)
Cxa.   *Caixa* (Box)
Pac.   *Pacote* (Package)
Doc.   *Documento* (Document)

Notes

PREFACE

1. Blackstone, *Commentaries* (1838), 1:374–75. Blackstone's strongest defense of English bastardy was leveled against legitimization by subsequent marriage in the civil law tradition. His defense of English law, distinguishing bastardy according to whether parents were either noble or commoner, finds analogous emphasis in this book for eighteenth-century Portugal.

2. In the United States, initially, the English common law rule denying legitimization by subsequent marriage was widely adopted. However, late eighteenth-century Virginia set the example of adhering to the civil (canon) law principle of legitimization by subsequent marriage that more states adopted in the nineteenth century. *Bracton on the Laws of England*, 1:635.

3. See O'Neill, Chap. 5 of *Social Inequality* (reviewing Livi Bacci's *A Century of Portuguese Fertility*, esp. p. 332); and Brettell, *Men Who Migrate*, pp. 52–58; Hajnal, "European Marriage Patterns," pp. 100–143, and "Two Kinds of Household Systems," p. 66; Laslett, "Family and Household," p. 531n15; and Kertzer and Brettell, "Advances in Family History," pp. 5–120.

4. "Nota preliminar" to *Dir. successões*, pp. 7–8.

5. Goody, *Family and Marriage*, pp. 244–45. Goody refers to the transmission of property between generations within a bilateral (cognatic) system of inheritance, i.e., where wealth passes to both sons and daughters.

6. Coelho da Rocha, *Ensaio*, p. 228.

7. See Lewin, "Natural and Spurious Offspring," pp. 379–89.

8. See Casey and Chacón Jiménez, eds., *Familia, España mediterránea*, especially Gacto's "El grupo familiar," pp. 36–64.

9. See Twinam, *Public Lives*.

10. Laslett, Oosterveen, and Smith (eds.) have perceived Europe, together with its "daughter societies" in the New World, as sharing a common understanding of bastardy, an assumption this book rejects. Laslett, Preface to *Bastardy*, p. 5. On the mistaken assumption that concubinage had ceased to be a significant institution in Europe during medieval times, see Goody, *Family and Marriage*, pp. 41 and 76; and Lewin, "Natural and Spurious Offspring," pp. 379–89.

LANGUAGE, ORTHOGRAPHY, AND NAMES

1. *Family and Marriage*, p. 7.

2. *Subsídios direito pátrio*, 4:37. Direct reference herein to laws applying in Brazil's colonial period draw on Delgado da Silva's comprehensive, nine-volume compilation spanning 1750–1820: *Collecção da legislação portugueza desde a ultima compilação das Ordenações*, abbreviated herein as "*CLP.*" Laws cited for imperial Brazil have been drawn from the government's overlapping *Collecção das leis do Imperio do Brasil de [year]*, whose title varies, abbreviated herein as *CLIB*. In addition, the verbatim texts of both colonial and imperial laws can be found in Candido Mendes' appendices to each book of the *Ordenações Filipinas*, or in legal commentaries.

3. The following abbreviations denoting the divisions of the Philipine Code are used in notes throughout this book: *Ord.* (*Ordenações*), L. (*Livro*), T. (*Título*), § (*Seção*), Art. (*Artigo*), and N. (*Número* or *Item*) or Par. (*Parágrafo*). References to "Candido Mendes, *Ord.*," followed only by page and/or footnote numbers, refer solely to Candido Mendes' annotative comments interpreting the *Ordenações*, esp. with regard to eighteenth- and nineteenth-century legal commentaries. Otherwise, direct references to the text of the *Ordenações Filipinas* are abbreviated "*Ord. Filipinas.*"

INTRODUCTION

1. Gouvêa Pinto, *Trat. testamentos*, Cap.3 (p. 10).

2. Among the most influential pioneering works are Ramos, "Marriage Vila Rica"; idem, "City and Country"; Nizza da Silva, *Sistema casamento*, esp. Chap. 6; idem, "Divorce Colonial Brazil"; Mesquita Samara, "O dote"; idem, "Família sociedade paulista"; idem, "Família, divórcio, partilha"; Mattoso, *Família Bahia*; Borges, *Family Bahia*; Nazzari, *Dowry*; Metcalf, *Family and Frontier*. Three anthropological works on Portuguese inheritance strategies are directly relevant for Brazil: O'Neill, *Social Inequality*; Brettell, *Men Who Migrate*; and Brandão, "Land, Inheritance, Family." See also Behar and Frye, "Property, Progeny."

3. On the intersection of ecclesiastical and civil law, see Vainfas, "Condenação adultérios"; Lewcowicz, "Fragilidade celibato"; Nizza da Silva, Chap. 4 of *Sistema casamento*; Vainfas, "Teia da intriga"; Mott, *Pecados*; Mello e Souza, *Desclassificados*; and Nazzari, "Concubinage."

4. Venâncio, *Ilegitimidade e concubinato*; Londoño, *Concubinato y iglesia*; Zenha, "Casamento e ilegitimidade"; Soihet, "Proibido ser mãe"; Novinsky, "Heresia, mulher, sexualidade"; O'Neill, *Jornaleiras*; Kuznesof, "Sexual Politics"; Nazzari, "Questionable Foundlings"; Marcílio, *Criança abandonada*; and Venâncio, *Famílias abandonadas*.

5. Exceptions include Moura's pathbreaking *Herdeiros da terra* and Paiva da Costa's "Herança." See also Nizza da Silva, "Legislação pombalina"; Ribeiro da Silva, "Marginais"; and Flusche's analysis of a major inheritance archive of the Spanish American *Juzgado de Beines de Difuntos, Tribunal Posthumous Estates*.

6. Lewin, "Natural and Spurious Children," pp. 354–56. NOTE: Some of the following historiographical remarks, together with portions of the explanation of inheritance as a legal system found in Chap. 1, first appeared in my "Natural and Spurious Children." However, that article's treatment of the legal position of natural and

spurious offspring has been somewhat revised, not to mention greatly enlarged, for Chaps. 2–4, especially where a parent's nobility mattered for heirship.

7. Glendon, Gordon, and Osakwe, *Comparative Traditions*, pp. 13, 16.

8. Moreira Alves, "Panorama," p. 87. The *Liber Judicorum* is better known in English as Fernando II's Spanish vernacular code: the *Fuero Juzgo.* Ibid., p. 87n3. Karst and Rosenn, *Law and Development*, pp. 20–21.

9. Watson, *Roman Law*, p. 85; Glendon, Gordon, and Osakwe, *Comparative Traditions*, p. 16.

10. Glendon, Gordon, and Osakwe, *Comparative Traditions*, p. 21.

11. Ibid.

12. Watson, *Roman Law*, p. 21.

13. MacDonald, "Alfonso's Reform," pp. 180–81; Merryman and Clark, *Comparative Law*, p. 117. On the *Siete Partidas*, see ibid., pp. 116–33.

14. Merryman and Clark, *Comparative Law*, pp. 116–18.

15. Watson, *Roman Law*, p. 91.

16. Karst and Rosenn, *Law and Latin America*, pp. 16–27; Moreira Alves, "Panorama," p. 89.

17. Gomes B. Câmara, *Subsídios direito pátrio*, 3:56–59, 65–69. This author rejects the conventional view, traceable to Paschoal José de Mello Freire, that exaggerates the early reception of Roman law in Portugal—an interpretation intended to undercut the authority of canon law in national legal development. Cf. Livermore, *New History*, pp. 34–85.

18. Gomes B. Câmara, *Subsídios direito pátrio*, 3:65–66, 68n28.

19. Mestre João das Regras (João Fernandes de Aregas) was also known as João ex-Regulus and de Legibus. Ibid., 3:69, 69n31. Candido Mendes, *Aux. juridico*, p. 771n.

20. Gomes B. Câmara, *Subsídios direito pátrio*, 3:61–62, 70. Candido Mendes, *Ord.*, p. xx. A list of all the royal jurisconsults appears in idem, *Aux. juridico*, pp. 771–73.

21. Evidence for the intellectual influence of D. João I on the *Ord. Afonsinas* is premature: his famous address to the Portuguese Cortes of 1385, delivered on the traditional date ascribed to the centralization of the monarchy. Gomes B. Câmara, *Subsídios direito pátrio*, 3:69n31–70.

22. Bevilaqua, *Dir. successões*, pp. 96–97, 99. The assimilation of Germanic vs. Roman (including classical) legal principles by the *Ordenações do Reino* is discussed ibid., pp. 95–118. See also Coelho da Rocha, *Inst. dir. civ. port.*, v.1, Sec.4, Cap.2, §335 (pp. 228–29).

23. Gomes B. Câmara, *Subsídios direito pátrio*, 3:100; Moreira Alves, "Panorama," p. 88.

24. The *Ord. Affonsinas* were published in 1787–1792. Candido Mendes, introduction to *Ord.*, p. xx.

25. Watson, *Roman Law*, p. 89. Moreira Alves, "Panorama," pp. 88–89.

26. Oliveira Marques, *Lusitania to Empire*, pp. 187–88; Moreira Alves, "Panorama," pp. 89–90; Watson, *Roman Law*, p. 91.

27. Watson, *Roman Law*, p. 156.

28. Moreira Alves, "Panorama," pp. 88–89. Neither the *Ord. Manuelinas* nor the succeeding *Ord. Filipinas* defined or spelled out the rules to determine right reason. Ibid., p. 89n4.

29. Candido Mendes, introduction to *Ord.*, pp. xxii, xxvi; Livermore, *New History*, p. 132.

30. Karst and Rosenn, *Law and Latin America*, p. 26.

31. Goody, *Family and Marriage*, pp. 136–39, 144.

32. Merryman and Clark, *Comparative Law*, pp. 72–74; Moreira Alves, "Panorama," p. 88.

33. Livermore, *New History*, pp. 151–52, 171. *Al.* of 12 Sept. 1564 and *cédula real* of 12 July 1565; cited in Candido Mendes, *Dir. civil ecclesiastico*, 2:xiii.

34. Candido Mendes, introduction to *Ord.*, p. xxiii.

35. Ibid.

36. Ibid.; Moreira Alves, "Panorama," p. 88. The principal Portuguese authors were Paulo Affonso and Pedro Barbosa, both high crown judges of the Desembargo do Paço, together with jurists Damião Aguiar and Jorge Cabedo. Candido Mendes, introduction to *Ord.*, p. xxii–iv (citing Mello Freire's *Hist. juris civ. port.*) and xxvi; Borges Carneiro, *Dir. civil Port.*, L.1, v. 1, Intro, Pt.1 (pp. 2(b)–3).

37. Introduction to *Ord.*, p. vii.

CHAPTER 1

1. "Nota preliminar," pp. 7–8.

2. Goody, *Family and Marriage*, p. 21.

3. *Ord. Filipinas*, L.4, Ts.94,96; Bevilaqua, *Dir. successões*, Pte.2, Cap.3, §32 (p. 98).

4. Although late colonial positive law might refer to canonical degrees in crown statutes treating marriage, strictly speaking, royal law reckoned degrees of kinship according to Roman, or civil, law. Lineal degrees were reckoned by counting each generation as one degree: a child and parent were first-degree lineals. Collateral degrees were reckoned by counting generations upward to a common ancestor and then downward to the individual to whom kinship was reckoned. Thus EGO's uncle was a third-degree collateral and siblings were second-degree collaterals. Canon law, however, reckoned kinship only by counting upward to a common ancestor, always taking the larger number of generations separating the reckoned individuals. Thus EGO's uncle was a second-degree collateral and his brother a first-degree collateral. Bevilaqua, *Dir. successões*, Pte.2, Cap.3, §31 (p. 92); idem, *Dir. familia*, Cap.3, §12 (p. 64).

5. Idem, *Dir. successões*, Pte.2, Cap.1, §28 (pp. 76–79).

6. Ibid., Pte.1, Cap.1, §15 (p. 39).

7. Ibid., Pte.2, Cap.1, §28 (pp. 78–79).

8. Candido Mendes, *Ord.*, p. 942n1. On a slave's incapacity to make a will, see Gouvêa Pinto, *Trat. testamentos*, Caps. 10,25 (pp. 51–52, 96). Cf. Mattoso, *Testamentos escravos*. Luso-Brazilian law followed classical Roman law, but, ironically and notably, following legal nationalism, the 1832 high court ruling reflected failure to incorporate the late imperial modification adopted under Justinian: "appointment of the heir [who was a slave] would in itself act as a gift of liberty." Watson, *Roman Law*, pp. 78–79.

9. *Av.* No. 16, 13 Feb. 1850, Joaquim José Rodrigues Torres replying to the *ofício* of the Treasury, Piauí, 4 Dec. 1849, *CLIB 1850*, pp. 15–16.

10. Law No. 2040 of 28 Sept. 1871, Art.4 and §1, in Silva Mafra, *Pomptuario*, pp. 192–93. Teixeira de Freitas, *Trat. testamentos Gouvêa Pinto*, Cap.1, §202, Art.1n342 (p. 286).

11. "Inheritance" (*herança*) and "heirs" (*herdeiros*) were used interchangeably with "succession" and "successors" in Portuguese legal commentaries, notwithstanding that inheritance connoted other forms of devolution than succession. Thus, the verb *"herder"* meant "to succeed" as well as "to inherit." Bevilaqua, *Dir. successões*, Pte.1, Cap.1, §4 (p. 17).

12. Davidson, "Inheritance Roman Law," p. 86. However, the ranking of surviving spouses as successors behind collateral relatives followed a Roman rule adopted in the fourteenth century. Ibid., p. 87.

13. Bevilaqua, *Dir. successões*, Pte.1, Cap.2, §10 (pp. 28–29).

14. Ibid., §11 (pp. 30–31).

15. Drawing on Mourton, Bevilaqua concluded that *saisine* (*seisen*) passed from Germanic law into "the customs of diverse nations." Ibid., §10 (p. 28).

16. Ibid. The key change tersely imposed by the Law of 9 Nov. 1754 was as follows: "A dita posse Civil terá todos os effeitos de posse natural, sem que seja necessario, que esta se tome; e havendo quem pretenda ter acção aos sobreditos bens, a poderá deduzir sobre a propriedade e pelos meios competentes. . . ." *CLP*, 1:342–43.

17. Bevilaqua, *Dir. successões*, Pte.1, Cap.2, §10 (p. 28–29, 28n3), citing *regs.* of 27 June 1845, 23 Nov. 1853, and 15 June 1859. See esp. the latter, part of *Dec.* No. 2.433 of the same date, Arts. 3–5, regarding collateral heirs not well known or distant and illegitimate children of contested eligibility: *CLIB 1859*, pp. 436–37.

18. Bert Barickman, communication to the author of June 1997. He found *"tornas"* used in the *partilhas* of eighteenth-century Bahian sugar mill owners, where certain heirs sought to keep land and grinding mills together by buying portions of their co-heirs.

19. *Dec.* No. 156, 28 Apr. 1842, Art.7, *CLIB 1842*, p. 221.

20. *CLIB 1809*, p. 85.

21. *Res.* No. 18 of 2 June 1819, Min. do Reino to Con. da Fazenda, *CLIB [Indice Decisões] 1819*, p. 13.

22. The standard clarification of the *res.* of 2 June 1819 was the Imperial Treasurer's order to the Inspector of the Treasury in the Province of Maranhão, 19 Dec. 1839, reiterating that "testamentary" successors, when not paternally recognized by notarized affidavit or, after 1828, legitimized by a judge, had to pay the inheritance tax. *CLIB 1839*, p. 307.

23. Surviving spouses had no place in *ab intestato* succession until the reign of Pedro I (1357–1367), when Roman law was employed to call them to *ab intestato* succession after all descendants, ascendants, and collateral heirs to the tenth degree. *Ord. Filipinas*, L.4, T.92&94; *Ord. Afonsinas*, L.5, T.95.

24. *Dir. successões*, Pte.1, Cap.2, §10 (p. 30).

25. On the disappearance of dower in England, see Staves, Chap. 2 of *Married Women's Property*; on widows in New England, see Ditz, *Property and Kinship*, p. 125.

26. See Lafayette, *Dir. familia*, Sec.1, Cap.1, §5; Sec.2, Cap.2, §§92–95 (pp. 7–8, 183–87, respectively).

27. Ibid.; Ditz, *Property and Kinship*, p. 125.

28. Bevilaqua, *Dir. familia*, Cap.7, §55 (p. 259).

29. Ibid. (citing Coelho da Rocha, *Inst. dir. civ. port.*, vol. 1, Note M, pp. 303–4).

30. Bevilaqua, *Dir. successões*, Pte.1, Cap.1, §8 (p. 22); Gouvêa Pinto, *Trat. testamentos*, Cap.4 (p. 11).

31. Although exclusively implying a noble father, this *ordenação* was interpreted as applying to both commoners and nobles, as well as to mothers and fathers. Candido Mendes, *Ord.*, p. 943n1&n5.

32. Law of 31 Jan. 1775, elaborating Pars. 3, 6&7 of the Law of 9 Sept. 1769. *CLP*, 4:6–8 & 3:419–30, esp. 427, respectively. The 1769 law regulated the use of wills for universal heirship and bequests from the *terça*. It restored some opportunity to leave patrimony to the church's charitable institutions in assigning bequests from the *terça*.

33. Teixeira de Freitas' historical retrospective of universal heirship, reaching to Pombal's era, appears in his annotated edition of Gouvêa Pinto: *Trat. testamentos Gouvêa Pinto*, T.2, Cap.1, §209 (pp. 301–5). The plural for "universal heir" was "co-heirs."

34. Due to the Philippine Code's "enigmatic" silence on adoption, Portuguese jurists resorted to Roman law to fill in the gap, using adrogation (*adrogação*), a device applying to adults. It had to be approved by the Tribunal of the Mesa do Desembargo do Paço. Commonly, couples lacking legitimate children resorted to nominating a foster child as a universal heir (*Ord.*, L.4, T.92, §1). The Law of 15 Dec. 1860 was the first to address adoption, followed by the Law of 31 Mar. 1874, conferring full *ab intestato* rights on adopted children vis-à-vis their adopted parents and retaining the same rights vis-à-vis biological parents. Bevilaqua, *Dir. successões*, Pte.2, Cap.5, §140 (pp. 126–27).

35. I am very grateful to Kathleen Higgins for permitting me to use this example and the two below, drawn from the full texts of Sabará wills, part of her primary research for *"Licentious Liberty."* E-mail communications of 7–8, 10 July 1997. NOTE: Legal commentaries always capitalized *"Alma,"* treating it as the given name of the *"herdeira"* (heir) to the *legítima*. *"Alma"* should not be confused with dispositions from the *terça* known as *"bens da alma,"* the customary payment for masses said for the decedent's soul.

36. Will of Francisco Gonçalves Pinheiro, 24 Mar. 1719. "Declaro e instituo por minha herdeira universal de tudo o que depois de pagos digo depois de pagas minhas dividas e compridos meus legados restar de minha fazenda a minha alma . . . ." Ibid. NOTE: In translating this extract and those below, I have inserted punctuation and rendered syntax less ambiguous.

37. Following the *al.* of 20 May 1769, the omnibus Law of 9 Sept. 1769 (§21) specifically identified "the *Alma*" as incapable of succeeding in universal heirship. *CLP*, 3:481. Teixeira de Freitas listed numerous *assentos* reiterating the same prohibition: N.1 of 29 Mar. 1770; N.4 of 5 Dec. 1770; N.22 of 21 July 1777; N.1 of 20 July 1780. *Trat. testamentos Gouvêa Pinto*, T.2, Cap.1, §§208–10 (pp. 294–304).

38. Will of Capt. João Lopes Freire, 5 Oct. 1790; courtesy of Higgins.

39. Will of Caetano Fernandes Silva, 27 Feb. 1771; courtesy of Higgins.

40. In one set of 155 eighteenth-century wills, Ramos found that 21 testators, nearly 14%, nominated their *Alma* a universal heir. Of the 16 men and 5 women, 20 were from Portugal or Africa. E-mail communication from Donald Ramos, 30 Dec. 1997.

41. Klein, "Colored Freedmen," pp. 40, 48–49.

42. Executed on 5 Oct. 1847, the will is reproduced in Sousa, *Bernardo de Vasconcellos*, pp. 285–87. Vasconcellos died on 1 May 1850.

43. 1864 Will of Francisca da Silva Costa, 1864, *fls. 8 e verso*. I am grateful to Dimas José Batista (a 1998 graduate student in history at Unesp/Franca) for permitting me to use this example from his primary research.

44. The *al.* of 20 May 1796 was the most important law to reaffirm the prohibition on nominating the *Alma* as a universal heir since Pombal's initial ban of 9 Sept. 1769. *CLP*, 6:281–83. Wherever testators nominated their *Alma*, both the *legítima* and *terça* would punitively revert to forced heirship for the benefit of the closest collateral heirs (Par.15). Teixeira de Freitas, *Trat. testamentos Gouvêa Pinto*, T.2, Cap.1, §208 (p. 296).

45. Law of 9 Sept. 1769, Pars.11–12,14; Law of 3 Aug. 1770, Par.5. *CLP*, 3:424–25, 427 & 478, respectively. Higgins found the *Alma do Testador* continued to be instituted a universal heir through 1806, in contravention of the Law of 9 Sept. 1769, Par.21. E-mail communications of July 7, 8, and 10, 1997.

46. *Trat. testamentos Gouvêa Pinto*, T.2, Cap.1, §208 (p. 296).

CHAPTER 2

1. Baptismal certificate of Col. Joaquim Francisco das Chagas Catete, reproduced in Walsh, *Notices*, 1:240–41.

2. Ibid., p. 241.

3. Lafayette, *Dir. família*, Sec.2, Cap.3, T.1, §103 (pp. 203–4); Sec.3, Cap.1, T.1, §120 (pp. 249–50).

4. Iraci de Nero da Costa, an exception, distinguished "natural" from illegitimate offspring in parish registers when he disaggregated abandoned children (*expostos*). In the 1804 census for the Province of Minas Gerais (combined populations of Vila Rica, Mariana, and Passagem), of those children under age 14 (3,044 individuals), 50.8% were freeborn; however, 62.2% of all free and slave births were natural offspring. *Estructuras populacionais*, p. 109. Marcílio found that 18% (1.4% of whom were foundlings) of Caiçara's children were born to "unmarried parents"—the lowest proportion recorded for late colonial Brazil (1790–1830). *Caiçara*, p. 172.

5. Gouvêa Pinto, *Trat. testamentos*, Cap.42, §1 (p. 145n1).

6. Ibid.

7. Fathers of natural children could be unmarried at either the moment of conception or the birth of the child. Candido Mendes, *Ord.*, p. 940n1; Lafayette, *Dir. família*, Sec.3, Cap.1, §120 (p. 250, citing Borges Carneiro, *Dir. civ. Port.*, L.1, v.2, T.20, §179); Bevilaqua, *Dir. família*, Cap.10, §67 (p. 440).

8. Title 92 nonetheless stipulated the important precondition that a natural child born of a slave mother had to be freed prior to the father's death—interpreted as posthumous manumission in his will. Gouvêa Pinto, *Trat. testamentos*, Cap.42, §1 (p. 147n1).

9. Although "this *ordenação* treats only paternal filiation," natural offspring were also the *ab intestato* successors of their mothers, unless maternity had been concealed. Candido Mendes, *Ord.*, p. 939n6.

10. In eighteenth-century Castilian law, recognized natural offspring might be forced heirs to the *legitim* (four-fifths of the estate), together with legitimate half-

siblings. Usually, the parent wrote a will so stipulating; however, customary recognition and tacit consent of the other heirs might permit succession to occur as in Portugal, without a will. Yet the father enjoyed greater latitude to exclude the child than in Portugal. Ordinarily, natural offspring were forced heirs only in the absence of legitimate children. I am grateful to Paloma Fernández Pérez for helping to clarify fine points in Spain's multiple systems of inheritance. See Chap. 5 of her *Rostro familiar*. Alternatively, a parent employed a will for disposing the one-fifth (*quinto*) of the estate falling under testamentary freedom (analogous to the Portuguese *terça*). On the inheritance position of natural or spurious offspring legitimized by the Spanish crown in the 1700s, see also Twinam, Chap. 8 of *Public Lives*, esp. pp. 218–22.

11. On the regional differences defining multiple systems of inheritance in eighteenth-century Spain, see Gacto's classic article, "El grupo familiar," pp. 56–57ff. See also Chacón Jiménez and Hernández Franco, eds., *Poder, familia y consanguinidad*; and Chacón Jiménez, Hernández Franco, and Peñafiel Ramón, eds., *Familia, grupos sociales y mujer*.

12. Gouvêa Pinto, *Trat. testamentos*, Cap.42, §1 (p. 145n1, citing *Ord. Afonsinas*, L.4, T.98.)

13. Borges Carneiro, *Dir. civ. Port.*, L.1, v.2, T.20, §179, N.3 (p. 250); Candido Mendes, *Ord.*, pp. 947n7–48. NOTE: References herein are to the 1844 reprint of Borges Carneiro's original edition (1826–1828) of L.1, published in two separate tomes (*tomos*), relabeled below as "volumes" 1 and 2.

14. Will of Capt. Manoel Alves da Costa, 6 Oct. 1826, quoted in the two following paragraphs and used with the permission of Hendrik Kraay, who provided his transcription.

15. When evidence for paternity was hearsay, the mother's exclusivity of sexual union with the alleged father was still determinative. Borges Carneiro, *Dir. civ. Port.*, L.1, v.2, T.20, §180, N.3 (pp. 253–54).

16. Ibid., Ns.5&10 (p. 254). See full text of §180, "Prova da Filiação dos Illegitimos," and §181, "Regras sobre Esta Prova" (pp. 253–55).

17. Schwartz, *Sugar Plantations*, pp. 319–320n20, citing MHN/CWP, pacote 1 (Santo Amaro, 1766).

18. Ibid., p. 320.

19. Ibid., p. 320n21, citing Juiz de Orfãos de São Francisco (1760), IHGBa, *pasta* 27, n.9.

20. For the case of a widow who contravened the will of her husband—freeing his slave paramour and their natural children—presumably by destroying the manumission certificates in order to succeed to her husband's *legítima*, see Metcalf, *Family and Frontier*, pp. 179–81.

21. Borges Carneiro, *Dir. civ. Port.*, L.1, v.2, T.20, §180, N.11 (p. 255).

22. Lafayette, *Dir. família*, Sec.2, Cap.3, T.1, §104 (pp. 205–6).

23. Coelho da Rocha, *Inst. dir. civ. port.*, v.1, Sec.3, Cap.2, §298 (p. 204).

24. Nazzari, "Women, Family, and Property," p. 184.

25. Idem, *Dowry*, p. 146.

26. Lustosa da Costa, *Senador dos bois*, p. 45. By 1858, law required a notarized declaration of paternity to guarantee Leocadio's patrimonial rights.

27. The *al.* of 18 Feb. 1763 conferred nobility on the *sargentos-mores* of the *orde-*

nanças (militias), and it was confirmed by the *al.* of 22 May 1805. Borges Carneiro, *Dir. civ. Port.*, L.1, v.1, T.4, §45, N.21 (p. 127).

28. Will of Sgt°-Mór Custodio Gomes de Almeida, 6 Sept. 1820, quoted extensively below and used with the permission of Hendrik Kraay, who provided his transcription.

29. All three are delineated in *Ord. Filipinas*, L.2, T.35. See Borges Carneiro, *Dir. civ. Port.*, L.1, v.1, T.4, §45, N.34 (pp. 130–31); v.2, T.23, §208, Ns.16–18 (pp. 332–33).

30. Gouvêa Pinto, *Trat. testamentos*, Cap.42, §1 (pp. 145–50).

31. *Ord. Filipinas*, L.1, T.4, §45.

32. Borges Carneiro, *Inst. dir. civ. Port.*, L.1, v.1, T.4, §45, N.34 (pp. 130–31). "*Perfilhamento em testamento*: The legitimization that a father enacts for a spurious offspring, nominating him for such in his will [*Ord.*, L.2, T.35, §12], in itself produces only the effect of conferring use of the father's name and house, the use of his arms and insignia, but *not succession to his estate nor any other effects*." Ibid., v.2, T.23, §208, N.18 (p. 333). Italics added.

33. Almeida e Souza de Lobão [henceforth, Lobão], *Notas*, L.2, T.5, §§17–19 (pp. 153–65); Coelho da Rocha, *Inst. dir. civ. port.*, v.1, Sec.4, Cap.2, §297 (pp. 203–4, 204n).

34. Lobão, *Notas*, L.2, T.5, §§17–19, N.7 (pp. 157–58), glossing Mello Freire's *Inst. juris. civ. lus.*, L.2, T.5, Pt.I, §§17–19.

35. Ibid.: "si a principe legitimetur." Lafayette, parsing Lobão: "se obtiver legitimação." *Dir. familia*, Sec.3, Cap.1, T.3, §129 (pp. 267n1).

36. Trigo de Loureiro, *Inst. dir. civ. bras.*, L.1, T.4, §66 (p. 38); Gouvêa Pinto, *Trat. Testamentos*, Cap.42, §1 (p. 151n2).

37. Candido Mendes, *Aux. juridico*, p. 778n1 (citing Mello Freire, *Hist. dir. civ. port.*, §72, and *Ord. Filipinas*, L.2, T.35, §12); Oliveira Marques, *Lusitania to Empire*, p. 187.

38. See also *Ord. Filipinas*, L.2, T.3, §1, and T.35, §12; L.4, Tit.36, §4. Coelho da Rocha, *Inst. dir. civ. port.*, v.1, Sec.4, Cap.2, §297 (pp. 203–4, 204n).

39. Gouvêa Pinto, *Trat. testamentos*, Cap.42, §1 (p.147n1).

40. Schwartz, *Sovereignty and Society*, p. 12. Reference herein to "the Tribunal" of the Mesa do Desembargo do Paço follows the verbal usage employed by legal commentators and legislators, who always construed crown legitimization as proceeding from the Desembargo do Paço convened as a judicial tribunal, not an administrative board.

41. Twinam, *Public Lives*, pp. 51–55.

42. Candido Mendes, *Aux. juridico*, p. 778–79; Schwartz, *Sovereignty and Society*, p. 10; Leal, "Historia judiciaria," pp. 76n155–77n164.

43. See esp. Mörner, *Race Mixture Americas*; Martínez Alier, *Marriage, Class, Colour, Cuba*; and Rípodas Ardanaz, *El matrimonio Indias*.

44. Of a total 232 petitions for *gracias al sacar* that Twinam unearthed for the eighteenth century—the full record—only 16 pertained to removal of the "defect" of non-European [Christian] ancestry. 216 sought removal of the "defect" of illegitimate birth. Appendix: Table 10, p. 356.

45. One trailblazing researcher thus far has tried, and failed, to locate this important archive in Lisbon's Torre do Tombo: Maria Beatriz Nizza da Silva. "Desembargo Paço," pp. 70, 72. Twinam's ingenious methodological extrapolation, enabling

her to locate the complete set of Spanish eighteenth-century legitimization petitions in the Archivo de las Indias, suggests that Lisbon's Torre de Tombo may yet yield the missing archive. *Public Lives*, pp. 345–47.

46. *Al.* of 22 Apr. 1808.

47. Law of 22 Sept. 1828, Art.2, §1. *CLIB 1828*, Pte.1ª, p. 47.

48. Crown legitimization of a noble's natural or spurious offspring derived from *Ord. Filipinas*, L.2, T.35, §12: "E o filho espurio não poderá haver o dito foro, salvo sendo legitimado por Nós em tal forma que possa succeder *ab intestato* e de outra maneira não." See also L.4, T.36, §4; L.1, T.3, §1, and T.85, §2; and Candido Mendes, *Ord.*, p. 269n. The basic statute on legitimization, from Pombal's era to 1847, was the Law of 7 Jan. 1770 (calling for a hearing with the *ab intestato* heirs where succession rights were involved), as explicated in the *ass.* of 9 Apr. 1772 and the *al.* of 29 Aug. 1776.

49. The *res.* of 16 Nov. 1798 appears in the table of contents of *CLP*, 6:513. However, the text was omitted due to erroneously dating the resolution as 16 Dec. 1798. Customarily, legal commentaries cited the *Prov.* of 18 Jan. 1799, but reiterated much of the 1798 resolution's text. Reproduced ibid., 6:517–18; Candido Mendes, *Ord.*, pp. 1053–54; and Borges Carneiro, *Add. leis desde 1603*, pp. 192–94. The Desembargo do Paço's *res.* of 17 Jan. 1770 required all legitimization certificates to contain either the names of the legitimate heirs, meaning the *ab intestato* heirs, when succession rights were not awarded, or those of the legitimized individual on whom the succession rights were bestowed. Ibid., p. 128.

50. *Res.* of 16 Nov. 1798, in Lobão, *Add. tract. morgados*, Cap.22, §62 (p. 477); and idem, *Notas*, L.2, T.5, §§17–19, N.8 (p. 158), citing Mello Freire (*Inst. jur. civ. lus.*, L.3, T.8, §14). Borges Carneiro, *Dir. civ. Port.*, L.1, v.2, T.23, §207, Ns.2–3 (p. 329); Trigo de Loureiro, *Inst. dir. civ. braz.*, L.1, T.4, §65 (p. 38); Lafayette, *Dir. familia*, Sec.3, Cap.1, T.3, §130 (p. 269n4). Gouvêa Pinto cited the "1ª *dissertação das sinco [dissertações] anonymas* [1808]," for a fuller explanation of procedures (*Trat. testamentos*, p. 148n).

51. At least the post-1808 cases from Rio de Janeiro support this conclusion. See the cases of Joaquim Manoel Gago da Camara (s/d) and Francisco de Assis Amorim Lima (1816), whose crown legitimization with succession rights depended solely on the evidence of private letters and informal affidavits for proving paternal intent. Cited in Nazzari, "Urgent Need To Conceal," pp. 115, 117; and Nizza da Silva, "Filhos ilegítimos," p. 123.

52. Lobão reported that the Desembargo Paço "is accustomed to require information on [the candidate's] filiation, that is heard from the *ab intestato* consanguines. The latter, for the most part, refuse [to waive their rights in heirship], but the legitimization certificate is always conceded." *Notas*, L.2, T.5, §§17–19, N.14 (p. 162).

53. Nizza da Silva, "Desembargo do Paço," pp. 70, 72–73; idem, "Filhos ilegítimos," p. 123.

54. Nizza da Silva, "Desembargo do Paço," p. 74.

55. Ibid., p. 71.

56. Lobão, *Notas*, L.2, T.5, §§17–19, N.6 (p. 155). The 1754 ladder of heirship, however, was confirmed in 1786 to extend to four canonical (ten civil) degrees. *Ass.* of 16 Feb. 1786.

57. Lobão, who was also a lawyer, described the technique, wherein *ab intestato*

heirs argued the legitimization candidate was not the offspring of the legitimizing father, or that his mother had sexual relations with other men, etc. *Notas*, L.2, T.5, §§17–19, N.14 (p. 162).

58. Nizza da Silva, "Filhos ilegítimos," p. 123.

59. The Law of 9 Sept. 1769, §10, abrogating the *Ord. Filipinas*, L.2, T.18, §1. *CLP*, 3:423. Teixeira de Freitas, *Trat. testamentos Gouvêa Pinto*, Pte.2, T.2, Cap.1, §208, Pars. 1&3 (pp. 295. 298–99). See also Gouvêa Pinto, *Trat. testamentos*, Cap.12 (p. 58n1), on the ability of clerics to write "passive" wills, sanctioned tacitly by the Philippine Code.

CHAPTER 3

1. *Trat. testamentos*, Cap.42, §1 (pp. 151n2–52).

2. *Dir. successões*, Cap.5, §41 (p. 129).

3. *Ord.*, p. 944n3.

4. *Ord. Filipinas*, L.4, T.93; Gouvêa Pinto, *Trat. testamentos*, Cap.42, §4 (pp. 155n3–56).

5. *Dir. civ. Port.*, L.1, v.1, T.1, §21, N.1b (p. 70n); and T.3, §43 (p. 121).

6. Papal legitimization in 1263 enabled D. Dinis the Farmer (Dinis I) to become king of Portugal in 1279, for he was the adulterine son of Affonso III and his paramour, Beatriz of Castile (the natural child of Alfonso El Sabio). MacDonald, "Alfonso's Reform," p. 161. On Pope John Paul II's similiar rescript of legitimization, see "Three Children Princess Caroline Declared Legitimate," *New York Times*, 6 Apr. 1993, Pt. B, p. 2:4. I am grateful to Carina Johnson for bringing this article to my attention. Borges Carneiro, *Dir. civ. Port.*, L.1, v.2, T.23, §209, N.3 (pp. 333–34).

7. Gouvêa Pinto, *Trat. testamentos*, Cap.42, §1 (pp. 145n1–46).

8. *Al.* of 26 Sept. 1769, specifying loss of office for any crown official who conducted investigations outside the standard prescribed: "E querendo obviar a um abuso de tal perniciosas consequencias . . . para o objecto das mesmas Devassas os concubinatos *com concubinas teúdas, e manteúdas* com geral, e publico escandalo . . ." (italics added). Adultery, like clerical concubinage, amounted to "qualified" concubinage, a union "damnable and prohibited." *CLP*, 3:432–33.

9. *Ord. Filipinas*, L.4, T.92, §3 & T.93; Gouvêa Pinto, *Trat. testamentos*, Cap.42, §1 (p. 147n1); Candido Mendes, *Ord.*, p. 944n3. In contrast, a noble father or mother whose parents were living could use the *terça* for endowing a recognized natural offspring, if legitimate children did not exist. *Ord. Filipinas*, L.4, T.92, §3.

10. Muriel Nazzari, personal communication on the will of Joaquim Elias da Silva, 1863; Arquivo do Ministério de Justiça, 2° Ofício da Família, São Paulo, No. 281. Nazzari, *Dowry*, p. 147n63.

11. "Fragilidade celibato," p. 63. Borges Carneiro, *Dir. civ. Port.*, L.1, v.1, T.4, §45, N.34 (pp. 130–31), citing Mello Freire, *Institutiones*, L.2, T.6, §6 & n. The *Ord. Filipinas* permitted simple legitimization, "*perfilhação em testamento.*" L.2, T.35, §12.

12. Originally applying to only noble fathers, this *ordenaçao* came to be interpreted as applying to all fathers. Candido Mendes, *Ord.*, p. 943n5.

13. Lafayette, *Dir. familia*, Sec.3, Cap.2, T.2, §130 (p. 269n2), citing *res.* 16 Nov. 1798 and Lobão's *Acções summarias*, §18, noting that parents alone could not institute their spurious offspring heirs.

14. Lewcowicz, "Fragilidade do celibato," p. 63.

15. Nizza da Silva, "Desembargo Paço," pp. 70–71, 75.

16. The reign of D. João I (1385–1433) witnessed a rise in royal legitimizations, 2000 petitions being granted. Between 1389 and 1438, crown legitimization was conceded to the children of 2 archbishops, 5 bishops, 11 archdeacons, 9 deans, 4 chanters, 72 canons, and nearly 600 priests, excluding minor orders. Oliveira Marques, *Daily Life Portugal*, pp. 176–77. In Spain, Ricardo Córdoba de la Llave's preliminary analysis for 1400–1420 indicated that about 70% of crown legitimizations pertained to spurious individuals: *sacrílegos* (54.7%), *adulterinos* (14.6%), and *incestuosos* (a negligible 1.04%); natural offspring were a minority (18.9%). Cited in Twinam, *Public Lives*, pp. 51 and 376n81.

17. Mello Freire, *Instituiçoens* (1834), L.2, T.6, §4 (p.80), citing the Law of 3 Jan. 1611. NOTE: All references to "*Instituiçoens* (1834), L.2," herein refer to Pereira Freire's Portuguese translation of Book 2 (*De jure personarum*, 1791) of Mello Freire's *Institutionum juris civilis lusitani*. Jurists frequently cited the 4-volume Latin edition by a hypothetical title rendered in Portuguese: "*Instituições de direito civil português* [or "*lusitani*"]," one appearing herein.

18. Cf. *Ord. Filipinas*, L.4, T.93: ". . . cuando algum filho de Clerigo, ou de algum outro danado ou punido coito per nossas Ordenações ou Direito Comum, a que o pai ou a mãe não pode succeder por assim ser nascido de coito danado ou punivel . . . ."

19. Baptismal entry for Diogo, "son of unknown parents," parish of Sé, São Paulo, 17 Aug. 1784, reproduced in Egas, *Feijó*, 1:3. On an equally celebrated Spanish American *exposto*—another *sacrílego*, Archbishop Juan de Palafox y Mendoza—see Brading, *First America*, p. 237 (citing Palafox's *Obras* I:15–45).

20. On the notion of heritable sin in eighteenth-century Spain, see Twinam, *Public Lives*, pp. 278–79.

21. Sousa, *Feijó*, p. 16; Freitas, "Notas filiação Feijó," p. 81. See Lewin, "'Body Vanishes.'"

22. *Cod. Penal Império 1830*, Arts. 249, 251, and 250, respectively. In 1990, adultery in the United States still remained a felony in three states and a misdemeanor in 23 others. "Treating Adultery as Crime," p. 1. See also Ireland, "The Libertine Must Die."

23. Babies were commonly abandoned by the poor in 1970s São Paulo—left in church pews, the center of a plaza, or cars and buses. *Jornal da Tarde* (São Paulo), 7 May 1975, cited in Lobo de A. Campos, "Configuração agregados," p. 69.

24. *Famílias abandonadas*, pp. 137–38. Venâncio found only 14 cases of legal adoption in nineteenth-century Salvador. A less systematic survey of Rio de Janeiro revealed one case.

25. Marcílio, *Criança abandonada*, p. 234; tables, pp. 232–35. See also Venâncio, *Famílias abandonadas*, Ch. 1, Tables I–V. In the Vila Rica de Ouro Preto census of 1804, Ramos calculated *enjeitados* at 8.7% of all offspring born of *agregados*, or household dependents. "Marriage Vila Rica," p. 233. In São Paulo's central parish of Sé baptismal registries from 1775/1782 through 1822, recording 2728 births, indicated 521, or 19.1%, were baptized of unknown parents. Lobo de A. Campos, "Configuração agregados," pp. 63, 67.

26. Venâncio has analyzed those notes. *Famílias abandonadas*, pp. 75–85.

27. *Al.* of 31 Jan. 1775, Par.7, "reducing" *expostos* to "simple orphans, like any

other people." Reprinted in Candido Mendes, *Ord.*, p. 1065. Karasch, *Slave Life*, p. 350n46.

28. Borges Carneiro, *Dir. civ. Port.*, L.1, v.2, T.19, §175, N.1 (pp. 238–39). Trigo de Loureiro, *Inst. dir. civ. bras.*, L.1, T.81 (p. 46).

29. See Twinam, *Public Lives*, pp. 18–20; on the crown *camara*'s failure to uphold presumption of legitimacy, p. 304.

30. D'Incao, "Amor romántico," p. 66.

31. Ibid.

32. Lobão, *Notas*, L.2, T.5, §§17–19, N.10 (p. 160), citing Law of 7 Jan. 1750.

33. Nazzari, "Urgent Need To Conceal," pp. 120–21.

34. Analysis of baptisms in São Paulo's parish of Sé, for 1700–1799, found that in 51 instances the mother of a natural offspring was known, but the father concealed, making the child paternally spurious (a *quaesito*). When the father of a natural offspring was known, in no instance was maternity concealed. In the three cases where priests identified infants as "adulterine," the mother's name was revealed, but the father's concealed. Lopes, "Bastardia São Paulo," Table 6 (p. 4).

35. *Con. primeiras*, L.1, T.20, Par.73.

36. Tavares Bastos, *Reg. civil* [*Regul.* No. 5604 of 25 Apr. 1874], Art. 52, on omitting both parents' names in birth registries "to avoid scandal"; and Art. 54, on the father's authorization as necessary for recording his name (pp. 70–71). Bevilaqua, *Dir. successões*, Cap.6, §82 (p. 300); Aguiar Souza, *Posição juridical*, pp. 4, 45–47.

37. "*Espúrios*, colloquially *quaesitos* . . . three more types . . . have to be noted, *adulterinos, incestuosos*, and *sacrílegos*." Gouvêa Pinto, *Trat. Testamentos*, Cap.42, §1 (pp. 145n1–46). Following the *Ord. Filipinas*, L.4, T.36, §4, Candido Mendes employed "*espúrio*" synonymously with "*quaesito*." *Ord.*, p. 814n2.

38. Candido Mendes, *Ord.*, p. 814n2; Borges Carneiro, *Dir. civ. Port.*, L.1, v.2, T.22, §196, N.7 (p. 310).

39. Candido Mendes, *Ord.*, p. 943n7. Cf. Gouvêa Pinto, *Trat. testamentos*, Cap.42, §1n1 (pp. 145–46).

40. On heirs "whose existence was completely unsuspected," even in the context of 1980s Salvador, Bahia, see Katia Mattoso, *Família Bahia*, p. 56n54.

41. *Ord. Filipinas*, L.4, T.36, §4.

42. *Dir. civ. Port.*, L.1, T.22, §196, N.7 (pp. 310–11).

43. Gouvêa Pinto, *Trat. Testamentos*, Cap.42, §1 (pp. 151n1–52).

44. *Ord.*, p. 814n2.

45. Gouvêa Pinto, glossing *Ord.*, L.4, T.36, §4, *Trat. testamentos*, Cap.42, §1 (pp. 151n–52).

46. The *Novo Regimento Desembargo Paço* (Law of 27 July 1582) remained in force until 1889. It is reprinted in Candido Mendes, *Ord.*, pp. 241–53; cf. Art. 118, on crown legitimization.

CHAPTER 4

1. 2:381. The list of Arco Verde's eight legitimized offspring was reconstructed from *partilhas*.

2. Ibid., 1:9, 206, 303–6. Catarina de Albuquerque was born c. 1544. Jeronymo's will is reproduced in Borges da Fonseca, *Nobiliarquia pernambucana*, 2:361–65.

3. *Ord. Filipinas*, L.4, T.92, §§1&2.; Candido Mendes, *Ord.*, p. 942n1; Gouvêa Pinto, *Trat. testamentos*, Cap.42, §1 (p. 147n1). On the first three ranks in late colonial Brazil (*moço-fidalgo*, *fidalgo-escudeiro*, and *fidalgo-cavalleiro*), see Lobo de A. Campos, "Configuração agregados," pp. 36–43.

4. Oliveira Marques, *Lusitania to Empire*, pp. 179–80.

5. On a noble's natural and spurious offspring, see *Ord. Filipinas*, L.4, T.36, §4. Borges Carneiro, *Dir. civ. Port.*, L.1, v.1, T.4, §45, Ns.33–34 (pp. 130–31). On the exception of the natural offspring conceived when the noble father was a commoner, and therefore called to *ab intestato* succession, see *Ord. Filipinas*, L.4, T.92, §2; and Gouvêa Pinto, *Trat. testamentos*, Cap.42, §1 (pp. 147n1, 151n1–52).

6. *Ord. Filipinas*, L.4, T.92, §2; Candido Mendes, *Ord.*, p. 814n2; idem, *Aux. juridico*, p. 823(IX). Liz Teixeira, *Curso dir. civ. port.*, Pte.1, T.6, §6 (p. 327).

7. Borges Carneiro, *Dir. civ. Port.*, L.1, v.1, T.4, §45, N.34 (p. 130). See Liz Teixeira, *Cur. dir. civ. port.*, Pte.1, T.6, §6 (p. 327).

8. The Law of 31 Jan. 1775 stipulated that nominations in universal heirship required confirmation by the Tribunal of the Mesa do Desembargo do Paço, following consultation with the legitimate heirs, but it deserves interpretation as a reinforcement of preceding law. *CLP*, 4:7

9. Lobão, *Notas*, L.2, T.5, §§17–19, N.7 (p. 157).

10. Will of Mathias de Crasto Porto, 5 Oct. 1742; used with permission of Kathleen Higgins (*supra*).

11. *Trat. Testamentos*, Cap.42, §1 (pp. 151n1–52).

12. *Ord.*, L.3, T.85, §2. The Law of 7 Jan. 1750, elaborating this *ordenação*, established fees for legitimization certificates: 3$200 *réis* for spurious offspring and 1$600 *réis* for "purely" natural offspring. Lobão, *Notas*, L.2, T.5, §§17–19, N.10 (pp. 159–60). On succession rights for non-legitimate offspring of the higher nobility (*bens de caroa*), see *Ord.*, L.2, T.35, §12.

13. Cf. Gouvêa Pinto, *Trat. testamentos*, Cap.42, §1 (p. 147n2). His bad syntax—"Those legitimized *per Rescriptum Principis* do not succeed their fathers *ab intestato*"—deserves rewording: "Prior to crown legitimization, those offspring do not succeed their fathers *ab intestato*." Cf. also *Ord.*, L.4, T.36, §4.

14. Borges Carneiro, *Dir. civ. Port.*, L.1, v.1, T.4, §45, Ns.8, 34 (pp. 124, 130–31); and L.1, v.2, T.23, §208, N.16 (p. 333).

15. Nizza da Silva, "Filhos ilegítimos, p. 123.

16. "Desembargo do Paço," p. 71.

17. Lobão, *Notas*, L.2, T.5, §§17–19, N.13 (pp. 161–62). The noble father could institute a family entail (*morgado*) on behalf of a legitimized child, who otherwise was prohibited from succeeding to an entail. Ibid.

18. Ibid., §§17–19, N.12 (p. 161); Borges Carneiro, *Dir. civ. Port.*, L.1, v.1, T.4, §45, Ns.8,33 (pp. 124, 130). Cf. ibid., §46, N.14 (p. 135b). Liz Teixeira differed, noting that "the only bastards conceded this right [*dom*]" were illegitimate children of the king and "no other." *Cur. dir. civ. port.*, Pte.1, T.6, §5 (pp. 325–26). The prohibition derives from the *al.* of 3 Jan. 1611 (reprinted in Pierangelli, *Cód. Penais*, pp. 154–55), reaffirming *Ord. Filipinas*, Bk.5, T.92, §7: "Those who are bastards, even legitimized, cannot use it [*dom*]." Section 7 restricted "*dom*" to bishops, counts, high judges, and legitimate descendants of men whose fathers or paternal grandfathers used it or per-

sonally enjoyed the privilege by direct royal grant. Their wives and legitimate children derived the right to use *"dona,"* just as other women did when their mothers or mothers-in-law used it.

19. Nascimento e Silva, *Synopse legislação militar*, 2:478.

20. Borges Carneiro, *Dir. civ. Port.*, L.1, v.2, T.23, §208, N.18 (p. 333).

21. Ibid., L.1, v.1, T.4, §49, Ns.14–15, 22, 24–25 (pp. 148–51).

22. Law school graduates of "low birth" could not clerk in the Desembargo do Paço, unless they demonstrated academic accomplishments and virtue, for minimal nobility still took precedence. Law of 10 Aug. 1625. *Dec.* of 24 June 1800, cited ibid. Abolished only on 9 May 1821, this legal barrier was reinstated in Portugal in 1823 (*Dec.* of 30 Sept.). Ibid., L.1, v.1, T.4, §47 (p. 155a).

23. Santos, "A legislação pombalina," pp. 155–56.

24. *Al.* 4 Apr. 1775, cited ibid.

25. Cunha Mattos, *Repertorio da legislação militar*, 2:328.

26. *Al.* of 17 Dec. 1802, §16, cited in Borges Carneiro, *Dir. civ. Port.*, L.1, v.1, T.1, §21, N.1b (pp. 69–70).

27. Koster, *Travels*, p. 391.

28. Ibid., p. 392. "It is to enable a man to become a cadet and then an officer without serving in the ranks, that requires nobility of birth." Ibid.

29. Nizza da Silva, "Filhos ilegítimos," p. 121.

30. For instance, in 1809, officers of color in Salvador's Third Military Regiment were typically artisans, practicing "low status trades," ergo without any claim to noble status. Kraay, "Black Militias," pp. 32, 38, 43. Borges Carneiro, *Dir. civ. Port.*, L.1, v.1, T.1, §20, N.1b (p. 70). In Portugal, during the 1820s, blacks (*pretos*) were still excluded from holding public office, except in town councils. Ibid., citing *dec.* of 20 Dec. 1693.

31. Barman, "New-World Nobility," pp. 40–41; Oliveira Marques, *Lusitania to Empire*, pp. 179–80.

32. *Honras de grandeza* implied the privileges of the *"Grandes do Reino"* in the metropole, prized for enhancing the rank of lesser titleholders who were barons and viscounts, the great preponderance of titleholders in imperial Brazil. Jansen, "Nobiliário," p. 167.

33. For a Brazilian perspective on these "commonly confused" terms, see Jansen's discussion. Whereas Iberians preferred *"fidalguia,"* beyond the Pyrenees *"nobreza"* was operative. Ibid., p. 166.

34. Borges Carneiro, *Dir. civ. Port.*, L.1, v.1, T.4, §45, Ns.4–5 (p. 123). *Fidalgos* were inscribed in the royal registers either by coat-of-arms, by special grace of the king, or as notable. Ibid., p. 123n(a). In Portugal, they admitted six legal ranks. *Escudeiros*, a step above *fidalgos*, admitted four gradations. Ibid., N.6 (p. 123 & 123b).

35. Jansen, "Nobiliário," p. 166.

36. Villaverde, *Cecilia Valdes*, p. 147.

37. Lobão, *Notas*, L.2, T.3, §15 (p. 26). Nobility was inherited from the mother or the father. Borges Carneiro, *Dir. civ. Port.*, L.1, v.1, T.4, §45, Ns.7,33,35 (pp. 122, 130–31), citing Law of 29 Jan. 1759. A husband transmitted his nobility to a non-noble wife, but a wife took the legal condition (estate) of her husband, causing a noblewoman who married a commoner to lose her nobility. Ibid., Ns.39–40 (p. 131), citing

Mello Freire, *Inst. dir. civ. lus.*, L.2, T.7, §6n1. But a noblewoman who married a commoner still transmitted nobility to her children, who received it from their maternal grandparent(s). Jansen, "Nobiliario," p. 166.

38. Pang, *Pursuit of Honor*, p. 51. Borges Carneiro, *Dir. civ. Port.*, L.1, v.1, T.4, §45, N.4 (p. 123). Jansen, "Nobiliário," p. 166.

39. Lobão, *Notas*, L.2, T.3, §15 (p. 27).

40. Ibid., §14 (p. 26); Barman, "New World Nobility," p. 41n6. In practice, titles "*de juro e herdade*" were hereditary. Ibid.

41. Lobão, *Notas*, L.2, T.3, §15 (pp. 26–27); Borges Carneiro, *Dir. civ. Port.*, L.1, v.1, T.4, §45, Ns.22–25 (pp. 127–28), citing *al.* of 8 June 1759, §12, and *prov.* of 29 Feb. 1778.

42. Lobão, *Notas*, L.2, T.3, §15, N.2 (p. 27). This and the following paragraph draw on ibid., Ns.1–8 (pp. 26–30).

43. Ibid., Ns.1–8 (pp. 27–29); Borges Carneiro, *Dir. civ. Port.*, L.1, v.1, T.4, §45, Ns.26–32 (pp. 129–30); on wholesalers, ibid., N.10 (p. 125), citing *als.* of 30 Aug. 1770, 29 Nov. 1775, 1 July 1776; and *als.* of 24 Nov. 1761, 10 Feb. 1757 (Par.3), and 6 Jan. 1802.

44. Borges Carneiro, *Dir. civ. Port.* L.1, v.1, T.4, §45, Ns.11,21 (pp. 125, 127). Cunha Mattos, *Repertorio legislação militar*, 2:191–92 (citing 1111 Foral of Coimbra and 1143 Cortes of Lamego). *Reg.* of 10 Dec. 1570; ibid.

45. Cunha Mattos, *Repertorio legislação militar*, 2:191–92. The Law of Military Enlistment and Militia Service (*prov.* of 30 Apr. 1758) stipulated that all officers and sergeants enjoyed the privilege of gentlemen (*cavalleiros*), even if they were not. Ibid. 2:328. The *al.* of 23 Feb. 1797, §1, declared that after completing military service all plebeians (*peões*) would cease to be so regarded, acquiring nobility ipso facto. Ibid. 2:249; 2:191 (citing *regul.* de 1763 e 1764, Cap.13, §7). The *al.* of 13 May 1789 conceded the treatment and all honors of the "privilege of *fidalgo*" to field marshals and lieutenant generals promoted from the ranks, where they did not already enjoy the latter. *CLP* 4:549.

46. Borges Carneiro, *Dir. civ. Port.*, L.1, v.1, T.4, §45, N.10 (p. 125), citing Law of 1 July 1776.

47. Ibid., N.33 (pp. 129n–30), citing *al.* of 6 Jan. 1802.

48. Ibid., Ns.14–18 (p. 126), citing *dec.* of 14 July 1758.

49. Lobão, *Notas*, L.2, T.3, §15, Ns.1–2,8 (pp. 26–27, 29); on the absence of "nobility in the half state" (Law of 29 Nov. 1775), see ibid., Ns.2,8. Borges Carneiro, *Dir. civ. Port.*, L.1, v.1, T.4, §45, N.43 (p. 132), citing *Ord.* L.4, T.92, §1.

50. Lobão, *Notas*, L.2, T.3, §15, N.9 (p. 30). A decree of 18 Dec. 1614 forbad nobles to marry New Christians of either Jewish or Muslim ancestry. Higher nobles needed the sovereign's permission to marry. Borges Carneiro, *Dir. civ. Port.*, L.1, v.1, T.4, §51, N.15 (p. 166).

51. Borges Carneiro, *Dir. civ. Port.*, L.1, v.1, T.4, §45, N.10 (pp. 124–25).

52. Ibid., N.43 (p. 132); Lobão, *Notas*, L.2, T.3, §15, N.9 (p. 30).

53. Vieira da Cunha, *Nobreza brasileira*, pp. 23–29 and notes.

54. *Al.* of 16 Mar. 1757, Arts.1–3, cited ibid., pp. 15–16.

55. Vieira da Cunha, *Nobreza brasileira*, p. 51.

56. *Dec.* of 1 Aug. 1821 [sic 1822], *CLIB 1821*, Pt.1, pp. 71–72.

57. An individual born 180 days following the parents' marriage, or 302 days after the father's death, was legally legitimate. Coelho da Rocha, *Inst. dir. civ. port.*, v.1, Sec.8, Cap.1, §290 (pp. 198–99).

58. *Instituições* (1834), L.2, T.6, §§1,4 (pp. 76, 79). "The name bastard also signifies *notos* and *espúrios*" (§4).

59. Ibid., §6 (p. 81), citing *Ord.*, L.4, T.92, §4, and concurring that for a noble parent's natural offspring, bastardy still had to be "broken."

60. *Trat. testamentos*, Cap.42, §1 (pp. 145n1–47n1).

61. *Dir. civ. Port.*, L.1, T.20, §79, N.2 (p. 250).

62. *Dir. familia*, Cap.10, §70 (p. 439).

63. Candido Mendes, *Ord.*, p. 943n7, quoting Mello Freire, *Inst. dir. civ. lus.*, L.2, T.6, §4.

64. Twinam, *Public Lives*, p. 278–80, 296.

65. *Ord.*, p. 943n7, citing Mello Freire, *Inst. dir. civ. lus.*, L.2, T.6, §4.

66. Blackstone, *Commentaries* (1915), 1:374–75. *Bracton on the Laws of England*, p. 186.

67. *Dir. familia* (1904), Cap.10, §68 (pp. 453–54). *Dir. successões*, Cap.5, §137 (p. 137). Blackstone, *Commentaries* (1915), 1:635. Candido Mendes, *Ord.*, p. 945n4. Cf. Lobão, "Analyse da ordenação," pp. 12–13; and Trigo de Loureiro, *Inst. dir. bras.*, L.1, T.4, §61 (pp. 34–35).

68. Trigo de Loureiro, *Inst. dir. civ. braz.*, L.1, T.5, §77 (p. 45).

CHAPTER 5

1. Law of 18 Aug. 1769, "A Lei da Boa Razão," §§10&12, "Declaring the Authority of Roman and Canon Law, *Assentos*, *Estilos*, and Customs." In Candido Mendes, *Ord.*, "Legislação portugueza," pp. 728–29; full text, pp. 725–30; also in *CLP* 3:476–83. Italics added. NOTE: The reference to "imperial" implies Justinian's juridical corpus.

2. 9 July 1829, *AS 1829*, 2:76.

3. 14 July 1829, ibid., 3:97.

4. The "Law of the *Morgado*" (Law of 3 Aug. 1770) rapidly followed that of 9 Sept. 1769, overhauling the inheritance system by amending and clarifying the 1754 basic law of *ab intestato* succession. *CLP* 3:419–30.

5. "Necrologia: Marquez de Caravellas, 8 Setembro de 1836," p. VII.

6. On the renewed force of regalism under Pombal, see Beal's excellent analysis: "Regalismo Brasil," pp. 38–57, 146 *passim*. See also Gérson, *Regalismo brasileiro*, and Coelho da Rocha, *Ensaio*, pp. 107–13, 159–66, 230–37.

7. Pires, "Teologia jansenista," pp. 331–34.

8. On D. João VI's clashes with papal nuncio Caleppi, and Caleppi's condemnation of the catechism authored by the future viscount of Cayru (José da Silva Lisboa), see Gerson, *Regalismo brasileiro*, pp. 19–32.

9. On the crown's mundane acceptance of Jansenist attitudes toward the Holy See, see Dauphinee, "Church and Parliament," pp. 20–25; and Beal, "O regalismo da caroa no Brasil, 1808–1850," Chap. 5 of "Regalismo Brasil."

10. "Epitome," p. 782n.

11. Moreira Alves, "Panorama," pp. 87–88. This discussion of "*boa razão*" draws directly on Moreira Alves' extremely lucid essay, translated by Keith Rosenn.

12. Ibid., p. 88.

13. Ibid., p. 89 and 89n4.

14. Lafayette, *Dir. familia*, pp. xviii–xix. Coelho da Rocha, *Ensaio*, p. 224 (citing

Mello Freire, *Hist. juridica*, §§117–18). On the Glossators, Commentators, and their legal humanist critics, see Cappelletti, Merryman & Perillo, *The Italian Legal System*.

15. Moreira Alves, "Panorama," p. 88.

16. Law of 18 Aug. 1769, §12.

17. Moreira Alves, "Panorama," p. 89 (citing Luis Antonio Verney, *Verdadeiro método de estudar*). See also Beal, "Regalismo Brasil," p. 10n23.

18. Miller, *Portugal and Rome*, p. 250. On the predominance of the canonists, see Ramos de Carvalho, *Reformas pombalinas*, pp. 72–74.

19. Barman and Barman, "Law School Graduates," p. 428 (Table 2)–429.

20. The idea was developed in Ribeiro Sanches' "Sobre a inhibição de se tomarem graus na Faculdade de Canônes em Coimbra," cited in Calazans Falcon, *Época pombalina*, pp. 48–49.

21. Moreira Alves, "Panorama," p. 89.

22. Ferreira Carrato, "Educational Reforms Pombal," p. 365.

23. Lafayette, *Dir. familia*, p. xix.

24. Bevilaqua, *Theoria geral*, p. 27 and 27n (citing the 1828 Judiciary Act), and p. 35n.

25. Moreira Alves, "Panorama," p. 89.

26. Law of 18 Aug. 1769, §12, in Candido Mendes, *Ord.*, p. 729.

27. Ibid. Italics added.

28. Beal, "Regalismo Brasil," p. 93 (citing 1772 New Statutes, L.2, T.8, Par.30).

29. Bevilaqua, *Theoria geral*, pp. 41–42.

30. Candido Mendes, "Epitome," p. 781n1. Mello Freire became professor extraordinary of *direito pátrio* by the decree of 11 Sept. 1772. Ibid.

31. Maxwell, *Pombal*, pp. 9–12, 102, 161.

32. Candido Mendes, "Epitome," p. 781n1. The decree of 12 July 1772 awarded him the benefice of the Collegiada de São João Baptista de Coruche. He was also a canon in the sees of Faro, Guardo, and Braga. Ibid., p. 783n1.

33. Candido Mendes, "Epitome," p. 781n1, citing Borja Garção Stockler, *Panegyrico*, eulogy delivered on 17 Jan. 1799, the primary source for Mello Freire's biography.

34. Appointed to the Committee for the Organization of the Civil and Criminal Codes (*dec.* of 31 Mar. 1787), Mello Freire served until the latter was extinguished (*dec.* of 3 Feb. 1789). Candido Mendes, "Epitome," p. 781n1.

35. Idem, "Bibliografia," p. XXXIV–XXXV.

36. Paschalis Josephi Mellii Freirii, *Historiae juris civilis lusitani (liber singularis)* (Lisbon: Ex Typ. Regalis Academiae Scientiarum Olisponensis, 1788).

37. Mello Freire's reply to the Royal Board of Censorship remained unpublished until the board was abolished during the French occupation: *Resposta de Paschoal José de Mello Freire contra a censura do compendio* (1809). See also: Freire de Mello [Carvalho], *Censura da obra "Historiae juris civilis lusitani"* (1821). After reprintings in 1794 and 1800, new editions of the *Historiae* appeared in 1815 and 1842.

38. Watson, *Roman Law*, pp. 159–60, 176. I have relied heavily on Watson's dates and interpretative analysis for the jurists publishing in German mentioned in this section.

39. Ibid., p. 160.

40. Ibid., p. 162.

41. Ibid., p. 163. Stryk's key work was the *Elementa juris Germanicitum verterus tum hodierni* (1735/36). Another key source "mined" by Mello Freire was the *Juris Feudalis Hypomnemata* (last published in Utrecht in 1747), authored by the Prussian Henricus Coccejus (1644–1719). Ibid., pp. 247–48.

42. Ibid., p. 163.

43. Ibid., pp. 160–61.

44. Ibid., p. 247. Book 2 of the *Institutiones* cited G. L. Boehmer's *Inst. Eccl. Protest.* and *Qui filii sint legitimi*; Stryk's *De ritu nuptiarum*, in *Dissert. de jure putativo*, and *Tract. de succes. ab intest.* It also used Henri Cocceu's *Diss. de lege morganatica.*

45. Ibid.

46. Pereira Freire, *Instituiçoens* (1834), L.2, T.9, §27 (p. 142). Quotations of Mello Freire in English for this chapter were translated by the author from this first Brazilian edition of *De jure personarum.*

47. Ibid., T.9, §7 (p. 124).

48. Ibid., T.4, §7 (p. 37).

49. Ibid., T.6, §§11,17,21 (pp. 86, 90–91, 93–94).

50. Ibid., T.4, §15 (pp. 44–45).

51. Ibid., T.5, §10 (pp. 56–57), citing *Ord. Manuelinas*, L.2, T.47, §1; and *Ord. Filipinas*, L.4, T.88.

52. Ibid., §9 (p. 55).

53. Ibid.

54. Ibid. (pp. 55–56).

55. The Congregation of the Index condemned the *Institutiones* (*dec.* of 7 Jan. 1836) and omitted the clause known as *Donec corrigantur*, which presumed error had been committed in good faith as a Catholic. Candido Mendes, "Bibliographia," p. LIII. See also Beal, "Regalismo Brasil," pp. 27, 48–50.

56. *Instituiçoens* (1834), L.2, T.5, §15 (p. 63).

57. Ibid., §16 (pp. 63–64), citing Boehmer's refutation "and that of Rieger, to whose opinion I subscribe . . . we also use this law in our courts." Italics added.

58. Twinam, *Public Lives*, esp. 233–36, 267, 275–79.

59. Nizza da Silva, "Desembargo Paço," p. 61.

60. Ibid., p. 74 (citing AN, Cxa.127, Pacote 2, *Doc.* 21: D. Josefa Maria Francisca de Paula, widow of Col. José Vaz Salgado, petitioner). See also idem, "Filhos Ilegítimos," pp. 121–24. Muriel Nazzari discusses the same case: "Urgent Need to Conceal," p. 26.

61. Nizza da Silva, "Desembargo Paço," p. 74 (citing *AN, Cxa.* 127, *Pac.* 2, *Doc.* 11: José de Mendonça Dormund e Vasconcelos and D. Rosa Mariana de Jesus Moreira, petitioners).

62. *Instituiçoens* (1834), L.2, T.5, §15 (pp. 62–63). Mello Freire referred to the *ordenação* of the *Ord. Filipinas* (L.2, T.35). He also cited that of the *Ord. Manuelinas* (L.2, T.17, §9), because its text admitted ambiguity and appeared to support popular opinions on the subject: "*Com tanto que este filho fosse tal, que com direito podesse ser legitimado por* [sic] *segundo matrimonio.*" Ibid., §16n(a) (p. 64).

63. Borges Carneiro (*Dir. civ. Port.*, L.1, v.2, T.23, §203, pp. 321(a)–22), Coelho da Rocha (*Inst. dir. civ. port.*, vol. 1, Sec.3, Cap.2, §296, p. 203), and Perdigão Malheiro (*Com. Lei N. 463*, pp. 61–62) defended legitimization by subsequent marriage for adulterine individuals in the nineteenth century, suggesting the Desembargo do Paço in Lisbon had established some precedent for it. By the 1920s it was more accepted

among jurists, although the authoritative commentator of the 1916 Civil Code, João Luiz Alves, disagreed, concurring with the Code that it applied exclusively to natural offspring (*Cod. civ. 1916*, p. 189). Arthur Vasco Itabaiana de Oliveira, *Elementos sucessões*, Cap.4, Sec.2, §241 (p. 145n426).

64. Menezes, *Pratica dos Inventarios*, Cap.2, §36 (pp. 69n45–70), citing Dr. Caetano Alberto Soares (in *Gazeta dos Tribunaes*, 30 Sept. 1848) in support of Mello Freire, Stryk, and Rieger (contra Lobão); and *Rev. Juridica*, N.2 (Mar.–Apr. 1868), p. 270, on an *accordão* issued by the Relação da Corte for 13 Nov. 1863, upholding a ruling of an orphans judge.

65. Quoted in Ferreira Carrato, "Educational Reforms Pombal," p. 393.

66. *Decs.* of 21 Aug. 1786 and 20 Jan. 1787, cited in Candido Mendes, "Epitome," p. 782. Mello Freire was also appointed honorary appellate judge for the Casa do Porto (*dec.* of 28 Mar. 1778). Ibid., p. 781n.

67. Candido Mendes, "Bibliographia," p. LIII. It was significant that Mello Freire's Criminal Code Project did not see vernacular publication until 1823: *Ensaio do Codigo Criminal à mandou proceder a Rainha D. Maria I.* A vernacular version of his civil code project appeared much later, in 1844: *O Novo Codigo de Direito Publico de Portugal.* Candido Mendes, "Epitome," p. 782.

68. Paschalis Josephi Mellii Freirii, *Institutionum juris civilis lusitani cum publici tum privati . . .* (Lisbon: Ex Typ. Regalis Academiae Scientiarum Olisponensis, 1789–1793). The *Institutiones* were published as four books in eight volumes; each book was reprinted several times during the 1790s: Book 1, *De jure publico*: 1789 (1794, 1797); Book 2, *De jure personarum*: 1791 (1794, 1799); Book 3, *De jure rerum*: 1791 (1794, 1800); Book 4, *De obligationibus, et actionibus*: 1793 (1795, 1800). Mellii Freirii, *Historiae juris civilis lusitani, liber singularis*, 5th ed. (Coimbra: Typis Academicis, 1860), p. XVIIn.

69. *Institutionum juris criminalis lusitani, liber singularis*, four tomes in one volume (Lisbon: Ex Typis Regia, 1794; reprinted 1795, 1796). The second edition circulated widely: Paschalis Josephi Mellii Freireii, *Institutionum juris criminalis Lusitani liber singularis. Editio secunda . . . .* (Conimbricae: Ex Typ. Academico-Regia, 1829). Alternatively, Book 5 sometimes consisted of the *Historiae juris civilis lusitani (liber singularis)* (Lisbon: Ex Typis Regalis Academiae Scientiarum Olisponensis, 1788; reprinted 1794, 1800). This explains why various editions of the *Institutiones* differ in having either four or five books. Candido Mendes, "Epitome," pp. 781–82.

70. In 1804, Francisco Freire de Mello, Mello Freire's nephew, published a subject index for the *Historiae* and the *Institutiones*: *Elenchus capitum . . . .*

71. His views contrasted starkly with those of his fellow Civil Code Project Committee member, Antonio Ribeiro Sanches, who had moved to a "more constitutionalist interpretation of state and the role of civil society." Maxwell, *Pombal*, p. 161. Candido Mendes "Bibliographia," p. XXXIV.

72. Maxwell, *Pombal*, p. 158, citing nuncio Bartolomeu Cardinal Pacca, *Memoires historiques*, pp. 269–74.

73. Mello Freire signed the New Statutes of Coimbra University as "Paschoal José de Mello," but the name he authorized for the title pages of the original editions of the *Historiae* and *Institutiones* was the one universally used by nineteenth-century jurists: "Paschoal José de Mello Freire." Francisco Freire de Mello [Carvalho] formally attached "dos Reys" to his surnames, although it had appeared in print before Mello Freire died in 1798. Candido Mendes, "Epitome," p. 782n.

CONCLUSION

1. *Cur. dir. civil braz.*, 2:342, quoted by Candido Mendes, "Epitome," p. 782n. NOTE: Ribas paraphrased what was the preceding judgment of Coelho da Rocha: *Esboço*, p. 228.

2. "Bibliographia," p. xxxiv.

3. Oliveira Marques, *Lusitania to Empire*, 1:402–6.

4. Pereira de Castro's (1571–1632) two-volume *De manu regia, tractatus* (1622–1625) had been placed on the Index in 1640, but published in a new edition in 1673. Its republication, in 1742, followed the original publication of his vernacular treatise on regalism in 1738: *Monomachia sobre as concordias que fizeram os Reis com os Prelados de Portugal*. Beal, "Regalismo Brazil," p. 28.

5. For instance, Caetano José de Aguiar Aragão e Vasconcellos, a lawyer and a leader of the 1817 "revolution" in Brazil's northeastern provinces, systematically cited the juridical works of "Desembargador Pascoal José de Mello" in his political writings. Sousa Montenegro, *Liberalismo radical*, p. 210.

6. *Curso direito civil brasileiro* (1865), 2:342; quoted in Candido Mendes, "Epitome," p. 782n.

7. *Dir. familia*, p. xxiv.

8. Manoel de Almeida e Souza de Lobão, *Notas de uso pratico, e criticas, addicções, e remissões (á imitação das de Müller á Struvio), sobre todos os titulos dos livros 1, 2 e 3 das Instituições de Direito Civil Lusitano do Dr. Paschoal José de Mello Freire* (Lisbon: Imprensa Regia, 1818–1824), 4 volumes in 8 tomes.

9. Instruction of 7 May 1805, count of Villa Verde to Regent D. João VI; in Mellii Freirii, *Institutiones*, 5th ed., Livro 1, *De jure publico* (1853), p. IV.

10. Coelho da Rocha, *Ensaio*, pp. 227–28.

11. Candido Mendes, "Epitome," p. 783n1.

12. Watson, *Roman Law*, pp. 163–64.

13. *Ensaio*, p. 228.

14. *Notas*, Bk.2, T.2, §9 (p. 21).

15. Nizza da Silva, *Cultura e sociedade*, pp. 118–19 (items 14, 18). Advertisements in the *Gazeta do Rio de Janeiro* freely edited the full title of the *Notas à Mello* in order to give prominence to Mello Freire, not Lobão. Furthermore, Lobão's dissertations were not necessarily attributed to his authorship in either the *Gazeta* or Nizza da Silva's list.

16. Important collections of Lobão's juridical opinions circulated prior to the era of independence, published in Lisbon on the royal imprint: *Tractado pratico de morgados*, 2nd ed. (1814); *Tratado, pratico compendiario de todas as acções summarias* (1817); *Fasciculo de dissertações juridico-praticas* (1816); and, especially, *Segundas linhas sobre o processo civil*, 2 vols. (1817). For the 1820s, see also his *Collecção de dissertações juridicas, e praticas* (1826) and the concordat guides to Lobão's works: Novaes e Souza, *Indice obras Lobão* (1829); Furtado Galvão, *Directorio obras Souza de Lobão* (1836); and the same author's 2nd ed. of the latter, *Continuação do Directorio* (1855). Republished in 1828–1835, the *Notas á Mello* appeared in two more editions, in 1861–1863 and 1883. Lobão's *Segundas linhas* (1817), a civil law commentary on Pereira e Souza's *Primeiras linhas* (1810), remained in print until the twentieth century (1910–1911), as did his *Acções summarias* (1903).

17. Manuel Borges Carneiro, *Direito civil de Portugal contendo três livros: I. Das pessoas; II. Das cousas; III. Das obrigações e acções* (Lisbon: Typ. de José Antonio da Rocha, 1826–1828, 1844). Only Book 1 (the law of persons), in 3 tomes, appeared in complete form in the 1820s. Book 2 (the law of things), in 4 tomes, was published posthumously, together with a reprinted Book 1 (Lisbon: Typ. de Antonio José da Rocha, 1844, 1851). Book 3 (law of obligations and actions) was never written. Silva, *Diccionario bibliographico portuguez,* 5:378.

18. Borges Carneiro, *Dir. civ. Port.,* Preface, L.1, v.1, p. VII.

19. Corrêa Telles, *Com. Lei Boa Razão;* reprinted in Candido Mendes, *Aux. juridico,* pp. 443–79. Corrêa Telles, "Ao leitor," in *Dig. portuguêz* (1860), 1:6.

20. "Ao leitor," in *Dig. portuguêz* (1860), 1:8.

21. Corrêa Telles, *Manual do tabellião, ou ensaios de jurisprudencia eurematica* (1819). Nizza da Silva, *Cultura e sociedade,* p. 119 (item 33). Pereira de Vasconcellos' *Nov. manual tabellião* (1864) was the first to adapt Corrêa Telles to Brazilian usage.

22. "Ao leitor," in *Dig. portuguêz* (1860), 1:6. The full title was *Digesto portuguêz, ou tratado das obrigações civis accommodado ás Leis e costumes da Nação Portugueza* (1835).

23. Statutes of the viscount of Cachoeira (Law of 11 Aug. 1827, Art.10), quoted verbatim in Bevilaqua, *Faculdade Direito Recife,* pp. 21–22.

24. Ibid., pp. 22–23.

25. Pereira Freire, "A Quem Ler," in *Instituiçoens* (1834), n.p. See n45.

26. Liz Teixeira, *Curso de direito civil portuguez para o anno lectivo de 1842–1843, ou commentario às Instituições do Sr. Paschoal José de Mello Freire,* 3 vols. (Coimbra: Imprensa da Universidade, 1845). M. A. Coelho da Rocha's *Instituições de direito civil portuguez* (Coimbra: Imp. da Universidade, 1844), also widely used, was not adapted to Brazilian practice until 1907.

27. Meira, *Teixeira de Freitas,* p. 53.

28. Gomes B. Câmara, *Subsídios direito pátrio,* 3:150–51; Meira, *Teixeira de Freitas,* p. 96. The second and third editions of the *Dig. port.* were published by Coimbra University Press in 1840 and 1845–1846, respectively, and a 4th edition in 1853–1858.

29. Gomes B. Câmara, *Direito pátrio,* 3:151.

30. Trigo de Loureiro, *Instituições do direito civil brasileiro, extrahidas das Instituições de direito civil lusitano do eximio jurisconsulto portuguez, Paschoal José de Mello Freire, na parte compativel com as instituições de nossa cidade, e augmentadas nos lugares competentes . . . com a substancia das leis brasileiras pelo. . .* (Pernambuco [Recife]: Typ. da Viuva Roma & Filhos, 1851). Bevilaqua, *Faculdade Direito Recife,* p. 36.

Legal Primary Sources Cited

I. JURIDICAL COMMENTARIES, TREATISES,
DISSERTATIONS, AND NOTARIAL MANUALS

Aguiar Souza. *Posição juridical dos filhos naturaes em face do nosso direito*. São Paulo: Typ. Hennies Irmãos, 1916.

Bevilaqua, Clovis. *Direito da familia*. 2nd ed. Recife: Ramiro M. Costa & Cia., 1904.

———. *Direito das Successões*. Bahia [Salvador]: Liv. Magalhães, 1899.

———. *Theoria geral do direito civil (actualizada por Achilles Bevilaqua)*. Rio de Janeiro & São Paulo: Liv. Francisco Alves, 1946.

Blackstone, Sir William. *Commentaries on the Laws of England in Four Books, with an Analysis of the Work. With a Life of the Author and Notes by Christian, Chitty, Lee, Hovendon, and Ryland*. New York: W. E. Dean, 1838.

———. *Commentaries on the Laws of England by Sir William Blackstone, K.T.* 2 vols., edited by William Casey Jones. San Francisco: Bancroft Whitney Company, 1915.

Borges Carneiro, Manuel. *Direito civil de Portugal contendo três livros: I. Das pessoas; II. Das cousas; III. Das obrigações e acções*. Lisbon: Typ. de Antonio José da Rocha, 1826–1828, 1844.

Bracton [Henry de]. *Bracton on the Laws and Customs of England*. Vol. 2. Translated by Samuel E. Thorne. Cambridge, Mass.: The Belknap Press of Harvard University Press.

Coelho da Rocha, M[anoel] A[ugusto]. *Instituições de direito civil portuguez por ... para o uso dos seus discipulos*. 3rd ed. Coimbra: Imp. da Universidade, 1852.

Corrêa Telles, José Homem. *Commentario critico a lei da boa razão em data de 18 de Agosto de 1769; e discurso sobre a equidade, para servir de supplemento ao preambulo desta lei*. Lisbon: Imp. Regia, 1824.

———. *Digesto portuguêz, ou tratado das obrigações civis accommodado ás Leis e costumes da Nação Portugueza para servir de subsidio ao novo codigo civil por ....* 3 vols. Lisbon: Coimbra: Imp. da Universidade, 1835.

———. *Digesto portuguêz ou tractado dos direitos e obrigações civis accommodado ás leis e costumes da nação portugueza para servir de subsidio ao novo codigo civil por ....* 3 tomes in 1 volume. 5th ed. Coimbra: Liv. J. Augusto Orcel, 1860.

———. *Manual do tabellião, ou ensaios de jurisprudencia eurematica, contendo a collecção de minutas dos contractos, instrumentos mais usuaes, e das cautelas mais precisas nos contratos, e testamentos, por ....* Lisbon: Imp. Regia, 1819.

Cunha Mattos, Raymundo José da. *Repertorio da legislação militar, actualmente em vigor no exercito e armada do Imperio do Brazil*, 3 vols. Rio de Janeiro: Typ. Imperial e Constitucional de Seignot & Plancer, 1834–1842.

Furtado Galvão, Luiz Guilherme Peres. *Continuação do directorio para presto se achar nos dez livros que ultimamente se publicaram das Obras do Jurisconsulto Souza de Lobão, a explicação, illustração, e combinação de todos os titulos, e paragraphos das Ordenações do Reino, e o que sobre elles discorreo breve ou extensamente o dito Jurisconsulto, feito para uso particular de seu author....* Lisbon: Imp. Nacional, 1855.

————. *Directorio para presto se achar nos vinte livros (que primeiro se publicarão) das obras do jurisconsulto Souza de Lobão, a explicação, illustração, e combinação de todos os titulos, e §§ das Ordenações do Reino, e o que sobre elles discorre, ou extensa, ou brevemente o dito Juris-Consulto, feito para uso particular de seu auctor....* Lisbon: Imp. Nacional, 1836.

Gouvêa Pinto, Antonio Joaquim de. *Tratado regular, e prático de testamentos, e successões, ou compendio methódico das principaes regras, e principios que se podem deduzir das leis testamentarias, tanto patrias, como subsidiarias, illustrados, e aclarados com as competentes notas.* Lisbon: Simão Thaddeo Ferreira, 1813.

Itabaiana de Oliveira, Arthur Vasco. *Elementos de direito das successões: Exposição doutrinaria do Livro IV da Parte Especial do Codigo Civil Brasileiro (Lei n. 3.071 de 1 de janeiro de 1916).* Rio de Janeiro: Typ. *Jornal do Commercio*/Rodrigues & Cia, 1929.

Liz Teixeira, Antonio Ribeiro. *Curso de direito civil portuguez, ou commentario às Instituições do Sr. Paschoal José de Mello Freire, sobre o mesmo direito, por ....* 3rd ed. Coimbra: J. Augusto Orcel, 1856.

————. *Curso de direito civil portuguez para o anno lectivo de 1842–1843, ou commentario às Instituições do Sr. Paschoal José de Mello Freire.* 3 vols. Coimbra: Liv. da Universidade, 1845.

Lobão, Manoel de Almeida e Souza de. "Analyse da *Ordenação* Livro 2, Titulo 35, Artigo 12." In *Collecção de dissertações juridicas, e praticas por ...* , 3–35. Lisbon: Imp. Regia, 1826.

————. *Collecção de dissertações juridicas, e praticas em supplemento ás Notas do Livro Terceiro das Instituições do dr. Pascoal J. M. Freire por ....* Lisbon: Imp. Regia, 1826.

————. *Fasciculo de dissertações juridico-praticas por ....* 2 vols. Lisbon: Imp. Nacional, 1849–1866.

————. *Notas de uso pratico, e criticas, addicções, e remissões (á imitação das de Müller á Stuvio), sobre todos os titulos dos livros 1, 2 e 3 das Instituições de Direito Civil Lusitano do Dr. Paschoal José de Mello Freire.* 3 vols. Lisbon: Imp. Regia, 1818–1824.

————. *Segundas linhas sobre o processo civil, ou antes addições as primeiras do bacharel Joaquim José Caetano Pereira e Souza, por ....* 2 vols. Lisbon: Imp. Regia, 1817.

————. *Tratado pratico compendiario de todas as acções summarias, sua indole e natureza em geral e em especial das summarias, preparatorias, provisionaes, incidentes, preconceitos comminatorios, etc. e requirisitos respectivos e excepções dos réus em cada das ditas acções e preceitos e practica d'estes contra os erros vulgares com appendice de dissertações por ....* Lisbon: Imp. Regia, 1817.

————. *Tractado pratico de morgados por ... editada, corregida e addicionada pelo autor.* 2nd ed. Lisbon: Imp. Regia, 1814.

Mellii Freireii, Paschalis Josephi. *Institutiones juris civilis lusitani, cum publici, tum privati.* 5th ed. Vol. 1, *De jure publico.* Conimbricae: Typis Academicis, 1853.

————. *Institutionum juris civilis lusitani, cum publici, tum privati.* 4 vols. Lisbon: Ex Typis Regalis Academiae Scientiarum Olisponensis, 1789–1793.

————. *Institutiones juris criminalis lusitani, liber singularis. Edito prima in usum Auditorii Conimbricensus juxta primam Olisiponensem an. 1794, sed auctior et emendatior, curante Joachimo Ignatio Freitasio.* Conimbricae: Typis Academicis, 1815.

————. *Regio Equestrium Ordinum Collegio olim collegae. Institutionum juris criminalis Lusitani liber singularis. Editio secunda in usum Auditorii Conimbricensis.* Conimbricae: Ex Typis Academico-Regia, 1829.

Mello Freire [de Carvalho], Francisco de. *Elenchus capitum, titulorum, et paragaphorum in Historia et Institutionibus juris civilis et criminalis Lusitani: quas Paschalis Josephus Mellius Freirus elucubravit, contentorum: adcedit index generalis rerum et verborum; studio Francisci Freirii Mellii pro desideratissimi avunculi scriptorum faciliori usu.* Editio secunda juxta primam Olisipon. Lisbon: Typ. Regia, 1804.

Mendes de Almeida, Candido. *Auxiliar juridico servindo de appendice a decima-quarta edição do Codigo Philippino ou as Ordenações do Reino do Portugal recopiladas por mandado de El-Rel D. Philippe I, a primeira publicada no Brasil aos que se dedicão ao estudo do direito e da jurisprudência patria por . . . .* Rio de Janeiro: Typ. de Instituto Philomathico, 1869.

————. "Bibliographia." In Candido Mendes de Almeida, *Ordenações Philippinas . . . ,* X–LXII. Rio de Janeiro: Typ. de Instituto Philomathico, 1870.

————. "Epitome dos trabalhos juridico-litterarios dos jurisconsultos." In Candido Mendes de Almeida, *Auxiliar juridico . . . ,* 781–88. Rio de Janeiro: Typ. de Instituto Philomathico, 1869.

Menezes, Alberto Carlos de. *Pratica dos inventarios, partilhas e contas. Primeira parte dos juizos divisorios, obra necessaria aos que começão no auditorio forense facilitando o uso da materia divisioria nas diversas questões . . . por . . . annotado pelo bacharel J. P. J. da S. C.* 6th ed. Rio de Janeiro: Liv. A. A. da Cruz Coutinho, 1878.

Nascimento e Silva, Manoel Joaquim do. *Synopse da legislação militar brazileira até 1874 cujo conhecimento mais interessa aos empregados do Ministerio da Guerra.* 2 vols. Rio de Janeiro: Typ. do *Diario do Rio de Janeiro*, 1874.

Novaes e Souza, Joaquim de Almeida. *Indice geral das obras de Manoel de Almeida e Souza de Lobão.* Lisbon: Imp. Regia, 1829.

Perdigão Malheiro [Augostinho Marques]. *Commentario à lei N. 463 de 2 de setembro de 1847 sobre successão dos filhos naturaes, e sua filiação.* Rio de Janeiro: Eduardo e Henrique Laemmert, 1857.

Pereira de Castro, Gabriel. *De manu regia tractatus, in quo explicantur omnes Leges Regiae Regni Lusitanae, in quibus Regi cognoscendi de materiis Ecclesiasticis potestas tributu.* 2 vols. Lisbon [Vlyssipone]: 1622–1625.

————. *Monomachia sobre as concordias que fizeram os Reis com os Prelados de Portugal, nas duvidadas de jurisdicção, ecclesiastica e temporal, e as breves de que forão tiradas algumas ordenações com as confirmações apostolicas que . . . .* Lisbon Occidental: 1738.

Pereira de Vasconcellos, F. M. P. *Novissimo manual do tabellião, ou collecão dos actos, attribuições e deveres d'estes funccionarios, contendo a collecção de minutas de con-*

tractos e instrumentos mais usuaes . . . ordenada sobre o Manual de José Homem Corrêa Telles por . . . . Rio de Janeiro: Liv. dos Editores Antonio Gonçalves Guimarães & C.ª, 1864.

Pereira e Souza, Joaquim José Caetano. *Classes de crimes, por ordem systematica: com as penas correspondentes, segundo a legislação actual.* Lisbon: J. F. M. de Campos, 1802.

———. *Primeiras linhas sobre o processo civil.* Lisbon: Typ. Lacerdina, 1810.

Pereira Freire, Francisco. *Instituiçoens de direito civil luzitano tanto publico como particular por Paschoal José de Mello Freire traducidas do latim por . . . livro segundo do direito das pessoas.* Pernambuco [Recife]: Typ. de Pinheiro & Faria, 1834.

Ribas, Antonio Joaquim. *Curso de direito civil brasileiro (parte geral).* 2 vols. Rio de Janeiro: Typ. Universal de Laemmert, 1865.

Rodrigues Pereira, Lafayette. *Direitos de familia por . . . .* Rio de Janeiro: B. L. Garnier, 1869.

Tavares Bastos, Cassiano Candido. *Registro Civil dos nascimentos, casamentos e obitos . . . Regul. N. 5604 de 25 de abril de 1874 e o N. 3069 de 17 de abril de 1863 . . . .* Rio de Janeiro: H. Garnier, 1887.

Teixeira de Freitas, Augusto. *Tratado dos testamentos, e successões por Antonio Joaquim Gouvêa Pinto accommodado ao fôro do Brasil até o anno de 1881 por . . . .* Rio de Janeiro: B. L. Garnier, 1881.

Trigo de Loureiro, Lourenço. *Instituições do direito civil brasileiro, extrahidas das Instituições de direito civil lusitano do eximio jurisconsulto portuguez, Paschoal José de Mello Freire, na parte compativel com as instituições de nossa cidade, e augmentadas nos lugares competentes . . . com a substancia das leis brasileiras pelo . . . .* Pernambuco [Recife]: Typ. da Viuva Roma & Filhos, 1851.

II. CONSTITUTIONS, CODES, AND COLLECTIONS OF LAWS

Borges Carneiro, Manoel. *Additamento geral das leis, resoluções, avisos, etc., desde 1603 até o presente, que não entrou no Indice Chronologico, nem no Extracto de Leis, e seu Appendice, pelo author destes . . . .* Lisbon: Imp. Regia, 1817.

Brazil. *Codigo Criminal do Império do Brasil [1830].* In *Códigos penais do Brasil: Evolução histórica,* edited by José Henrique Pierangelli, 167–265. Bauru, São Paulo: Edição Jalovi Ltda., 1980.

———. *Collecção das leis do imperio brazileiro.* [Title varies.] Rio de Janeiro: Typ. Nacional, 1808–1889.

Delgado da Silva, Antonio. *Collecção da legislação portugueza desde a ultima compilação das ordenações, redigida pelo Desembargador . . . .* 9 vols. Lisbon: Typ. Maigrense, 1825–1847.

Mello Freire, Paschoal José de. *Ensaio do Codigo Criminal á que mandou proceder a Rainha D. Maria I.* Lisbon: 1823.

———. *O Novo Codigo de Direito Publico de Portugal, com as provas, compilado pelo desembargador . . . .* Coimbra: Imp. Universitaria, 1844.

Mendes de Almeida, Candido. *Codigo Philippino ou Ordenações e Leis do Reino de Portugal recopiladas por mandado d'El-Rey D. Philippe I, decima-quarta edição, segundo a primeira de 1603, e a nona de Coimbra de 1824.* Rio de Janeiro: Typ. do Instituto Philomathico, 1870.

────. *Direito civil ecclesiastico brazileiro, antigo e moderno, em suas relações com o direito canonico ou collecção completa chronologicamente disposta desde a primeira dynastia portugueza até o presente comprehendendo . . . por . . . .* 2 vols. Rio de Janeiro: B. L. Garnier, 1873.

"Novo Regimento da Mesa do Desembargo do Paço (Lei de 27 de julho de 1582)." Reprinted in Candido Mendes de Almeida, *Codigo Philippino . . .* , 241–53. Rio de Janeiro: Typographia Philomathico, 1870.

Pierangelli, José Henrique, ed. *Códigos Penais do Brasil: Evolução histórica.* São Paulo: Edição Jalovi, 1980.

Portugal. *Ordenações do Senhor Rey D. Affonso V.* In *Collecção da Legislação Antiga e Moderna do Reino de Portugal.* Pt. I, *Da Legislação Antiga.* 5 vols. in 3. Coimbra: Real Imp. da Universidade, 1787–1792.

────. *Ordenações do Senhor Rey D. Manoel.* In *Collecção da Legislação Antiga e Moderna do Reino de Portugal.* Pt. I, *Da Legislação Antiga.* 5 vols. in 3. Coimbra: Real Imp. da Universidade, 1797.

Silva Mafra, Manoel da. *Pomptuario das leis de manumissão, ou indice alphabetico das disposições da Lei N. 2040 de 28 de setembro de 1871 . . . regulamentos . . . avisos . . . e da jurisprudencia do Conselho de Estado dos Tribunaes das Relações e Supremo Tribunal de Justiça, por . . . .* Rio de Janeiro: Typ. Nacional, 1877.

Teixeira de Freitas, Augusto. *Codigo civil: Esboço.* Rio de Janeiro: Typ. Nacional, 1860–1861.

────. *Consolidação das leis civis.* Rio de Janeiro: Typ. Universal de Laemmert, 1857.

Vide, Sebastião Monteiro da. *Constituições primeiras do Arcebispado da Bahia feitas, e ordenadas pelo illustrissimo, e reverendissimo senhor D. Sebastião Monteiro da Vide, 5º Arcebispo do dito Arcebispado, e do Conselho de Sua Magestade: propostas, e aceitas em o synodo diocesano, que o dito senhor celebrou em 12 de junho do anno de 1707.* São Paulo: Typ. 2 de Dezembro, 1853.

Other Sources Cited

WILLS IN MANUSCRIPT

Arquivo Histórico Municipal, Franca, Estado de São Paulo. Courtesy of Dimas José Batista:
  Silva Costa, Francisca da. 1864. Caixa 0086, No. 10; *Ofício Civil, folhas* 8 *e verso.*
Arquivo Público do Estado da Bahia, Seção Judiciária, Registro de Testamentos e Inventários. Courtesy of Hendrik Kraay:
  Alves da Costa, Capt. Manoel. Oct. 6, 1826. Vol. 17, No.312.
  Gomes de Almeida, Sgt°-Mór Custodio. Sept. 6, 1820. [04/1748/2218/01], No. 154.
Museu de Ouro, Sabará, Estado de Minas Gerais. Courtesy of Kathleen Higgins:
  Crasto Porto, Mathias de. 6 Oct. 1742. *Inventários* (1740–1746).
  Lopes Freire, Capt. João. 5 Oct. 1790. Livro de Testamentos, 18 Jan. 1791, *folhas* 156–57 *verso.*
  Pinheiro, Francisco Gonçalves. Mar. 24, 1719. Livro de Testamentos (1716–1725), *folha* 7.
  Silva, Caetano Fernandes da. Feb. 27, 1771. Livro de Testamentos, 22 May 1770, *folha* 56 *verso.*

BOOKS AND ARTICLES

Barman, R. J. "A New-World Nobility: The Role of Titles in Imperial Brazil." In *University of British Columbia Hispanic Studies*, edited by Harold Livermore, 39–50. London: Tamesis Books Limited, 1974.
Barman, Roderick J., and Jean Barman. "The Role of the Law Graduates in the Political Elite of Imperial Brazil." *Journal of International Studies and World Affairs* 18 (1976): 423–50.
Beal, Tarcisio. "Os Jesuítas, a Universidade de Coimbra e a Igreja Brasileira, subsídios para a história do regalismo em Portugal e no Brasil, 1750–1850." Ph.D. diss., The Catholic University of America, 1969.
Behar, Ruth, and David Frye. "Property, Progeny, and Emotion: Family History in a Leonese Village." *Journal of Family History* 13 (1988): 13–32.
Bevilaqua, Clovis. *História da Faculdade de Direito do Recife, edição comemorativa do Sesquicentenário da Instauração dos Cursos Jurídicos no Brasil (1827–1977).* 2nd ed. São Paulo: Instituto Nacional do Livro/Conselho Nacional da Cultura, 1977.
Borges, Dain. *The Family in Bahia, Brazil, 1870–1940.* Stanford: Stanford University Press, 1992.

Borges da Fonseca, Vitoriano. *Nobiliarchia pernambucana*. 2 vols. In *Annaes da Biblioteca Nacional* [Rio de Janeiro], vols. 47 (1925) and 48 (1926).

Brading, D. A. *The First America: The Spanish Monarchy, Creole Patriots, and the Spanish State, 1492–1867*. Cambridge: Cambridge University Press, 1991.

Brandão, Maria de Fátima. "Land, Inheritance and Family in North-West Portugal: The Case of Mosteiro in the Nineteenth Century." Ph.D. diss., School of Modern Languages and European History, University of East Anglia, 1988.

Brettell, Carolyn B. *Men Who Migrate, Women Who Wait: Population and History in a Portuguese Parish*. Princeton: Princeton University Press, 1986.

Bruschini, Cristina, and Fúlvia Rosemberg, eds. *Vivência: História, sexualidade e imagens femininas*. Vol. 1. São Paulo: Brasiliense, 1980.

Burns, Robert I., ed. *The Worlds of Alfonso the Learned and James the Conqueror: Intellect and Force in the Middle Ages*. Princeton: Princeton University Press, 1985.

Calazans Falcon, Francisco. *Época pombalina: Política econômica e monarquia ilustrada*. São Paulo: Editora Ática, 1980.

Cappelletti, M., J. Merryman, and J. Perillo. *The Italian Legal System: An Introduction*. Stanford: Stanford University Press, 1967.

Casey, James, and Francisco Chacón Jiménez, eds. *La familia en la España mediterránea, siglos XV–XIX*. Barcelona: Centre d'Estudis d'Història Moderna "Pierre Vilar"/Editorial Crítica, 1987.

Chacón Jiménez, Francisco, and Juan Hernández Franco, eds. *Poder, familia y consanguinidad en la España del antiguo régimen*. Barcelona: Anthropos, Editoral del Hombre, 1992.

Chacón Jiménez, Francisco, Juan Hernández Franco, and A. Peñafiel Ramón, eds. *Familia, grupos sociales y mujer en España (S. XV–XIX)*. Murcia: Universidade de Murcia, 1991.

Coelho da Rocha, M[anoel] A[ugusto]. *Ensaio sobre a historia do governo e da legislação de Portugal para servir de introducção ao Estudo do direito patrio por . . . .* 2nd ed. Coimbra: Da Imp. da Universidade, 1843.

Dauphinee, Bede A[nthony]. "Church and Parliament in Brazil During the First Empire, 1823–1831." Ph.D. diss., Georgetown University, 1965.

Davidson, Theresa Sherrer. "The Brazilian Inheritance of Roman Law." In *Brazil: Papers Presented in the Institute for Brazilian Studies, Vanderbilt University*, edited by James B. Watson, Theresa Scherrer Davidson, and Earl W. Thomas, 59–90. Nashville: Vanderbilt University Press, 1953.

D'Incao, Maria Angela, ed. *Amor e família no Brasil*. São Paulo: Contexto, 1989.

———. "O amor romántico e a família burguesa." In *Amor e família no Brasil*, edited by Maria Angela d'Incao, 57–71. São Paulo: Contexto, 1989.

Ditz, Toby. *Property and Kinship: Inheritance in Early Connecticut, 1750–1820*. Princeton: Princeton University Press, 1986.

Egas, Eugenio. *Diogo Antonio Feijó (Estudo)*. S. Paulo: Typ. Levi, 1912.

Fernández Pérez, Paloma. *El rostro familiar de la metrópoli: redes de parentesco y Lazos mercantiles em Cadiz, 1700–1812*. Madrid: Siglo XXI de España, 1997.

Ferreira Carrato, José. "The Enlightenment in Portugal and the Educational Reforms of the Marquis of Pombal." In *Studies on Voltaire and the Eighteenth Century*, vol. 167, edited by James A. Leith, 359–92. Oxford: The Voltaire Foundation at the Taylor Institution, 1977.

Flusche, Della M. *The Tribunal of Posthumous Estates in Colonial Chile, 1540–1769.* Della M. Flushche, 1998.

Freire de Mello, Francisco. *Censura da obra "Historiae juris civilis lusitani do illustre mestre Paschoal José de Mello" por um theologo eristico, resposta do autor da obra censurada, resposta de Manuel Francisco da Silva e Veiga Magro de Moura, adjutante do procurador da coroa publicado pelo . . . .* Lisbon: Imp. Nacional, 1821.

Freitas, Affonso A. de. "Notas sobre a filiação, puericia e adolescência do Padre Feijó." *Revista do Instituto Historico e Geografico de São Paulo* 23 (1925): 72–95.

Gacto, Enrique. "El grupo familiar en la Edad Moderna en los territorios mediterráneos: una visión jurídica." In *La familia en la España mediterránea, siglos XV–XIX,* edited by James Casey and Francisco Chacón Jiménez, 36–64. Barcelona: Centre d'Estudis d'Història Moderna "Pierre Vilar"/Editorial Crítica, 1987.

Gama Lima, Lana Lage da, ed. *Mulheres, adultérios e padres.* Rio de Janeiro: Raymundo Paula de Arruda, 1987.

Gérson, Brasil. *O regalismo brasileiro.* Rio de Janeiro: Liv. Editôra Cátedra, 1978.

Glass, D. V., and D. E. C. Eversley, eds. *Population in History: Essays in Historical Demography.* London: Edward Arnold, 1965.

Glendon, Mary Ann, Michael W. Gordon, and Cristopher Osakwe. *Comparative Legal Traditions,* Nutshell Series. St. Paul: West Publishing Co., 1982.

Gomes B. Câmara, José. *Subsídios para a história do direito pátrio,* vol. 3, *1822–1889.* Rio de Janeiro: Liv. Brasiliana Editôra, 1966.

Goody, Jack [John Rancine]. *The Development of the Family and Marriage in Europe.* Cambridge: Cambridge University Press, 1983.

Hajnal, J. H. "European Marriage Patterns in Perspective." In *Population in History: Essays in Historical Demography,* edited by D. V. Glass and D. E. C. Eversley, 100–143. London: Edward Arnold, 1965.

———. "Two Kinds of Pre-Industrial Household Formation Systems." In *Family Forms in Historic Europe,* edited by Richard Wall, Jean Robin, and Peter Laslett, 65–104. Cambridge: Cambridge University Press, 1983.

Higgins, Kathleen. *"Licentious Liberty" in a Brazilian Gold-Mining Region: Slavery, Gender, and Social Control in Eighteenth-Century Sabará, Minas Gerais.* University Park: The Pennsylvania State University Press, 1999.

Instituto Historico e Geographico Brasileiro. *Diccionario historico, geographico e ethnographico do Brasil (Commemorativo do Primeiro Centario da Independencia).* 2 vols. Rio de Janeiro: Imp. Nacional, 1922.

Ireland, Robert M. "The Libertine Must Die: Sexual Dishonor and the Unwritten Law in Nineteenth-Century United States." *Journal of Social History* 23, 1 (1989): 27–44.

Jansen, José. "Introdução ao nobiliário maranhense." *Anais do Museu Histórico Nacional* 21 (1969): 165–69.

Johnson, Lyman L., and Sonya Lipsett-Rivera, eds. *The Faces of Honor: Sex, Shame, and Violence in Colonial Latin America.* Albuquerque: University of New Mexico Press, 1998.

Karasch, Mary. *Slave Life in Rio de Janeiro, 1800–1850.* Princeton: Princeton University Press, 1987.

Karst, Kenneth L. and Keith S. Rosenn. *Law and Development in Latin America: A Case Book.* UCLA Latin American Studies Series, vol. 28. Los Angeles & Berkeley: University of California Press, 1975.

Kertzer, David I., and Caroline Brettell. "Advances in Italian and Iberian Family History." *Journal of Family History* 12 (1987): 85–120.

Klein, Herbert S. "The Colored Freedmen in Brazilian Slave Society." *Journal of Family History* 3 (1969): 30–52.

Koster, Henry. *Travels in Brazil*. London: Longman, Hurst, Rees, Orme, and Brown, 1816.

Kraay, Hendrik, ed. *Afro-Brazilian Culture and Politics: Bahia, 1790s–1990s*. Armonk, New York: M. E. Sharpe, 1998.

———. "The Politics of Independence-Era Bahia: The Black Militia Officers of Salvador, 1790–1840." In *Afro-Brazilian Culture and Politics: Bahia, 1790s–1990s*, edited by Hendrik Kraay, 30–56. Armonk, NY: M. E. Sharpe, 1998.

Kuznesof, Elizabeth Anne. "Sexual Politics, Race and Bastard-Bearing in Nineteenth-Century Brazil: A Question of Culture or Power?" *Journal of Family History* 16 (1991): 241–60.

Laslett, Peter. "Family and Household as Work Groups and Kin Groups: Areas of Traditional Europe Compared." In *Family Forms in Historic Europe*, edited by Richard Wall, Jean Robin, and Peter Laslett, 513–63. Cambridge: Cambridge University Press, 1983.

Laslett, Peter, Karla Oosterveen, and Richard M. Smith, eds. *Bastardy and Its Comparative History: Studies in the History of Illegitimacy and Marital Nonconformism in Britain, France, Germany, Sweden, North America, Jamaica, and Japan*. Cambridge: Harvard University Press, 1980.

Lavrin, Asunción, ed. *Sexuality and Marriage in Colonial Latin America*. Lincoln: University of Nebraska Press, 1989.

Leal, Aureliano. "Historia judiciaria do Brasil." In *Diccionario historico, geographico e ethnographico do Brasil (Commemorativo do Primeiro Centario da Independencia)*, 2 vols., edited by the Instituto Historico e Geographico Brasileiro, 1:1107–87. Rio de Janeiro: Imp. Nacional, 1922.

Leith, James A., ed. *Studies on Voltaire and the Eighteenth Century*, vol. 167. Oxford: The Voltaire Foundation at the Taylor Institution, 1977.

Lewcowicz, Ida. "A fragilidade do celibato." In *Mulheres, adultérios e padres*, edited by Lana Lage da Gama e Lima, 53–68. Rio de Janeiro: Raymundo Paula de Arruda, 1987.

Lewin, Linda. "Natural and Spurious Offspring in Brazilian Inheritance Law from Colony to Empire: A Methodological Essay." *The Americas* 48 (1992): 351–96.

———. "'The Body Vanishes': The Secret Birth and Strange Death of a Brazilian Regent—Or, the True Story of Diogo Antonio Feijó's Bill to Abolish Clerical Celibacy." Paper for the Latin American Studies Association Meeting, 19 Apr. 1997; Guadalajara, Mexico.

Livermore, H. V. *A New History of Portugal*. Cambridge: Cambridge University Press, 1969.

Livermore, Harold, ed. *University of British Columbia Hispanic Studies*. London: Tamesis Books Limited, 1974.

Lobo de A. Campos, Alzira. "A configuração dos agregados como grupo social: marginalidade e peneiramento (o exemplo da cidade de São Paulo no século XVIII)." *Revista de História* (Nova Série [SP]), Nº 117 (July–Dec. 1984): 27–69.

Lopes, Eliane Cristina. "A bastardia na São Paulo setecentista." *Populações (Boletim de CEDHAL)*. No. 2 (Aug. 1995): 1–6.

Lustosa da Costa. *O senador dos bois: Correspondência do Senador Paula Pessoa*. Sobral, Ceará: Edições UVA, 2000.

MacDonald, Robert A. "Law and Politics: Alfonso's Program of Political Reform." In *The Worlds of Alfonso the Learned and James the Conqueror*, edited by Robert I. Burns, 150–202. Princeton: Princeton University Press, 1985.

Marcílio, Maria Luiza. *Caiçara: terra e população (estudo de demografia histórica e da história social de Ubatuba)*. São Paulo: CEDHAL, 1986.

———. *História social da criança abandonada*. São Paulo: HUCITEC, 1998.

Martínez Alier, Verena. *Marriage, Class, and Colour in Nineteenth-Century Cuba*. London: Oxford University Press, 1974.

Mattoso Queirós, Kátia de. *Família e sociedade na Bahia do século XIX*. São Paulo: Editora Corrupio, 1988.

———. *Testamentos de escravos libertos do século XIX: Uma fonte para o estudo de mentalidades*. Estudos Bahianos, No. 85. Salvador: Universidad Federal de Bahia, 1979.

Maxwell, Kenneth. *Pombal: Paradox of the Enlightenment*. Cambridge: Cambridge University Press, 1995.

Meira, Silvio. *Teixeira de Freitas, o jurisconsulto do império: Vida e obra*. Rio de Janeiro: José Olympio Editora/MEC, 1978.

Mellii Freirii, Paschalis Josephi. *Historiae juris civilis lusitani (liber singularis)*. Lisbon: Ex Typis Regalis Academiae Scientiarum Olisponensis, 1788.

Mello e Souza, Laura de. *Desclassificados de ouro: A pobreza mineira no século XIX*. Rio de Janeiro: Graal, 1982.

Mello Freire, Paschoal José de. *Resposta de Paschoal José de Mello Freire contra a censura do compendio—Historiae juris civilis lusitani feita por Antonio Pereira de Figueiredo, deputado da extincta Real Mesa Censoria*. Lisbon: 1809.

Merryman, John Henry, and David S. Clark. *Comparative Law: Western European and Latin American Legal Systems*. Indianapolis and New York: The Bobbs-Merrill Co., Inc., 1978.

Mesquita Samara, Eni. "O dote na sociedade paulista do século XIX." *Anais do Museu Paulista* 30 (1980/1981): 41–53.

———. "A família na sociedade paulista do século XIX, 1800–1860." Ph.D. diss., University of São Paulo, 1980.

———. "Família, divórcio e partilha de bens em São Paulo no século XIX." *Estudos Econômicos* 13 (1983): 787–97.

Metcalf, Alida. *Family Power and Frontier in Colonial Brazil: Santana de Parnaíba, 1580–1822*. Berkeley and Los Angeles: University of California Press, 1992.

Miller, Samuel J. *Portugal and Rome, c. 1743–1830: An Aspect of the Catholic Enlightenment*. Rome: Université Gregoriana Editrice, 1978.

Moreira Alves, José Carlos. "A Panorama of Brazilian Civil Law from Its Origins to the Present." In *A Panorama of Brazilian Law*, edited by Keith S. Rosenn and Jacob Dolinger, 87–120. Miami: University of Miami Press, 1992.

Mörner, Magnus. *Race Mixture in the Americas*. Boston: Little, Brown, and Co., 1967.

Mott, Luiz R. B. *Os pecados de família na Bahia de Todos os Santos (1813)*. Salvador: Centro de Estudos Baianos/Universidade Federal da Bahia, 1982.

Moura, Margarida. *Os herdeiros da terra: Parentesco e herança numa área rural.* São Paulo: HUCITEC, 1978.

Nazzari, Muriel. "Concubinage in Colonial Brazil: The Inequalities of Race, Class, and Gender." *Journal of Family History* 21 (Apr. 1996): 107–24.

———. *The Disappearance of the Dowry: Women, the Family, and Property in São Paulo (1600–1900).* Stanford: Stanford University Press, 1991.

———. "Questionable Foundlings: The Fake Abandonment of Infants in Colonial Brazil," 31p. Paper presented for the American Historical Association Annual Meeting, 1995.

———. "An Urgent Need To Conceal: The System of Honor and Shame in Colonial Brazil." In *The Faces of Honor: Sex, Shame, and Violence in Colonial Latin America*, edited by Lyman L. Johnson and Sonya Lipsett-Rivera, 103–26. Albuquerque: University of New Mexico Press, 1998.

Nazzari, Muriel Smith. "Women, the Family and Property: The Decline of the Dowry in São Paulo, Brazil (1600–1870)." Ph.D. diss., Yale University, 1986.

"Necrologia, 8 de Setembro de 1836: Marquez de Caravellas." *Jornal do Commercio* [Rio de Janeiro], 15 Sept. 1836. Reprinted in *Annaes da Câmara do Senado de 1837*, VII–XVI.

Nero da Costa, Iraci de. *Minas Gerais: Estructuras populacionais típicas.* São Paulo: EDEC, 1981.

Nizza da Silva, Maria Beatriz, ed. *Cultura e sociedade no Rio de Janeiro (1808–1821).* São Paulo: Cia. Editora Nacional, 1977.

———. "Divorce in Colonial Brazil: The Case of São Paulo." In *Sexuality and Marriage in Colonial Latin America*, edited by Asunción Lavrin, 313–40. Lincoln: University of Nebraska Press, 1989.

———. "A documentação do Desembargo do Paço e a história da família." *Ler História* [Lisbon] 20 (1990): 61–77.

———. "Os filhos ilegítimos no Brasil colonial." In *Anais da Sociedade Brasileira de Pesquisa Histórica, XVª Reunião* (1995): 121–24.

———. "A legislação pombalina e a estrutura da família no antigo regime português." In *Pombal revisitado*, edited by Maria Beatriz Nizza da Silva, 405–14. Lisbon: Editora Estampa, 1984.

———. *Sistema de casamento no Brasil colonial.* São Paulo: Editora da USP, 1978.

———, ed. *Pombal revisitado.* Lisbon: Editora Estampa, 1984.

Novinsky, Ilana W. "Heresia, mulher e sexualidade (algumas notas sobre o Nordeste Brasileiro nos séculos XVI e XVII)." In *Vivência: História, sexualidade e imagens femininas*, v. 1, edited by Maria Cristina A. Bruschini and Fúlvia Rosemberg, 227–56. São Paulo: Brasiliense, 1980.

O'Neill, Brian Juan. *Jornaleiras e Zorros: Dimensões da ilegitimidade numa aldéia transmontana, 1870–1978.* Paris: Fondation Calouste Gulbenkian, 1985.

———. *Social Inequality in a Portuguese Village: Land, Late Marriage, and Bastardy, 1870–1978.* Cambridge: Cambridge University Press, 1987.

Oliveira Marques, A. H. de. *Daily Life Portugal in the Late Middle Ages.* Translated by S. S. Wyatt. Madison: The University of Wisconsin Press, 1971.

———. *From Lusitania to Empire.* Vol. 1 of a *History of Portugal.* New York & London: Columbia University Press, 1972.

Pacca, Bartolomeu Cardinal. *Memoires historiques du cardinal Pacca sur les affaires ecclesiastiques d'Allemagne et de Portugal pendent ses nonciatures. Traduits de l'Italien, augmentes de pieces justificatives termines par le bref de Pie VI sur* . . . . 3rd ed. Paris: P. J. Camus, 1844.

Paiva da Costa, Dora Isabel. "Herança e cíclo de vida: um estudo sobre família e população em Campinas, São Paulo 1765–1850." Ph.D. diss., Federal University Fluminense Niterói, 1997.

Pang, Eul-Soo. In *Pursuit of Honor and Power: Noblemen of the Southern Cross in Nineteenth-Century Brazil.* Auburn: University of Alabama Press, 1988.

Pires, Heliodoro. "Uma teologia jansenista no Brasil." *Revista Eclesiástica Brasileira* 8 (June 1943): 331–34.

Ramos, Donald. "City and Country: The Family in Minas Gerais, 1804–1838." *Journal of Family History* 3 (1978): 361–75.

————. "Marriage and the Family in Colonial Vila Rica." *Hispanic American Historical Review* 55 (1975): 200–225.

Ramos de Carvalho, Laerte. *As reformas pombalinas da instrução pública. Boletins da Faculdade de Filosofia, Ciências e Letras [Universidade de São Paulo]*, No. 160. São Paulo, 1952.

Ribeiro da Silva, Francisco. "Marginais e marginalizados à luz das *Ordenações Filipinas.*" *Revista de Ciências Históricas* [Universidade Portocalense] 11 (1996): 69–76.

Rípodas Ardanaz, Daisy. *El matrimonio en Indias: Realidad social e regulación jurídica.* Buenos Aires: Fundación para la Educación, la Ciencia y la Cultura, 1977.

Rosenn, Keith S., and Jacob Dolinger, eds. *A Panorama of Brazilian Law.* Miami: University of Miami Press, 1992.

Santos, Eugenio dos. "A legislação pombalina e os novos marginalizados do Brasil: Uma abordagem." *Revista de Ciências Históricas* [Universidade Portocalense] 11 (1996): 151–61.

Schmidt, William E. "Treating Adultery as Crime: Wisconsin Dusts Off An Old Law." *New York Times*, 30 Apr. 1990, 1, 9.

Schwartz, Stuart B. *Sovereignty and Society in Colonial Brazil: The High Court of Bahia and Its Judges, 1609–1751.* Berkeley and Los Angeles: University of California Press, 1973.

————. *Sugar Plantations in the Formation of Brazilian Society: Bahia, 1550–1835.* Cambridge University Press, 1985.

Soihet, Rachel. "É proibido ser mãe; opressão e moralidade da mulher pobre." In *História da sexualidade no Brasil*, edited by Ronaldo Vainfas, 191–212. Rio de Janeiro: GRAAL, 1986.

Sousa, Octavio Tarquínio de. *Bernardo Pereira de Vasconcellos e seu tempo.* Rio de Janeiro: José Olýmpio Editora, 1937.

————. *Diogo Antonio Feijó (1784–1843).* José Olýmpio Editora, 1942.

Sousa Montenegro, João Alfredo de. *O liberalismo radical de Frei Caneca.* Rio de Janeiro: Tempo Brasileiro, 1978.

Staves, Susan. *Married Women's Separate Property in England, 1660–1833.* Cambridge: Harvard University Press, 1990.

Stockler, Franciscus de Borja Garção. *Panegyricus historicus sempiternae memoriae: Paschalis Josephi de Mello Freire dos Reis . . . die 17 januarii 1799* . . . . Reprinted in Paschalis Josephi Mellii Freirii, *Historiae juris civilis lusitani; liber singularis*, 5th ed., IX–XXXII. Coimbra: Typis Academicis, 1860.

"Three Children of Princess Caroline of Monaco Are Declared Legitimate by the Vatican, Making Them Eligible To Succeed to the Throne." *New York Times*, 6 Apr. 1993, Pt. B, 2:4.

Torres Londoño, Fernando. *El concubinato y la iglesia en el Brasil colonial*. ESTUDOS CEDHAL, No. 2. São Paulo: CEDHAL/USP, n.d. [1988?].

Twinam, Ann. *Public Lives, Private Secrets: Gender, Honor, Sexuality, and Illegitimacy in Colonial Spanish America*. Stanford: Stanford University Press, 1999.

Vainfas, Ronaldo. "A condenação dos adultérios e padres." In *Mulheres, adultérios e padres*, edited by Lana Lage da Gama e Lima, 35–52. Rio de Janeiro: Raymundo Paula de Arruda, 1987.

————, ed. "A teia da intriga; delação e moralidade na sociedade colonial." In *História da sexualidade no Brasil*, edited by Ronaldo Vainfas, 41–66. Rio de Janeiro: GRAAL, 1986.

————. *História da sexualidade no Brasil*. Rio de Janeiro: GRAAL, 1986.

Venâncio, Renato Pinto. *Famílias abandonadas: Assistência à criança de camadas populares no Rio de Janeiro e em Salvador, séculos XVIII e XIX*. Campinas, São Paulo: Papirus Editora, 1999.

————. *Ilegitimidade e concubinato no Brasil colonial: Rio de Janeiro e São Paulo*. ESTUDOS CEDHAL, No. 1. São Paulo: CEDHAL/USP, 1988.

Verney, Antonio Luis. *Verdadeiro método de estudar*. Lisbon: Liv. Sá Costa, 1952.

Vieira da Cunha, Rui. *Estudo da nobreza brasileira: I—Cadetes*. Rio de Janeiro: Min. da Justiça e Negócios Interiores/Arquivo Nacional, 1966.

Villaverde, Cirilo. *Cecilia Valdes, or Angel's Hill: A Novel of Cuban Customs*. Translated by Sydney G. Gest. New York: Vantage Press, 1962.

Wall, Richard, Jean Robin, and Peter Laslett, eds. *Family Forms in Historic Europe*. Cambridge: Cambridge University Press, 1983.

Walsh, Robert. *Notices of Brazil in 1828 and 1829*. 2 vols. Boston: Richardson, Lord & Holbrook, William Hyde, Crocker & Brewster, *et al.*, 1831.

Watson, Alan. *Roman Law and Comparative Law*. Athens, Georgia: The University of Georgia Press, 1991.

Watson, James B., Theresa Scherrer Davidson, and Earl W. Thomas, eds. *Brazil: Papers Presented in the Institute for Brazilian Studies, Vanderbilt University*. Nashville: Vanderbilt University Press, 1953.

Zenha, Celeste. "Casamento e ilegitimidade no cotidiano da justiça." In *História da sexualidade no Brasil*, edited by Ronaldo Vainfas, 125–42. Rio de Janeiro: GRAAL, 1986.

Index

In this index an "f" after a number indicates a separate reference on the next page, and an "ff" indicates separate references on the next two pages. A continuous discussion over two or more pages is indicated by a span of page numbers, e.g., "57–59." *Passim* is used for a cluster of references in close but not consecutive sequence.